DATE DUE

MAY 1 3 2009			
AUG 1 7 2009			
			Printed in USA

HIGHSMITH #45230

North Africans in Contemporary France: Becoming Visible

Richard L. Derderian

DC
34.5
N67
D47
2004

For Shoko
Through it all

First published 2004 by
PALGRAVE MACMILLAN™
175 Fifth Avenue, New York, N.Y. 10010 and
Houndmills, Basingstoke, Hampshire, England RG21 6XS
Companies and representatives throughout the world

PALGRAVE MACMILLAN is the global academic imprint of the Palgrave Macmillan division of St. Martin's Press, LLC and of Palgrave Macmillan Ltd. Macmillan® is a registered trademark in the United States, United Kingdom and other countries. Palgrave is a registered trademark in the European Union and other countries.

ISBN 1–4039–6566–8

Library of Congress Cataloging-in-Publication Data
Derderian, Richard L.
    North Africans in contemporary France : becoming visible / by Richard L. Derderian.
        p. cm.
    Includes bibliographical references and index.
    ISBN 1–4039–6566–8
    1. North Africans—France. 2. North Africans—France—Social conditions. 3. North Africans—France—Political activity. 4. Minorities—France. 5. Pluralism (Social sciences)—France. I. Title.

DC34.5.N67D47 2004
305.896'044—dc22   2003064781

A catalogue record for this book is available from the British Library.

Design by Newgen Imaging Systems (P) Ltd., Chennai, India.

First edition: July 2004
10 9 8 7 6 5 4 3 2 1

Printed in the United States of America.

Contents

Acknowledgments

T here are many people who deserve recognition for making this book possible. I am deeply indebted to all those who so generously shared their time, experiences, and hospitality with me. It was their willingness to engage in lengthy and sometimes multiple interviews and to lend their own archival holdings that allowed me to move toward an understanding of an important chapter in the largely unwritten story of France's ethnic minority past. Oral histories are about learning from the living. The many contacts and acquaintances I had the opportunity to make in the course of my research were unquestionably what made this such a rewarding and enjoyable experience.

A number of lasting friendships took shape during my research in France. I had the pleasure to come to know Latifa Benabou, Christopher Jones, Ratiba and Jaoud Hachani, and Amina and Zineb Derbal. Latifa, Ratiba, and Amina were especially generous in translating a number of Arabic language songs into French. Zineb's assistance at the Algerian Cultural Center was invaluable. Roger and Marie-France Bâcle helped make Paris a home by offering their studio apartment and extending their hospitality throughout the year in France.

This book grew out of a doctoral dissertation completed at the University of North Carolina at Chapel Hill. My advisor, Don Reid, merits special recognition for his tireless reading and unfailingly constructive criticism throughout the long graduate process. I was equally fortunate to benefit from the support and kindness of Jay Smith, Lloyd Kramer, Wendy Perry, and John Rutledge who have all left me with only fond memories of my years in North Carolina. I would also like to acknowledge the much-appreciated assistance offered by Alec Hargreaves whose work on North Africans and ethnic minorities in France has always been a source of inspiration.

Most of the research for this book was completed during the 1993–1994 academic year in Paris funded by a Fulbright-Hays Dissertation Research

Grant and a Gilbert Chinard Scholarship from the Institut Français de Washington. In Paris, Suzel Anstett at the Direction de la Population et des Migrations, Christine Pelloquin at the Centre d'Information et d'Études sur les Migrations Internationales, and the staff at the Agence pour le Développement des Relations Interculturelles all provided invaluable support and resources for this study. The National University of Singapore (NUS) made it possible to make a number of subsequent return trips to France. The staff at NUS's Central Library, and Ms. Tey Lin Lin in particular, have been very helpful in purchasing necessary secondary sources. My colleagues Bruce Lockhart and Anne Raffin in Singapore have been especially generous in reading and commenting on new and revised additions to my work. Of course, all of the shortcomings are my own.

Although the desire to embark on an academic odyssey is often unfathomable from the outside, I was always fortunate to benefit from the support and encouragement of my parents, Robert and Gail Derderian. In the course of my journey I was blessed with a marriage to my loving wife Shoko and the birth of three healthy and heartwarming children, Nicholas, Mitchell, and Natalie. It has been a journey that has taken me from Massachusetts to North Carolina, France, and finally to Singapore. Through it all my wife Shoko has helped me weather countless storms and rough seas encountered along the way. For this I am forever grateful and to her I dedicate this book.

Introduction

Since the early 1980s France's North African community has been at the center of ongoing debates about French citizenship and the prospects for incorporating new ethnic minorities into the nation. From the tightening of traditionally generous citizenship laws to the media frenzy surrounding the wearing of Islamic headscarves in public schools, North Africans reveal profound French anxieties about the strength and vitality of the nation. Long targeted by the far-right National Front and disproportionately affected by racially motivated acts of violence, numerous public opinion polls express serious reservations about the ability of Muslim North Africans to find a place in French society.

France is certainly not the only nation grappling with the challenge of integrating new immigrant populations. Given the reality of global migration flows and ever more heterogeneous populations debates about immigration and national identity have become quite common. Yet for many observers what makes France exceptional is the emotional level of these debates and the intense fears that new ethnic minorities could potentially unleash the kind of ethnic and racial strife witnessed in Lebanon, Yugoslavia, or the ghettos of America. Caught in the grips of a kind of national hysteria, France's particular inability to cope with its multiethnic present is often diagnosed as the result of an outmoded national identity that produces profound anxieties about ethnic diversity.

In her recent series on Muslims in Europe National Public Radio's Sylvia Poggioli begins her segment on France by contrasting racial tensions and popular support for the xenophobic National Front with the country's egalitarian traditions and its refusal to extend official forms of recognition to France's ethnic minority populations. The conclusion is clear, if the some three million Muslims who live in France today, four-fifths of whom are from France's former empire in the Maghreb (Algeria, Morocco, and Tunisia), represent a dilemma for the nation it has much to do with the continued valence of older conceptions of national identity rooted in the Enlightenment and the French Revolutionary past.[1]

While agreeing that France is mired in the past, Maxim Silverman locates French resistance to ethnic diversity in the Third Republic. Humiliated by the Franco-Prussian War and surrounded by enemies on the left and the right, the Third Republic sought allies and legitimacy by cloaking itself in the rhetoric and symbolism of the French Revolution. This mode of imagining the nation, Silverman argues, is now out of sink with the times. "Today a republican political culture still profoundly attached to those modern ideals is frequently at odds with the post-colonial and postmodern reality of contemporary France." While the expression of cultural difference is becoming a common feature of everyday life, French political culture clings to the old ideals of "a division between the (universalistic) public and the (particularistic) private sphere where they have manifestly broken down."[2]

What we are witnessing in France today, claims Michel Wieviorka, is not the survival of an older national identity but a nostalgic retreat from an unsettling present. The process of deindustrialization and the collapse of the working class, globalization, European integration, and the rise of particularist forms of identity are all part of the shifting postwar landscape that creates a desire to seek refuge in an imagined past. The Republican model, closely associated with the public school system of the Third Republic, is a central component of French nostalgia. The Republican model is based on the belief that integration functioned successfully in the past because of the values of *laïcité*, or the separation of church and state, and the promotion of an individual form of inclusion prioritizing shared rights and obligations and the restriction of particularlist identities to the private sphere. Pointing out the important concessions made to the Catholic Church in Alsace-Lorraine and long-standing policies of sex-segregation in French schools, Wieviorka argues that this myth of the Republican model does not hold up to serious scrutiny.[3]

Jean-Philippe Mathy cautions us not to be misled by the common opposition between French and Anglo-Saxon models of citizenship. France has never been the kind of Jacobin steamroller depicted in studies like *Peasants into Frenchmen*.[4] On both sides of the Atlantic there is a common concern about forging unity while respecting diversity. The works of American and Canadian scholars who have grappled with these questions are now widely read and debated in France. "Richard Rorty, John Rawls, Michael Walzer, and Charles Taylor have replaced German philosophers as some of the Parisian intelligencia's favorite foreign imports." Mathy claims that there is growing support in France for a "Third Way" that has much in common with the ideas advocated by scholars such as Walzer and Appiah. "What I call in this book *la troisième voie*, the middle way between assimilation and exclusion that many French intellectuals and public figures are trying to imagine today (they call it integration), seems to me quite akin to Walzer and Appiah's attempts to preserve the plurality of accepted social identities and individual behaviors in a democratic society while preserving a common, cohesive public culture that is the cornerstone of a republican form of government."[5]

The aim of this book is to explore the prospects for greater recognition and acceptance of ethnic diversity in contemporary France. I do so by focusing primarily on the North African community and by looking at several novel developments that took place from the mid-1970s and during the Mitterrand years (1981–1995). In particular I consider the rise of ethnic minority political and cultural initiatives, the first French television series featuring North Africans and multiethnic casts and the first national museum exhibition devoted to the creative work of immigrant youth. Lastly I examine how the progeny of North African workers are both caught up in and help to reimagine prominent sites of national memory such as the working-class suburbs or banlieues and the Algerian War.

The French Melting Pot

Given France's long history of immigration one might expect the country to be better prepared to contend with new immigrant populations in the present. Whereas large-scale immigration in much of Europe is a relatively recent post–World War II phenomenon, mass migration to France began at least a century earlier. As population growth slowed in France well before that of its neighbors, immigration provided a much-needed solution to the country's demographic and economic needs. According to statistics from the Ministry of the Interior more than one-third of France's present-day population is of immigrant origin. "Together with the United States and Canada, France is one of the industrialized countries whose population owes the most to immigration."[6]

The first wave of immigrants to wash across France in the mid-nineteenth century came from neighboring countries such as Belgium and Italy. By the interwar years second wave immigrants were already coming from new regions such as Central and Eastern Europe with certain groups such as Polish workers becoming especially numerous. In contrast to the first two waves of immigration post–World War II arrivals were predominately from France's former imperial territories in Asia, North, and sub-Saharan Africa. Whereas Europeans accounted for 72.3 percent of all foreign workers as late as 1968, by 1990 they represented only 40.7 percent of the immigrant population. In particular, the percentage of North Africans (primarily from the Maghreb) grew from 24 percent of the foreign population in 1958 to 45.4 percent in 1990.[7]

The size of the immigrant population in France grew rapidly from the mid-nineteenth century to the interwar years. In 1851, the date of the first official census, foreigners accounted for only 1 percent of France's total population. During the first wave, between 1851 and 1886, the number of foreigners grew to over one million, reaching nearly 3 percent of the total population, helping to fuel the process of industrialization and modernization in the nineteenth century. The second wave, from 1921 to 1931, witnessed the arrival of approximately one million immigrants in a single decade, providing a much-needed human infusion following the bloodletting and material destruction caused by World War I. By 1931 immigration peaked at 6.4 percent of the total population and France became the leading per capita immigration country in the world, surpassing even the United States. A third and final wave of immigration responded to the continued shortage of labor and nearly 30 years of postwar economic growth. Between 1954 and 1974, the immigrant population grew from 1.7 to 3.5 million, reaching 6.5 percent of the total population—approximately the same percentage as today.[8]

Yet despite the long history and central role of immigration in the making of modern France, the history of immigration is marked by cycles of xenophobia and intolerance. During the economic downturns that invariably followed periods of growth and expansion immigrants were singled out for their cultural incompatibility and their unwelcome competition with French workers. Earlier waves of Italian and Polish immigrants, whose more conservative Catholic beliefs placed them at odds with an increasingly secular French workforce, were often seen as being poorly suited to life in France.[9] Violence targeting foreigners and xenophobic rhetoric in the press and political circles reached unparalleled levels during the late nineteenth century and the interwar years. In 1893 riots in the mining community at Aigues-Mortes in southern France claimed the lives of at least ten Italian workers.[10] During the 1930s depression years French authorities deported thousands of unwanted Polish workers.

Gérard Noiriel asserts that these economic downturns actually contributed to the stabilization and integration of France's foreign populations. As the myth of returning to the home country begins to collapse, turnover rates decrease, family reunification increases, and the weight of the immigrant community begins to shift from the first to the second generation. It is the growing presence of immigrant families in French communities, social services, and institutions (schools, hospitals, etc.) that gives rise to ethnic tensions between minority and majority populations. Ironically, xenophobia becomes commonplace at the very moment when immigrants begin to conform to the dominant norms of French society (family strategies, occupational diversification).[11]

The inclusion of foreign populations has always been a gradual process that often stretches out over several generations. The allure of the French nation or the power of its normalizing institutions did not simply cause immigrants to discard their deeply rooted ties to the home country. Immigrants often settled in the same regions, cities, or towns. Through clubs, associations, and religious activities foreign workers and their families forged a sense of community based on social exchanges, shared values, customs, and beliefs. In some cases communal life was encouraged by French employers or foreign governments as a means of isolating foreign workers from the influence of unionized and politicized French workers and maintaining national ties. This was true for interwar Polish immigrants who worked in the mines of Northern France. With the help of French employers and the Polish government, immigrants established tightly knit communities characterized by a highly complex network of social, cultural, and religious activities.[12]

Despite the persistence of ties to the home country, most immigrants and their families gradually assimilated into French society. Statistical measurements such as the rise of mixed marriages, job diversification, the acquisition of French citizenship, and the shrinking size of immigrant families demonstrate that over time past waves of immigrants adopted the dominant norms of French society.[13] North Africans today, much like earlier immigrant groups regarded as being particularly attached to their community of origin, are showing signs of successful assimilation.[14] In contrast to widely help popular beliefs, North African youth are experiencing a successful cultural and economic integration into French society. Over half of all immigrant youth have enjoyed a rise in social status.[15]

Algerian Exceptions

Given the politically charged nature of debates about immigration in the French present it is important not to lose sight of parallels with the past. However, such parallels also threaten to obscure the particularities of the Algerian experience by conflating them with a larger immigration history. Without looking at the specificity of this experience it is impossible to fully grasp French attitudes toward North Africans today or the impetus behind struggles for recognition by North African workers and their children in France.

As early as the interwar years we see a number of striking differences between Algerians and European immigrants. Algerians were typically assigned to the very bottom rungs of the occupational ladder in positions even lower than those taken by other immigrant groups. "Overall those types of unhealthy work which involved great heat, toxic gases, acids, dust, hot metals, and dyes had a predominance of immigrant workers among which North Africans made up the largest group."[16] When it came to wages Algerians were usually classified as unskilled or semiskilled workers by their employers placing them at the lowest end of the pay scale. "Even when migrants, after many decades in France, had achieved work skills on a par with those of the French and European workers, they continued to be categorized in the lowest levels." Moreover, when the economy slumped Algerians were often the first to be fired.[17]

As colonial subjects Algerians were at more of a disadvantage than their European counterparts. They lacked the protection of their own national government and the kinds of agreements that brought about improvements for European immigrants. "Those foreigners whose governments were strong in protecting their nationals interests through bi-lateral accords and contracts (Italy, Poland, Spain) no longer provided cheap labor compared to the Maghrebians."[18] Moreover, fearful that contact with metropolitan French might weaken Algerian obedience, during the interwar years a powerful colonial lobby did much to fabricate and anchor negative stereotypes in the minds of a French public that was by no means predisposed against North Africans. "The proliferation of such stereotypes, particularly through the press, played no small part in the creation of a climate of racism which was to continue into the postcolonial period."[19]

Failing to halt the flow of Algerians workers to France between the wars, influential colonial administrators and settler organizations successfully lobbied for special control and surveillance mechanisms. Quite often these mechanisms were run by colonial officials and staffed by people who had a thorough knowledge of Algerians. Founded in 1925, SAINA (Service de Surveillance, Protection et Assistance des Indigènes Nord Africains), for example, was a joint police and welfare agency established by a group of ex-administrators from Algeria. The police unit, administered by the Prefecture of Police, established a special brigade of men typically born or raised in Algeria and fluent in Arabic or Berber. Targeting criminal elements and nationalists within the Algerian community, the brigade launched raids on Algerian cafés, carried out identity checks, and disrupted political meetings.[20] Masked by the rhetoric of the civilizing mission, the welfare unit used its advisory and repatriation services, job location, unemployment benefits, housing, healthcare, and other services as a means of compiling files and exerting pressure on Algerians in France. "Thus while most immigrant nationalities, the Italians, Poles, Spaniards and others, aroused xenophobic responses in the

French public during the inter-war years, the targeting of the relatively small group of North Africans was far more intense and sustained."[21]

During the Algerian War similar techniques of control and surveillance were brought to bear on the Algerian community. To combat the FLN Maurice Papon, former Prefect of Constantine, recruited specially trained army officers from Algeria to form the SAT (Service d'assitance technique aux français musulmans d'Algérie). Much like the SAINA, the SAT used the guise of a welfare agency to collect intelligence on the Algerian community. As with the SAINA, the SAT also put together a special police brigade to fight against Algerian nationalists. The FPA (Force de Police Auxiliaire) made up of Algerians, known as harkis, "soon achieved notoriety for their ruthless methods, including the use of torture, and their success in taking the battle into the FLN bastions like the Goutte d'Or."[22] The SONACOTRA (Société Nationale de Construction de lodgements pour les Travailleurs Algériens), which built housing for Algerian workers, was established in 1956 to remove Algerians from the FLN-dominated *bidonvilles* (shantytowns) where they could be subjected to closer surveillance. "SONACOTRA hostels, managed by former policemen, army officers or native administrators were part of a wider system of political surveillance."[23]

The empire hinged on the creation and maintenance of artificial dividing lines. As Edward Said has shown the production of knowledge was instrumental in forging the many binary relations that defined and justified the relationship between colonizers and colonized.[24] The introduction of Algerian workers to France, during and after World War I, threatened to erode these divisions together with the very fabric of colonial society. It was by imposing new security and control mechanisms, often through an active exchange of personnel and surveillance techniques with Algeria that French authorities sought to protect "French Algeria" against the breakdown of the imperial divide.

Racializing Practices

Immigration policy makers were also active in the process of demarcating and distancing North Africans from European immigrants. The High Committee for Population and Families, entrusted by de Gaulle in 1945 with the mission of formulating an immigration policy, had envisioned an approach that would favor the arrival of "more assimilable" European workers while discouraging the introduction of less ethnically desirable elements (i.e., North Africans, Asians, Slavs, etc.). Although ethnic preferences were never officially adopted, they remained an important priority in postwar immigration policy.[25] In 1946, The National Immigration Office (ONI), a state-run agency created the previous year to take charge of the regulation of immigration to France, aggressively began to recruit Italian workers. Between 1950 and 1954 Italians represented 75 percent of the workers recruited by the ONI.[26] Despite these figures, the number of Italians was far less than hoped for. Economic growth in Europe and the rise of the iron curtain shut down more traditional sources of immigration from countries such as Italy and Poland.

In contrast, North African immigration from Algeria experienced almost unparalleled growth in the postwar period. Technically, until France ended its over 130-year-presence in Algeria in 1962, Algerians were not immigrants because Algeria was officially an integral part of metropolitan France. In fact, the spectacular postwar growth of the Algerian population in France was due to the special travel and work privileges granted to Algerians, first as residents of France's overseas departments, then as beneficiaries of the Evian Accords that brought an end to French rule in Algeria. While some 20,000 Algerians resided in France in 1946, the number increased to 210,000 by 1954—a 32.5 percent annual rate of growth at a time when immigration as a whole increased by only 1.3 percent.[27] In the first decade after World War II, the largest number of immigrants came from Algeria.[28] Algerian immigration to France slowed during the war for independence (1954–1962) but once again began to accelerate following the end of the conflict. Between 1962 and 1975, the Algerian population in France more than doubled from 350,484 to 710,690.[29] By 1982, Algerians represented the single most important national group in France—some 21 percent of the immigrant population.

Little was done to accommodate Algerians who arrived in France during the 1950s and 1960s. Mud cities comprising makeshift homes without electricity or plumbing, little different from Third World shantytowns, sprung up across the country. In 1966 the Ministry of the Interior reported that these *bidonvilles* housed some 75,000 people—a number that may in reality have been three times higher.[30] The last of the *bidonvilles* were finally torn down in the 1970s and replaced by supposedly temporary, transitional housing or *cités de transits* (transit cities) where immigrant families could be "educated" about modern French lifestyles and homes before moving on to more permanent HLM (*Habitation à Loyer modérée*) or public housing.[31] Prefabricated communities erected on vacant lots in the urban periphery, cut off from the surrounding towns and cities, devoid of basic infrastructural resources, the transit cities were only a marginal improvement over the *bidonvilles*. Originally built to last no more than two years, many families found themselves parked in transit cities for over two decades.[32]

While doing little to promote the integration of new immigrant populations French officials began to voice their alarm by the late 1960s. Policy makers frequently adopted a racialized discourse when discussing postcolonial populations, singling out North Africans as especially problematic. For example, the 1969 Calvez report, written by Correntin Calvez for the Economic and Social Council, referred to postwar immigrants as an "unassimiable island," and pointed out the need to stop the flow from the Maghreb in particular.[33] Not unlike their British counterparts, French policy makers were especially concerned about maintaining an ethnic balance.[34] France simply could not, in their opinion, continue to maintain an open-door immigration policy given the predominantly non-European origins of the new immigrant populations. Voicing what has since become a popularized retrospective rereading of France's immigration history, these officials suggested that it was the cultural proximity of previous waves of immigrants that facilitated their integration into French society and the cultural distance of postwar immigrants that complicated their inclusion. It was concerns about fostering a greater ethnic balance, "not the economic slow-down and manpower surplus which provided the initial justification for immigration controls in the modern period."[35]

Guided by these concerns French immigration strategies since the late 1960s have centered on a two-pronged integration and control policy. However, government policy makers have placed far more emphasis on controlling the influx of immigrants and reducing the number of foreigners already living in France than devising and enacting plans to integrate immigrants and their families into the fabric of French society. In 1972 the Marcellin-Fontanet Circulars, named after the Ministers of the Interior and Labor, created a catch-22 situation for immigrants by linking work permits to proof of adequate housing.[36] Pressure to control immigration intensified during the presidency of Valéry Giscard d'Etaing (1974–1981) as the French economy began a protracted recession following the 1973 oil shock. North Africans, and Algerians in particular, were singled out by a series of measures intended to stem the tide of unemployment. In 1974, the Giscard administration officially closed the door to non-European Union immigration and attempted to block family reunification. In 1977, Lionel Stoléru, secretary of state for immigrant workers, established a 10,000 franc financial incentive for the voluntary repatriation of foreign workers and their families. In 1979, Minister of the Interior Christian Bonnet strengthened police powers to deport illegal aliens or foreigners who transgressed French laws. The Bonnet Law resulted in the deportation of hundreds of North African youths—many of whom had spent all or most of their lives in France.[37] By the end of the decade, the forced repatriation of several hundred thousand Algerians became the centerpiece of an official French plan, never actually implemented, to boost the number of jobs for French workers and to combat the problem of economic stagnation.[38]

While parties and unions of the Left may have condemned these anti-immigrant policies they often cooperated on the local level. A number of Communist municipalities objected to receiving what they saw as a dispro-portionate share of the immigration population. "By the late 1970s it had become commonplace in Communist and Socialist-government municipali-ties to exclude immigrant families from housing, schools and even social services, actions often justified by notions of a 'threshold of tolerance.'"[39] One of the most notable and often-cited incidents was the decision by the Communist mayor of Vitry outside Paris to take matters into his own hands by ordering the bulldozing of an immigrant hostel on Christmas Eve in 1980.[40] By presenting the problems and dangers of immigration in their public statements and public meetings, local officials helped pave the way for Jean-Marie Le Pen and the National Front's emergence on the national scene in the early 1980s.[41]

A National Dilemma

No doubt the National Front and its flamboyant leader were instrumental in catapulting immigration into the limelight of national politics during the 1980s. Prior to the 1980s immigration had largely been a technical affair excluded from the realm of electoral competition. Under the banner of the "national preference" Le Pen made immigration the lynchpin of his political platform. Calling for the forced reparation of immigrants in France as a means of opening up jobs for French workers and reinvigorating an embattled French culture, Le Pen has consistently garnered between 10 and 15 percent of the national vote over the past two decades—making it as far as the second and final round of the presidential elections in 2002.

Much of the rhetoric of the National Front has centered on France's Muslim community. "The nature of immigration has changed," writes Le Pen. "What we are witnessing on our national soil is the shock of two fun-damentally different cultures. Islam, which is already the second religion in France, is opposed to any kind of assimilation and threatens our own iden-tity, our Occidental and Christian civilization."[42] Benefiting from a context of uncertainty caused by the end of the miracle years, the process of dein-dustrialization, and the seemingly inexorable rise of unemployment Le Pen provided a simple and powerfully appealing racial reading and solution to France's problems.

A number of scholars explain the success of Le Pen and the surge of racial violence targeting North Africans during the 1980s as a direct consequence of the Algerian past. Benjamin Stora points out that Le Pen, a veteran of the Algerian War, deploys rhetoric that taps into memories of the Algerian past. Moreover, many of Le Pen's rank and file supporters, including those who staff the National Front, are members of France's *pied noir* community (European settlers who fled Algeria after independence).[43] Opting for a Freudian explanatory Anne Donadey argues that what we are witnessing today is the violent return of a repressed colonial past. Triggered by a period of change and uncertainly, the still bitter and unresolved memories of the Algerian War are resurfacing with a vengeance—often in the form of hostility toward the North African immigrant community.[44]

Whether or not we accept notions of repressed memory the escalation of French hostility toward North Africans during the 1980s is undeniable. Racially motivated attacks on North African workers began even before the first oil shock in 1973 causing the Algerian government to suspend immigration to France that same year. However, it was in the next decade that racial acts of violence became commonplace. Although North Africans represented no more than 40 percent of the foreign population, between 1980 and 1993 they accounted for 78 percent of all officially recorded racial crimes. Typically pointing to their religion or way of life, public opinion polls reveal profound doubts about the prospects for integrating North Africans into French society.[45]

These doubts have manifested themselves in debates about the need to reinforce the laws and institutions that shape the process of integration. During the conservatives' return to power in 1986–1988, Prime Minister Chirac's government proposed a revision of the nationality code specifying that citizenship should no longer be granted automatically to those born in France. Briefly passed into law during the early 1990s, the revisions were at odds with the historical French confidence about the integrative abilities of the nation and its traditionally generous citizenship policies.[46] The more restrictive policies suggested that in contrast to previous waves of primarily European immigrants tougher measures and safeguards were required for postwar and predominantly non-European immigrants.[47]

In the wake of the nationality debate a new controversy erupted in October 1989 when three junior high school girls were expelled by their public school principal for wearing Islamic headscarves to class. Ostensibly about the infringement of the secular principles of the public school system, what became known as the "headscarves affairs" quickly escalated into national debate about the ability of France's most revered normalizing institution to integrate Muslim minorities into French society. Dividing both the left and the right and leading to the formation of strange alliances and partnerships, the headscarves affair provided clear evidence that anxieties about France's Muslim community, most of whom are North African, remained one of the nation's most central concerns.[48]

Not unlike blacks in Britain, North Africans have been subjected to a form of cultural racism. Similar to biological racism discredited by the Nazi past, cultural racism posits absolute cultural differences or ethnic divides that negate the possibility of integration or peaceful coexistence. Prominent public institutions, such as public schools or the justice system, function as symbols and sources of national culture that are at odds with or threatened by particular ethnic minority communities. Paul Gilroy's comments on Britain seem especially applicable to France. "Schools are defined by the right as repositories of the authentic national culture which they transmit between generations. They mediate the relation of the national community to its youthful future citizens. Decaying school buildings provide a ready image for the nation in microcosm."[49]

Cultural racism, in the case of Algerians, stretches back to the period of conquest. In their efforts to distinguish between Algeria's Kabyle and Arab populations French administrators, intellectuals and military officers stressed the relative proximity of the Kabyle language, gender roles, and sedentary way of life that, in contrast to the Arab majority, made them more likely prospects for assimilation and a more promising source of labor. Most importantly, it was the perceived secular proclivities of Kabyles that set them apart from what were regarded as the entrenched and alien Islamic beliefs of the Arab population.[50]

Cultural racism in the French present works in connection with an array of disqualifying labels. For example, with the advent of the term "beur" to designate the progeny of North African workers, it is the first time that second-generation members of an immigrant community have been assigned an ethnic label.[51] *Beur* refers to young people between 15 and 30 who have a North African look, and consequently are unlike the French. A spatially and usually gender-specific term, *beurs* are males who populate a much-demonized world of France's working-class suburbs or *banlieues*. There is also the less frequently employed term *beurette* for women but it does not conjure up the same emotions of suspicion and fear. Regarded as harder working and more successful in school, less inclined to associate with gangs, and more constrained by a traditional patriarchal family structure, *beurette* generally inspires sentiments of sympathy for immigrant daughters.[52]

Beurs, second-generation immigrants, children of North African workers, are among the many designations that operate as distancing devises.[53] Born or raised in France, it is precisely because there is little to distinguish North African youth from "French natives" that these distancing devises must be invented and deployed. "Since the 1970s the term '*immigré*' (immigrant) is used less often to designate someone from another geographic space than to evoke origins, ancestry, and blood ties." Labels such as second-generation immigrant or immigrant children are effective in erecting and maintaining cultural divisions when real differences have broken down.[54]

Immigration Studies

Although immigration has become one of the nation's major preoccupations scholarship remained quite limited until the 1970s. Historian Gérard Noiriel explains that this is because France never considered itself an immigration country. While one-third of all French citizens today need only go back three generations to find an immigrant relative, immigration has been marginalized in the writing of French history. According to Noiriel, historians, who interpreted the French Revolution as the defining moment in French history, contributed to the marginalization of immigration. Whereas the American Revolution represented the birth of the nation, the French Revolution was seen to mark its completion. The French nation-state was the culmination of events leading up to, including, and defined afterward by the French Revolution. Social relations, institutions, and ideals were regarded as being largely intact by the time of the Revolution or shortly afterward—long before the first wave of immigration to France in the mid-nineteenth century. Immigrants who came to France were not invited to take part in the building of the nation but rather to become part of the finished product that was the nation.

This holistic view of French society has made for the invisibility of successive waves of immigration to France. Moreover, the absence of references to race, ethnicity, or religion in national statistics and censuses, another legacy of the French Revolution, has made it difficult for scholars to trace the presence or evolution of minority communities. Once a foreigner acquires French citizenship his or her origins vanish from state records—with the notable exception of the Vichy Period. Noiriel remarks that even those historians who became immigration specialists typically came to the subject indirectly, through the study of related topics such as labor relations or political movements.[55]

Until the 1980s, immigration was considered a temporary economic phenomenon, not a permanent structural feature of French society. A handful of specialists studied immigration primarily from an economic, legal, or demographic perspective. Maxim Silverman argues that immigration generated more scholarship and public interest in the 1970s, and especially in the 1980s, because it took on new meanings. Immigration became a means of explaining unemployment, urban violence, delinquency, and a host of other social problems. The social, economic, and political significance that immigration acquired over the past two decades has pushed it on to center stage as one of the nation's most polemical and contentious issues.[56]

The dramatic growth of immigration research was accompanied by a shift in focus from studies of single, first-generation laborers to works on immigrant families and the children of foreign workers. This evolution in immigration research reflected the changing demographic reality of France's foreign population. Following President Valéry Giscard d'Estaing's 1974 decision to close French borders "temporarily" to non-European Union immigration, a policy that remains in force today, migratory flows to France have been characterized by the arrival of family members, not new foreign workers. Between 1976 and 1978, family reunification accounted for 95 percent of all non-European Union immigration to France.[57] The increased numbers of families, the appearance of immigrant children in the educational system, and the growing tensions between French natives and foreigners cohabiting the same communities gradually changed the volume and focus of immigration research. From 1981 to 1988 three times as many immigration studies were published than during the preceding decade. Immigrants were now regarded as a permanently settled minority communities, not transitory workers. Scholars focused on the problems of cohabitation between immigrants and French natives (usually limited to the working class). Questions about the compatibility of lifestyles and cultures as well as school failure, deviance, and identity problems of the second generation dominated much of the academic work. The rediscovery of the Chicago School of sociology (which pioneered the study of race relations in the United States), the development of urban ethnology, and the adoption of ethnographic methods shaped much of the research on immigration.[58]

Immigration studies is a somewhat misleading category to describe much of the current body of research on France's minority communities. A large number of the so-called immigration studies examine the status of families and children and their "integration" into French society, not the condition of foreign workers or the character of population flows to France. As Alec Hargreaves observes, the French understanding of immigration studies is closer in meaning to what English speakers would refer to as race-relations. However, the French avoid terms such as race or ethnicity that legitimize and reinforce the existence of autonomous identity-based groups. Integration refers to the inclusion of all those, French or foreign, who find themselves marginalized by social and economic change. Integration implies the elimination of differences, not their perpetuation.[59]

Overview

My study is part of the shift from primary immigrants to ethnic minorities in France. I am also interested in examining the inclusion of North Africans into French society. However, the focus here is less on measuring integration variables than examining the prospects for constructing broader narratives of belonging in France. To do so I look at a number of unprecedented developments that took place from the mid-1970s and during the Mitterrand years (1981–1995). More specifically, I consider the collective and individual efforts by the sons and daughters of North African workers to mobilize both culturally and politically in the public sphere and the first French initiatives to convey the experiences of ethnic minorities to French television and museum audiences. There is no denying that cultural expression has long been a facet of France's diverse immigrant communities. What seems novel about this specific time period is that growing numbers of ethnic minorities began to take their experiences and aspirations beyond the confines of their community. Moreover, during the Mitterrand years the French government and French cultural institutions became exceptionally supportive of projects to make the past and present experiences of ethnic minorities visible to the French public.

Chapters 1–3 look comparatively at the political and cultural initiatives by the children of North African workers in France. Chapter 1 takes up the rise and demise of the associational movement spearheaded by North African youth during the 1980s. Here I stress the importance of nonrecognition and disrespect in accounting for the emergence of ethnic minority political actions. In particular, I draw from Axel Honneth's *The Struggle for Recognition* to argue how various forms of nonrecognition have the potential to trigger movements for equal rights. However, I also suggest that the denial of recognition, especially physical forms of disrespect that affect our trust and confidence in others, can complicate efforts to forge much-needed alliances. It was the legacy of distrust that made it difficult for the children of North African workers to build and sustain a national associational movement.

Memory has long been regarded as an important element in the past failure and future solution to building a sustainable ethnic minority movement in France. I conclude this chapter by commenting on the recollections of North African activists and their efforts to share their critical reflections on past political struggles. Contrary to the frequent criticisms of ethnic minority memory as invariably divisive, skewed, or detrimental to the nation, I point out how activists from the North African community engage critically with the past and attempt to situate the associational movement within the context of French history. I contend that laying claim to the past can also be a means of fostering critical awareness and attempting to renew rather than break with the nation.

Chapter 2 examines the trajectory of collective forms of cultural expression from the mid-1970s through the Mitterrand years. My intention here is not to posit the emergence of a homogenous ethnic minority or *beur* culture, a highly mediatized theme in the early 1980s, but to draw attention to the shared concerns and strategic choices that cut across an otherwise disparate body of amateur and professional cultural actors. In particular, I discuss the importance of lived experiences and testimonial memory, the use of comedy to address sensitive subjects, and the interactive, participatory relationship with French and minority audiences.

I point out how the evolution of North African cultural expression during the Mitterrand years parallels that of the associational movement. Just as many former associational leaders sought ways to transform their experiences into professional career tracks by joining the ranks of the "beurgoisie," cultural actors often gravitated from militant forms of voluntary-based cultural expression to more professional, career-oriented ambitions. In some cases this transition proved too ambitious while in others it has entailed a tendency to shy away from or to soften the treatment of sensitive issues that might offend newly targeted mainstream French audiences.

I conclude by emphasizing the serious constraints experienced by North African artists in France. Whether or not their work has any relation to their North African descent, North African artists are frequently categorized and marginalized because of their ethnicity. It is this particularizing tendency of French society that partly explains why North African cultural actors are often inclined to distance themselves from their ethnic milieu while preferring to define themselves in terms of their professionalism or their craft rather than their ethnicity.

Chapter 3 offers a more focused study of the 11-year history of Radio Beur, the first radio station in Paris created and operated by members of the North African immigrant community. The history of Radio Beur offers a microcosm in which to examine the difficulties experienced by ethnic minorities in their struggles for recognition in France. The external and internal forces that cut short the life of Radio Beur are similar to those that crippled numerous minority-run associations during the 1980s. Externally, the political openness toward minorities and cultural diversity that existed in the early 1980s proved short-lived. By the late 1980s, the willingness to embrace a more inclusive French society had given way to concerns about combating growing problems of unemployment, urban violence, and drugs. In the realm of social and economic policy, the Socialist government realigned itself more closely with the positions of the right. Internally, Radio Beur was structurally too weak to accommodate the disparate interests of its members. In the absence of larger unifying objectives, Radio Beur collapsed under the weight of the same diversity of individual interests it tried to encompass and promote.

Chapters 4 and 5 turn to French efforts to bring the immigration past and present to mainstream French audiences. Chapter 4 examines the 1983 exhibition *Les enfants de l'immigration* (Immigrant Children) at the Georges Pompidou Center. Featuring the creative work of a diverse body of artists and cultural actors from France's ethnic minority communities, in many respects *Les enfants de l'immigration* was a landmark event. It challenged reductionist notions of ethnic minorities as problems, shed light on France's still-unrecognized immigration history, and empowered the children of immigrant workers to become actors in a prominent public space in the nation's capital. The exceptionally high rates of attendance among North Africans in particular, a first at Beaubourg, attest to how members of France's most marginalized ethnic minority community identified with and laid claim to the exhibition.

Nevertheless, *Les enfants de l'immigration* demonstrates many of the difficulties of extending recognition to ethnic minorities in France. The reluctance of French institutions to support the exhibition, the failure to attract French visitors, and the decision to abandon plans for several follow-up exhibitions, suggest that *Les enfants de l'immigration* failed to resonate with official organs of the state and the general public. Moreover, the emphasis placed by the exhibition on the condition of ethnic minorities in the urban present and the exclusion of references to the colonial past raise questions about the willingness of the organizers to confront what many scholars argue are the institutional and popular roots of racist attitudes toward postcolonial populations in France today. If museums are often criticized for being feel-good institutions that bolster national self-esteem but do little to encourage critical reflection, this too may be one of the shortcomings of *Les enfants de l'immigration*.

Chapter 5 centers on two sitcoms, *La Famille Ramdam*, which aired on M6 in 1990 and was the first French series to features a North African immigrant family, and *Seconde B*, broadcast on France 2 in 1993 and was the first to showcase the friendship of five friends from diverse ethnic horizons in the same suburban high school. Although both shows are to varying degrees affiliated with

Vertigo Productions, founded and operated by Farid Lahouassa and Aïssa Djabri, the focus here is less on minorities who diffuse culture, as in the Radio Beur chapter (chapter 3), and more on the diffusion of minority cultures. In particular, this chapter details how the demands of French "broadcasting," which caters to the tastes and consumption habits of a mainstream French audience, caused both shows to lose much of their ethnic specificity. While sometimes attempting to exploit commercialized forms of exoticism, neither show did much to delve into the tensions and daily realities confronting ethnic minorities in France.

Finally, chapters 6 and 7 borrow from and challenge Pierre Nora's conception of sites of memory or *lieux de mémoire*. Rather than threatening to undermine the shared sites of memory that bind together the nation through their own search for roots, as Nora suggests, the chapters 6 and 7 reveal some of the ways in which ethnic minorities participate in and add complexity to France's *lieux de mémoire*. Chapter 6 takes up the suburbs or *banlieues*, a demonized space that is now intimately associated with French anxieties about the inclusion of ethnic minority populations and North Africans in particular. This chapter underscores how French perceptions of Franco-Algerian youth are colored by diverse representations of the urban fringe and its inhabitants going back to the early nineteenth century. It is the weight of accumulated knowledge about marginalized suburban populations and peoples that is currently being brought to bear on North African youth in the French present. Yet as Paul Gilroy notes is the case with some black artists in Britain and the United States, cultural actors from France's North African community challenge essentialized depictions of the suburban communities in their own creative works.[60] By featuring the diversity of lifestyles and life trajectories, artists from the North African immigrant community defy attempts to lock the suburbs into fixed frameworks of meaning that often reduce ethnic minorities to the status of victims or perpetrators.

Similarly, if racism and intolerance are on the rise in France with North Africans as their primary target, the surfacing of memories of the Algerian War are often deployed as the chief explanatory. Borrowing from Freudian theories of repressed memory, Algerian youth become the victims of past failures to work through the turmoil of the imperial past. Chapter 7 rejects the notion that it was ever possible to repress the Algerian War from active memory. While successive French administrations have preferred to forgive and forget, this chapter supports Benjamin Stora's reading that the sheer number of groups affected by the conflict made forgetting impossible. What has happened, however, has been what Stora describes as the cloistering of memory into mythologized narratives custom-tailored to each group's preferred reading of the past.

Rather than contributing to the further fragmentation of memory, I argue that the memory work of second-generation Algerians has the potential to challenge the cloistered remembering of the Algerian past.

In summary, this book attempts to reveal both the difficulties of going public with ethnic minorities experiences for both North Africans and mainstream French cultural institutions. Immigration gained visibility in France but as this book demonstrates it was by no means a smooth and unobstructed process. However, my contention is that the kinds of individual and collective projects that were undertaken are a means of potentially enriching French narratives of belonging. Rather than threatening to undermine the unity of the nation, efforts to make ethnic minority experiences visible can help to reinforce the ties between the nation and its newest members.

CHAPTER 1

Ethnic Minority Struggles for Recognition

N orth Africans in France have not been passive recipients of exclusionary measures and discriminatory policies. Algerian nationalism and the long struggle for independence have their roots within France's North African immigrant community. It was during the early 1920s that French Communists, inspired by Lenin's anticolonial ideology, helped mobilize North African workers in France. By founding organizations such as the Intercolonial Union and its newspaper *le Paria* (Pariah) in 1922, and convening the first congress of North African workers in 1924, French Communists were influential in politicizing and encouraging North Africans to articulate their grievances about French colonial rule.

With the organizational skills and funding provided by French Communists, militants from the North African immigrant community were able to establish the *Étoile nord-africane* (North African Star) in 1926. The goal of the *Étoile nord-africane* (ENA), founded by Messali Hadj and Hadj Ali Abdelkader, was to "fight for the total independence of three countries: Tunisia, Algeria, and Morocco, and for the unity of North Africa." Dissolved on several occasions by French authorities, the ENA tapped into the resources of Algerian "notables" who ran restaurants, cafés, and hotels within the immigrant community to denounce the evils of imperialism. Through its newspapers and meetings the ENA took an active stand against the special security and control measures imposed on North Africans during the interwar years.[1]

With the outbreak of the Algerian War in 1954, the Algerian community in France became an important source of funding and the site of violent clashes between rival nationalist organizations. At the start of the war over

200,000 Algerians resided in France—a number that would increase to more than 350,000 by the end of the conflict.[2] By the late 1950s approximately half of all Algerian earnings returned to Algeria in the form of remittances—a figure that in 1957 equaled "a third of the total Algerian budget or a quarter of all earnings."[3] Faced with the escalating costs of war, the ability to exploit this wealth was critical to the struggle for independence.

It was precisely because the Algerian immigrant community grew in importance during the war that violent clashes erupted between the leading nationalist organizations. The newly created National Liberation Front (FLN), whose actions launched the war in Algeria, was little known in France. Far more established was the Algerian National Movement (MNA). Its leader, Messali Hadji, was one of the founding fathers of Algerian nationalism and a living icon within the Algerian immigrant community. At the start of the conflict a rhetorical war raged in the pages of newspapers belonging to the FLN and the MNA.[4] It was only after several years of internecine bloodletting, costing the lives of at least 3,800 Algerians and wounding nearly twice that number, that the FLN was eventually able to displace the MNA.[5]

After contributing their blood and money to the cause of independence Algerian immigrants found their rights and privileges severely restricted during the postcolonial period. In keeping with concerns about maintaining an ethnic balance French authorities began to ratchet up controls on North Africans during the 1970s. Making it harder for immigrants to acquire work permits, change jobs, or reunite with their families, French authorities ultimately elaborated plans to deport several hundred thousand Algerians from France. Although immigration controls were supposed to be counterbalanced by an array of integration policies, little was done "to treat immigrants as a part of French society or to encourage immigrants' emergence as autonomous actors."[6]

Facing an increasingly hostile French government, immigrants were not able to count on the protection of home governments and were uneasy about support offered by leftist organizations. Rather than alleviating the sentiment of insecurity, home governments often worked in collaboration with French authorities to keep tabs on the immigrant community. Just as North African regimes sought to control the working class at home, "the role of associations and other societies more or less officially established in France is to intimidate, control, even denounce political and militant elements."[7] On the left immigrants were always at risk of being caught up in political and class struggles that were not their own. Although many immigrants were attracted to extreme left movements, "they were wary of the political motivations of their guachiste allies and resented serving as symbols of exploitation and oppression for a movement which did not always treat them with equal respect."[8] It was precisely because they felt threatened from all sides that it became paramount to establish autonomous immigrant worker movements.

During the early 1970s militant North African students took the lead in mobilizing the immigrant community. Already organized in response to the Six Day War and the Palestinian question, these militant students quickly adopted the cause of oppressed immigrant workers in France. Clandestine organizations such as the Palestinian Committee and the Arab Workers Movement organized hunger strikes, work stoppages, and demonstrations against repressive anti-immigration measure and the escalation of racial violence targeting North African workers. A series of "Festivals of Immigrant Worker Popular Theater" took place between 1975 and 1979 to "express their culture and experience as immigrants through drama, film, music, dance, and print."[9] During the last half of the 1970s massive and prolonged rent strikes were launched by the residents of the SONACOTRA foreign worker hostels. While sparked by sharp and sudden rent increases, the much broader demands included "greater privacy guarantees, the designation of Islamic prayer sites, the right to sign a lease and be recognized as tenants rather than simple residents, and most crucially, the right to elect their own recognized representatives in negotiations with the authorities."[10]

While immigrants devised their own often unconventional forms of mobilization, their success in securing important housing concessions and workplace rights hinged on the support of a broad range of French allies. Through their autonomous actions immigrants were able to generate a considerable degree of awareness and support among left-wing political parties and trade unions. "The French left as a whole gradually grew more sensitive to the needs of non-native workers. Its organizations exhibited greater tolerance for the specific nature of many of their demands, and less for discrimination."[11] Traditionally harboring somewhat paternalist attitudes toward immigrant communities in their care, Catholic and Protestant solidarity groups together with other church-based organizations gained a newfound respect for postcolonial minorities. "Cooperation was facilitated to the extent that French allies during this period demonstrated a growing responsiveness and respect for immigrants' aspirations to become full participants in their own destiny." Humanitarian organizations and trade unions offered a greater degree of representation to immigrants and the Socialist party backed autonomous forms of protest, the freedom of association and the right to vote at the municipal level. Church-based groups were especially active in supporting and encouraging immigrant initiatives.[12] "But despite the objections voiced by some immigrant activists to their treatment by the French left and their crusade for a genuinely autonomous movement, in practice, virtually all efforts at collective action were based on sustained cooperation and interaction between immigrants and allies."[13]

Mobilizing North African Youth

By the late 1970s the children of North African workers came of age and became involved in the struggle for recognition. However, many North African youth had trouble identifying with the plight and struggles of immigrant workers. They frequently rejected the humiliations experienced by their parents and refused to be bound to a working-class status. Nationalist sentiments were even less important. Algerian sons and daughters were often shocked by the degree of corruption and abusive authoritarianism they discovered on visits to Algeria. Although they shared strong attachments to their parents' homeland and took pride in Algerian independence, they distrusted the FLN government and its political wing in France, the Amicale des Algériens en Europe (Association of Algerians in Europe).

The older generation of militants also failed to recognize the particular concerns of North African youth.

> First-generation immigrant associations and groupings were built on the dominant idea of returning to the country of origin. Their struggles were therefore centered on juridical questions, on the workplace, and on democratic alternatives in their home countries. They failed to see that this new generation had come of age and didn't understand its specificities. Foreign students who came to France to complete their studies were often cut off from the reality of the cities. They lived in their university residences and their attention was centered on supporting "immigrant workers."[14]

There were some prominent attempts to bridge the generational divide. Most notably was the news magazine *Sans Frontière* (1979–1985). Casting itself as a magazine "for and by immigrants," *Sans Frontière* journalists included a number of North African youth active in or who went on to become involved in a variety of cultural endeavors. However, most of the direction remained tightly controlled by former militants of the Arab Workers Movement whom North African youth from France continued to regard as a distinct group with very different sensibilities. It was the failure to bridge this generational divide and the ultimate decision by North Africans from France to leave *Sans Frontière* that contributed to the final demise of the magazine.[15]

Didier Lapeyronnie and François Dubet argue that collective political action by North African youth was not the product of national or class-consciousness but rather a successful assimilation of mainstream French values and cultural practices. By just about every measure—mixed marriages, birthrates, cultural practices—North African youth have adopted the norms and forms of French culture.[16] Yet despite this successful process of acculturation they still remain second-class citizens. In particular, institutional forms of racism and discrimination (educational tracking, police oppression, judicial prejudice), racially motivated assaults, or more ordinary difficulties (job or apartment searches) serve as daily reminders of the reality of exclusion. Racism targeting North Africans, Lapeyronnie explains, is an attempt to artificially construct new boundaries and dividing lines precisely because real cultural differences have become negligible. The gap between the hopes and expectations for social mobility and the reality of racial discrimination generates a deep sense of frustration or moral indignation among the progeny of North African workers that can trigger diverse forms of protest.

Lapeyronnie is correct to point out that discrimination, racism, and other forms of disrespect can trigger various kinds of protest. Drawing from Gunnar Myrdal's 1944 study of race relations in America, Lapeypronnie notes that it is precisely because ethnic minorities have embraced the dominant values that racial discrimination generates sentiments of hatred, anger, frustration, or moral indignation capable of fueling revolt.[17] While it is an exaggeration to claim that North Africans raised in France have been whitewashed leaving them with no attachments to their cultural heritage, they have certainly adopted French egalitarian values and aspirations that make the fear of deportation, substandard housing, school tracking, police harassment, and an often-biased justice system particularly unacceptable. Moreover, when social mobility is blocked, when equal opportunities are denied, this frustration can spark diverse forms of protest.

Building on the work of Friedrich Hegel and George Herbert Mead, Axel Honneth posits that mis- or nonrecognition, which can also be understood as disrespect, can damage our psychological health. In the modern age when group identities have given way to the triumph of individualism we are all vulnerable and dependent on others in forming our own sense of self.

What the term "disrespect" refers to is the specific vulnerability of humans resulting from the internal interdependence of individualization and recognition, which both Hegel and Mead helped to illuminate. Because the normative self-image of each and every individual human being—his or her "me," as Mead put it—is dependent on the possibility of being continually backed up by others, the experience of disrespect carries with it the danger of an injury that can bring the identity of the person as a whole to the point of collapse.[18]

Our psychological integrity hinges on the recognition extended by others. When recognition is denied, when we are disrespected, the results are similar to those of a disease or infection. "The experience of being socially denigrated or humiliated endangers the identity of human beings, just as infections with a disease endangers their physical life."[19] However, as with an illness the symptoms of disrespect, such as shame, rage, hurt, or indignation can also alert us to the malady and inspire a course of healing.

Nacer Kettane, himself a medical doctor, writes that during the Giscard presidency (1974–1981) a deepening climate of insecurity and intolerance created a kind of psychosis among North African youth. "The arbitrary expulsions, racial attacks, vexing measures against workers nurtured an understandable insecurity psychosis within the North African community." However it was precisely this sentiment of fear and insecurity, according to Kettane that motivated the first collective actions. Subject to what Kettane described as the "double tutelage" of the Algerian government and French antiracist movements, autonomous forms of mobilization nevertheless took some time to emerge.[20]

Cultural initiatives were among the earliest collective projects by immigrant youth. Beginning in the mid-1970s, amateur theater provided an important outlet for youth to organize and present individual and group experiences within a structured and coherent discourse. In the early 1980s, rock concerts in Paris (Rock Against Police) and Lyon areas (Zaâma de banlieue) allowed immigrants artists to express their grievances while attempting to inform and mobilize other French and minority youths against the rise of intolerance toward foreigners in France.[21]

Some youth chose to express themselves through more violent forms of confrontation. In summer 1981, riots broke out in the Lyon area suburb of Les Minguettes pitting immigrant youth against French police. In one of the first urban riots covered by the national media, a shocked French public viewed pictures of immigrant youth joyriding in stolen cars, which they defiantly set ablaze in front of French police. It was the completely spontaneous and uncontrolled nature of these events, known as the *rodéos*, that distinguished Les Minguettes from other popular revolts linked to working-class structures and more traditional forms of protest.[22]

Initiatives taken by the newly elected Socialist government following the riots at Les Minguettes brought an end, at least temporarily, to violent forms of confrontation. An array of social measures helped quell tensions in cities such as Les Minguettes with high concentrations of ethnic minorities, few social outlets, and disproportionate exposure to the problems of unemployment, drugs abuse, and delinquency. Yet perhaps even more effective in mitigating urban/ethnic tensions was the decision to extend equal rights of association.[23]

For decades foreigners had been subject to a 1939 decree law enacted during the turbulent months prior to the outbreak of World War II. This law required any association in which foreigners represented more than one quarter of the members, or with one foreigner on the administrative council, to receive authorization from the Ministry of the Interior.[24] Such authorizations were limited in duration and "could be revoked at any time."[25] The abrogation of the 1939 decree law precipitated an explosion of minority associations specializing in everything from sports to social work. According to Saïd Bouziri, vice president of the National Council of Immigrant Populations, some 300–350 associations were created from 1981 to 1982 and 500–600 from 1990 to 1991.[26]

Granting equal rights of association was just one of several gestures by the Socialist government that seemed to herald a radical departure from previously confrontational relations and the possibility of more far-reaching forms of recognition. Since the 1970s the Socialists had lent their support to the immigrant workers movements. From legislation sponsoring the right to vote and a ten-year combined residency and work permit to its public support for the SONACOTRA rent strikers and the vow to end the expulsion of immigrant youth convicted of minor offences, the Socialists and their presidential candidate François Mitterrand had long been important advocates for ethnic minority rights in France.[27]

This support was part of a larger effort by the Socialist leadership to transform and broaden their shrinking electoral base during the 1970s. In competition with the Communist party the Socialists targeted not only advocates of ethnic minority rights but also feminists, ecologists, and women's rights advocates who formed the "New Left." "What is most striking and original about PS action during the first half of the 1970s," notes Robert Ladresh, "was the significance given to incorporating various movement activities into the party."[28] Among the New Left elements integrated into the Socialist party leadership were a number of those involved in the immigrant workers movement. Newly incorporated members of the New Left fostered greater awareness of immigrant issues, "encouraged the intervention of party leaders and activists in immigrant struggles, and cultivated ties between the party and anti-racist, solidarity and immigrant associations."[29]

Once in power in 1981, after over 20 years of unbroken conservative rule, the Socialists made good on a number of promises. In addition to granting equal rights of association, the government ordered a halt to the deportation of immigrant youths for minor offences and regularized over 100,000 illegal aliens. The infusion of government social support into beleaguered cities like Les Minguettes was part of a general reformist spirit and a greater willingness to address the exclusionary socioeconomic conditions affecting French and ethnic minority residents alike.[30] The Social Action Fund (FAS), the government agency chiefly responsible for subsidizing ethnic minority associations, experienced a doubling of its funds between 1980 and 1983.[31]

Writing during the early 1980s it was possible for scholars to conclude that the Socialist government was embracing a new policy of "ethnocultural accommodation" and moving away from a traditional Jacobin suspicion of group cultures and identities. The massive introduction of postcolonial populations during the 1960s and 1970s had made France a multicultural society where more emphasis would have to be placed on ethnic minority rights and cultures. "The immigrant problem could no longer be dealt with by expulsion or 'law-and-order,' France had become a multiethnic and multicultural society."[32] "With the election of the Socialists in 1981, who pursued a policy of decentralization, and with the rejuvenation of regionally based social movements, France appeared to be moving down the road toward a more pluralist society."[33]

The March for Equality and Against Racism

It was within this political context that North African youth stepped into the national limelight by organizing a series of protest marches on Paris. The 1983 March for Equality and Against Racism, the first and most prominent of the marches, grew out of a heightened sense of insecurity among North African youth. Since fall 1982, North African youth had become the target of an alarming number of racially motivated assaults. According to Radio Beur, an influential station with the Paris-area North African community, between October 1982 and September 1983 there were at least 44 violent attacks on immigrant youth, with 19 dead and 45 injured.[34] During the municipal elections of March 1983 the far-right National Front scored its first electoral victories on a virulent anti-immigration platform. National Front leader Jean-Marie Le Pen influenced French politics with a level of unabashed racist rhetoric not seen since the Vichy period.

In his personal account Bouzid recalled the sense of anxiety among North African youth just prior to the March. The series of racial murders, "forty-eight within eighteen months," seemed like a wave of terrorism. "One more drop of additional racist horror would suffice to trigger an explosion…Which is what some were most certainly waiting for so they could massacre us *legitimately*."[35] Pushed by what he described as a growing sense of paranoia, Bouzid felt a need to do something. This paranoia, Bouzid added, was shared by many others. "I think that paranoia is, like an inferiority complex, the lot of all those who suffer from racism: you reach the point where everything can be explained in terms of the *bête immonde* (horrible beast)."[36]

Within this climate of mounting tensions and insecurity, the wounding of Toumi Djaïdja, shot in the chest by a French police officer, provided the final spark that ignited the March. Djaïdja was one of the leaders of the association SOS Avenir Minguettes, which only a few months before had lead a successful hunger strike against French police actions in the Lyon suburb. In the weeks following the shooting, members of SOS Avenir Minguettes rallied around Djaïdja. With the advice of Father Christian Delorme plans were elaborated for a peaceful cross-country protest march on Paris. The March for Equality and Against Racism ultimately became a national event in which North African youth and their French allies converged on Paris on December 3, 1983.

The media attention and popular support generated by the March catapulted North African youth into the national spotlight. Some 100,000 demonstrators participated in the festivities that followed the arrival of the March in Paris. President Mitterrand himself greeted some of the leaders at the Elysée Palace and promised to respond to their key demands—a ten-year combined work and residency card for foreign workers and their families, a plan to study more severe forms of punishment for racially motivated crimes, and a more serious consideration of the right of foreigners to vote in local elections. Mitterrand's decision to issue a ten-year combined work and residency card for foreign workers was widely regarded as the crowning achievement of the March.[37]

Distrust and the Unraveling of the Associational Movement

Yet what becomes evident throughout Bouzid's account of the March are the lingering suspicions, doubts, and general lack of confidence and trust among North African youth in their French allies and supporters. From the outset Bouzid comments that he was shocked and surprised that French natives could ever feel any compassion for North African youth. "White and French, living in France, he had all that was necessary to possess a sense of superiority. He could have, at the least, been indifferent to the problems of immigrants. But no, he didn't hesitate to take to the street to fight against the injustices affecting them while I hesitated."[38] Despite this revelation Bouzid comments repeatedly on the fear among the marchers that their movement might be manipulated or co-opted by outsiders. After being treated to a warm reception by a conservative community Bouzid wonders whether they were only using the marchers to ease their guilt. In short, Bouzid is never able to shake his doubts and uncertainties about the sincerity of the March's French supporters.

Using the examples of rape and torture victims Axel Honneth argues that our trust and confidence in others can be fundamentally damaged by those who disrespect our physical integrity. Assaults on our physical freedom represent what Honneth describes as the "most fundamental sort of degradation. This is because every attempt to gain control of a person's body against his or her will—irrespective of the intention behind it—causes a degree of humiliation that impacts more destructively than other forms of respect on a person's practical relation to self." When we are disrespected physically we loose our basic confidence and trust in ourselves and others acquired from relations of love within the family. "Physical abuse represents a type of disrespect that does lasting damage to one's basic confidence (learned through love) that one can autonomously coordinate one's own body." It is a form of disrespect that results in "social shame" and "the loss of trust in oneself and the world, and this affects all practical dealings with other subjects, even at a physical level."[39]

Central to the March was an attempt to speak out against racial violence by remembering the dead. Bouzid notes how t-shirts and posters were made with the faces of victims of racist murders. Several victims of particularly onerous crimes received special attention. The marchers sent a delegation to visit the mother of Taoufik Ouannes, a nine-year-old boy shot to death by a French neighbor just prior to the March—the motive for the murder was the noise made by Ouannes and his friends playing in their housing development. During the March another delegation laid a wreath at the Lunéville train station in memory of Habib Grimzi, a young Algerian thrown to his death from the window of a moving train by French Foreign Legion recruits. Both *Sans Frontière*'s special volume devoted to the March and Bouzid's account include chronological lists of North African victims of racist assaults.[40]

The paranoia and psychosis referred to by Kettane and Bouzid are references to the racial crimes and threats of deportation that quite literally threatened the legitimacy and permanence of North African bodies in France. This context, together with the very real efforts to organize the mass repatriation of North African families in France, created a powerful source of anxiety among immigrant youth that both fueled diverse forms of protest and undermined trust and confidence in French society. Identifying himself with stateless Palestinians, Bouzid repeatedly comments that he is in search of the "planet dignity," a place where he will be free from racism, where he will finally be able to belong.[41]

The unwillingness or inability to maintain alliances with French supporters is foremost among explanations for the failure to sustain the momentum generated by the March. Even before the end of the March several associations were critical of its "missionary character." The crux of their discontent was the influential role played by religious and humanitarian associations. Moreover, they denounced French politicians for using the March as a means of creating a more progressive public image.[42] The choice between autonomy and the formation of a broader coalition became the chief bone of contention at the Lyon Assises (June 9–11, 1984)—a national conference held after the March to debate the future course of the associational movement. The 400 representatives from 50 associations who attended the conference agreed on the need to advance the process of social and political inclusion of immigrant youth into French society. They were unanimous in rejecting both the French assimilationist model of citizenship and the formation of an ethnically entrenched and consequently "ghettoized" movement. However they failed to reach any kind of operational consensus and their objectives remained vague.

The Lyon Assises split into two principal groupings of associations—the Paris and Lyon collectives. Members of the Lyon collective, responsible for organizing and hosting the conference, supported an autonomous movement. They argued that the March, designed to combat right-wing forces of exclusion and marginalization, had been manipulated by the left that sought to influence and exploit a nascent ethnic minority political movement. Only by consolidating an autonomous political force could the movement preserve its integrity. The Paris collective and its supporters warned that any effort to fight against the surge of racism and xenophobia in France could only succeed with the help of strong allies within the context of a larger social struggle. They argued for a broad alliance that would include other minority communities as well as progressive political and social forces.[43] The Lyon conference ultimately ended in failure. Unable or unwilling to reach a consensus the representatives disbanded and returned home. Both the Paris and the Lyon collectives eventually broke apart and a planned follow-up conference at Saint-Etienne drew only a small number of followers.

The success of the March was its fusion of three elements—solidarity movements, immigrant associations, and the political left. However, this was the first and last time this fusion was achieved.[44] What surfaced at the Lyon meeting was a general distrust and unwillingness to collaborate with larger movements. "Many associational activists, although willing to participate in assemblies that allowed for an exchange of experiences and ideas, distrusted formal organization structures and were unwilling to associate with a formal movement." With the failure to elaborate a clear agenda, power struggles, and the absence of any leader with a broad following the meeting broke down into "personal quarrels dividing Paris and Lyon, 'communitarians' and 'multiculturalists,' 'Beurs' and 'banlieue youth.'"[45]

A second march, entitled Convergence 84, was organized in an attempt to consolidate and strengthen a rapidly disintegrating movement. Convergence consisted of five groups on mopeds departing from five French cities (Dunkirk, Strasbourg, Marseilles, Toulouse, and Brest) on November 3 and converging on Paris on December 1, 1984. Each of the five groups took shape around a core of North African, Antillean, Portuguese, African, Asian, and French riders who represented France's ethnic diversity. The theme of Convergence—"France is like a moped, it takes a mixture to work (oil and gasoline)," or "let's live together with our commonalities, regardless of our differences,"—and its diverse ethnic composition reflected the more inclusive, alliance-based philosophy of its leaders.[46]

In many respects Convergence represented a retreat to a Republican position. By grounding their movement in a broad coalition of French and ethnic groups, the leaders of Convergence tried to distance themselves from the more ethnically specific 1983 March, also known as the Beur March due to the preponderant role played by North African youth. The title of the demonstration was an explicit renunciation of the call for the right to difference that had been a prominent theme in the 1983 March. Farida Belghoul, one of the leaders and initiators of Convergence, argued that a defense of ethnic, racial, or religious differences would only result in the segregation and exclusion of France's diverse minority groups.[47]

But Convergence was unable to live up to its ideals. Not long after it began some of the protestors grew resentful of the influence of French militants and became frustrated by the disinterest of urban minorities.[48] Following an altercation between a North African participant and a French militant, the movement split into two groups: those who remained faithful to the alliance-based approach and those who argued for an autonomous, North African movement. When the protestors arrived in Paris, Farida Belghoul, leader of the Marseilles–Paris contingent, switched her support from the original alliance concept to those who warned against the growing influence of external parties.[49] In a scathing speech delivered to a crowd of over 30,000 supporters at the Place de la République, Belghoul rebuked the

French militants who, in her opinion, were too personally detached to understand the reality of immigrant youth. In Belghoul's opinion, Convergence had only revealed the widening gap between a socially and economically estranged French left and an increasingly marginalized immigrant youth relegated to a rapidly deteriorating urban universe.[50]

A third and final March, entitled Divergence, took place in 1985. With the goal of promoting a greater degree of electoral participation among immigrant youth, Divergence adopted a more autonomous organizational strategy. While praised in some North African accounts for refusing to submit to the authority of French allies, the low turnout on the arrival of Divergence in Paris revealed the need to forge broad coalitions. In contrast to the "meager crowd of some 4,000 in Paris," SOS-Racisme, the newly created broad-based antiracist movement, drew over 50,000 supporters to its own celebration following the conclusion of its "Tour de France" one week after Divergence. While Divergence was snubbed by the political elite SOS was welcomed by a delegation of dignitaries including Prime Minister Laurent Fabius and Minister of Social Affairs Georgina Dufoix.[51]

A Movement Co-opted?

SOS-Racisme became a convenient scapegoat among North Africans to explain the failure of the associational movement. SOS has been charged with lifting the tactics of the associational movement (support concerts, antiracist themes) while reducing and simplifying the earlier struggle to the combat against racism. Accused of being a tool of the Socialist government, SOS has also been discredited for its supposed ties to the French Jewish Students Union—a group that supports the Israeli state and is hostile to the PLO.[52] Nacer Kettane, one of the initiators and organizers of Divergence, writes that SOS-Racisme "was an organization perceived by almost all the youth associations as a mechanism for depersonalizing and dismantling their movement still in its infancy." Kettane adds that SOS was regarded as a media machine, gravitating to the newsworthy people and issues of the day but with little real interest in the real problems confronting immigrant youth. "To some," Kettane notes, "SOS seemed like a leveraged buyout by the Jewish community to build voter support for the left in the next legislative elections, for others, as a machine to divert the beur movement."[53]

Writing in *Sans Frontière*, Farida Belghoul accused SOS-Racisme of being both detached from the history of the North African youth movement and exploiting inoffensive morsels of the movement. Referring to the 1983 March, Convergence and initiatives going back to Rock Against Police, Belghoul claimed that SOS had little to do with the history of North African struggles. Instead, she argued that SOS had reduced this history to the fight against racism. "By addressing immigration only in terms of a single moral point of view," Belghoul concluded that SOS-Racisme had become the "source of all kinds of misunderstandings, confusion, and solidarities emptied of their social content." For Belghoul SOS was simply another manifestation of external solidarity seeking to expropriate and limit the struggle of North African youth to its own moral agenda without being willing to take on the real inequalities and injustices plaguing ethnic minorities in France. Citing the African American militant Eldrige Cleaver Belghoul concluded with the following quote:

> There are many people who are eager to think for us, even if we are the ones doing the dying. But they are not ready to go all the way and die for us. If we want to die for our ideas, they should at least be our own; we need to end this servility that inspires us to die for the all the causes and all the mistakes...except our own.[54]

It would be unfair to dismiss the charges and accusations leveled at SOS-Racisme by North African political actors simply as the ravings of paranoid and distrustful individuals suffering from the psychologically ravaging effects of disrespect and nonrecognition. Both SOS-Racisme and its rival France Plus benefited from strong ties to various political currents with the Socialist government.[55] Long-time supporters of the immigrant workers movement, the Socialists found themselves deprived of viable intermediaries following the rise of the North African youth movement. In the absence of such intermediaries different currents within the Socialist party struggled over the "symbolic control of the beur movement."

Vincent Geisser offers two scenarios for how this struggle played out. The first is that one fringe group within the Socialist party, led by Julian Drey, created SOS-Racisme as the vehicle for taking over the associational movement and forged an alliance with Laurent Fabius and his supporters to achieve this goal. The second scenario is that Lionel Jospin, then secretary general of the Socialist party, backed the creation of France Plus to block the Fabius group. While SOS, at least in its early years, sponsored a multicultural society, France Plus adopted a counter discourse promoting civic participation through a traditional assimilationist Republican discourse.[56] State funding for both SOS-Racisme and France Plus increased throughout the 1980s, even after the Socialists lost their parliamentary majority to a center–right coalition between 1986 and 1988.[57]

The French state does possess tremendous power to channel, block, or facilitate social movements in France. Following the failure of Convergence, the Socialist leadership provided funding and logistical support that helped

SOS-Racisme fill the void. "From the start, SOS-Racisme benefited from the logistical, financial, and moral support of the government, the PS, and the left-leaning press."[58] Whereas the Socialists cut off support for many new social movements following their rise to power, SOS-Racisme was one of the exceptions in receiving generous state support. Not surprisingly, most of the new social movements languished during the 1980s while SOS thrived.[59]

While SOS certainly benefited from the financial support and political patronage of the Socialist party, such connections do not fully account for the organization's success. SOS was able to build support on the right and left precisely because it focused on building a moral consensus against the rise of racial intolerance and did not attempt to stake out specific, militant positions toward French immigration policies. Moreover, its moral stand against racism appealed to a new civically minded generation of French youth that took shape during the 1980s. Distanced and suspicious of the realm of traditional politics, this so-called moral generation was eager to engage in new approaches to the problems of inequality and injustice. Casting itself as a pluri-cultural movement, SOS appealed to generational unity and avoided the criticisms of the *Beur* movement often criticized for representing only a single ethnic minority community. From the several hundred thousand yellow "hands off my buddy" (Touche Pas à Mon Pot) badges sold for one dollar a piece in the months after its creation to the crowd of over 300,000 that turned out for its star-studded concert at Paris' Place de la Concorde, SOS's marketing and media skills were recognized by all. SOS certainly enjoyed support in high places; however, "it is exaggerated and misleading to understand SOS as the pure product of the intervention and manipulation of the Elysée and the Socialist party, as many critics later charged, or to account for its success solely on the basis of its ties to political elites."[60]

If one of SOS's greatest strengths was its ability to reach out and forge broad alliances this was also one of the North African associational movements most obvious weaknesses. If Mitterrand and influential figures within the Socialist party were willing to work with SOS-Racisme, it was because they recognized its potential. By contrast, "the Beur movement showed itself to be divided, prone to insistence on radical demands, mistrustful of political support and protective of its autonomy, which made it a difficult partner especially during a period when immigration was considered a major political risk."[61]

The Republican Consensus

It was the rise to national prominence of Jean-Marie Le Pen and the far right National Front in the 1983 municipal elections that made immigration such a political risk. Capitalizing on the disarray of the right following the Socialist victory in 1981 and the uncertainty caused by the failure of the Socialists to reverse the economic downturn, the far right cast immigration as the source of the nation's perceived ills. Beyond its charges that immigrants and their children were weighing on the welfare system, taking French jobs, and fueling the growth of crime and insecurity, the far right raised fundamental questions about French national identity. By skillfully appropriating the right to differ- ence discourse previously associated with the left, the far right suggested that what was at risk was the preservation of France's cultural identity. Immigrant communities, especially Muslim North Africans, were too culturally different to be assimilated and posed a direct threat to French culture. Only by restor- ing and preserving the integrity of French culture, namely by repatriating postcolonial minorities and reinforcing national sovereignty, was there any hope for a recovery and restoration of national greatness.[62]

In propagating its message the far right received considerable assistance from the mainstream right in search of a response to the Socialist victory. The publications of "new Right" intellectuals and conservative clubs such as Alain Griotteray's *Les Immigrés: Le Choc* and *La Préférance Nationale: Réponse à l'Immigration* by Jean-Yves Le Gallou and le Club de l'Horloge helped circu- late and lend legitimacy to the far right's differentialist discourse. Cover issues of conservative magazines, such as the October 1985 issue of *Le Figaro* featuring a bust of Marianne draped in a headscarf and veil with the caption—"will we still be French in 30 years?"—only served to further enflame xenophobic sentiments.[63]

During the campaign for the 1983 municipal elections the far right was not alone in exploiting the theme of immigration. "In dozens of cities" main- stream conservative candidates also "played on the fear of growing crime and disorder, closely associated with the presence of immigrants, as a way to cap- ture popular disenchantment with the country's economic and social condi- tions."[64] While the actual impact of immigration on the outcome of the elections is unclear, it was perceived to be of crucial importance by the Socialist leadership. It was the sentiment that the left's favorable positions toward immigration had made them especially vulnerable that would have an important impact on future immigration policies.[65]

The Socialist response was ultimately to adopt a tougher stance toward immigration, to distance themselves from the right to difference, and finally to embrace the new concept of Republican integration. By 1984 the Socialists were reversing their earlier position and adopting more rigid immi- gration policies—tightening controls on illegal aliens, erecting new restric- tions to complicate the process of family reunification, and reintroducing financial incentives for the repatriation of foreign residents.[66] In response to both the "divisiveness of second-generation politics and the rise of Le Pen," the Socialists moved away from their earlier support for the right to difference and began to emphasize commonalities with new campaigns such as *vivre ensemble* (living together).[67]

We need to be careful not to exaggerate the Socialist's support for the right to difference. While this discourse certainly became popular on the left in the 1970s "one finds few if any official references to notions such as 'difference,' 'ethnic pluralism' or a 'multicultural society,'" once the Socialists came to power. However, it is equally important to recognize that the Socialists were also not committed to any particular national model of incorporation. Yet as the right rose to prominence on a differentialist discourse and elements of the left rejected difference as potentially segregationist "the New Left factions associated with cultural pluralism declined in favor of a resurgent Jacobinism."[68] By the mid-1980s both the left and the right had embraced a supposedly traditional Republican model of integration that served their mutual interests.

The concept of Republican integration, as articulated by the Nationality Commission's response to the proposed reforms to the Nationality Code in 1986, expressed a deep suspicion of the tribalizing effect of group identities. Instead, the Commission advocated a supposedly traditional model of integration based on shared rights, duties, and values and the relegation of difference to the realm of the private sphere. For the right, integration offered the possibility of differentiating themselves from the intolerance of the extreme right. For the left, integration allowed them to deflect earlier charges that their support for cultural pluralism risked undermining the unity of the nation. "But from 1987 on, all the mainstream political parties, along with most intellectual elites and important immigrant rights activists, backed a conception of the nation that was open but unitary, in which immigrants could participate but exclusively on an individual basis and not as members of communities with particular rights or status."[69]

Localization and the "Beurgeoisie"

Since the end of the 1980s, minority associations have become increasingly protective of their autonomy and detached from the events of the early 1980s. Jocelyne Ceasari's research on North African associations in Marseille and its environs reveals that most associations are rooted in specific neighborhoods and centered on a variety of leisure activities—sports, music, dance. These associations demonstrate considerable skepticism and reticence toward initiatives extending beyond the local community. Efforts to form larger federations, even at the local or regional level, have been largely unsuccessful. Moreover, most of these associations have no strong connection to the earlier protest movements. Their members, usually men between the ages of 16 and 25, are either too young or chose not to participate in events like the 1983 March or Convergence 84. Furthermore, worsening urban conditions, mounting unemployment, and the proliferation of drugs, lead them to view these earlier struggles as complete failures.[70]

Despite the emphasis minority associations place on their autonomy, they have gradually become more dependent on state and local subsidies. Support from municipal governments or state agencies such as the FAS provides the means to pay for permanent or part-time staff, to secure suitable facilities and equipment, and to engage in larger, more ambitious projects. The role of the FAS, the chief source of subsidies for minority associations, has grown dramatically since the early 1980s. The number of minority associations subsidized by the FAS increased from 300 in 1983 to 4,000 in 1991. During this same period, between 1980 and 1990, the FAS budget doubled from 600 million to 1.2 billion francs. While the vast majority of FAS resources have traditionally targeted noncultural activities such as housing and job training, it has considerably beefed up its support for minority associations.[71]

The increasingly prominent role played by state agencies in relation to minority associations has created a number of problems. Saliha Amara claims that government support has had a debilitating effect on minority initiatives. Minority activists no longer know how to survive without recourse to state subsidies. Moreover, rather than devising and engaging in meaningful social or cultural activities, associational leaders devote more and more of their time to administrative duties (i.e., applying for subsidies).

> I came to realize that I was spending all my time filling out forms, writing letters, I had become an administrator. I was managing a big machine and while I was managing I couldn't do other things, or at least I couldn't give them my full attention. We all became administrators of associations... and no longer intervened in the real social and political conflicts.

Many associational leaders have converted their positions into full-time jobs. Amara, who works has a high school literature teacher, was quick to point out that her managerial responsibilities at ANGI were strictly voluntary.[72]

Some minority leaders have either been directly absorbed into mainstream political parties or have been elevated to the status of intermediaries. On the one hand, intermediaries facilitate and make possible a dialogue between their community and the political establishment, helping to mitigate potentially explosive problems or mounting tensions. On the other hand, increased interaction or collaboration with French authorities undermines the legitimacy and credibility of minority intermediaries among their supporters and constituents. Immigrant youth, who experience worsening economic and social conditions and the persistence of racism and discrimination, often regard these intermediaries as a new "beurgoisie" motivated more by individual career interests and professional sensibilities than what they perceive to be the real needs and concerns of their community. The failure of these elites to prevent or control a series of riots that exploded in a number of French cities in the early 1990s (Vaulx-en-Velin, Sartrouville, Mantes-La-Jolie) offered some indications of their fragile positions among urban minorities.

North Africans did not withdraw from the struggle for recognition during the last years of the Mitterrand administration. From the fight against the deportation of North African youth convicted of minor crimes (*double peine*) to efforts to articulate a new citizenship detached from traditional nationality requirements, activists from the North African community continued to advocate their vision of a more just and inclusive society. However, these and other initiatives have typically been limited in scope, duration, and participation. As the minority news agency IM'média reports, "the effectiveness of these specific struggles is always shaped by their conjuncture with events and never a real political perspective." "Immigrant youths," IM'média laments, "remain dispersed and without representation."[73]

Collective Memory

For veteran activists from or close to the North African community there is little hope of surmounting the explosive tensions in French cities or the fragmented and dispersed character of ethnic minority political actions without forging a collective identity. Rather than attempting to create a sense of solidarity out of past experiences of victimization, building a collective memory is understood as an effort to forge a greater critical awareness of the strengths, weakness, achievements, and failures of past struggles for recognition. This is a fundamentally present- and future-oriented notion of collective memory based on a desire to learn and benefit from past struggles for recognition. It stems from the need to avoid what is often perceived as a cyclical history of perpetual beginnings.

As early as the mid-1980s North African activists were warning of the need to forge a stronger intergenerational memory. If North African youths were to escape the assimiliationist fate of earlier waves of Polish and Italian immigrations, if they hoped to withstand the force of Jacobin traditions in France and to be recognized for their cultural specificity like the Armenian or Jewish community, Nacer Kettane argued that they needed to gain a greater understanding of their shared heritage. "The necessary affirmation of a cultural memory assumes that we must also lay claim to the past struggles of generations that preceded us in France as well as the cultural, social and political history of our countries of origin." Forging a clear and lucid memory, Kettane added, was essential to one's "mental and cultural health." Conversely, neglecting the past and heading down the road of assimilation "would simply be a denial of a part of ourselves."[74]

Yet in the wake of the 1983 March and Convergence 84, *Sans Frontière* editor Driss El Yazami claimed that forgetting past struggles was exactly what was happening. "It is amazing to see over these last few years how each movement presents itself as the initiators of the first immigrant struggles and it is distressing to see them happily take up the media refrain: the parents accepted everything and the children—look out—are going to revolutionize everything." For El Yazami, North African youth stood little chance of confronting the rise of racial intolerance without learning from the experience of past struggles. From Kabyle strikers in Marseille at the turn of the century and the formation of the Algerian nationalist movement during the interwar years to the immigrant workers moving in the 1970s, El Yazami stressed the rich history of North African struggles in France. "Rejecting this past, the beur movement has deprived itself of a part of its future, and without re-appropriating this patrimony, it will remain diminished."[75]

In the "Saga of the Beur Movement" IM'média comments that immigrant youth are locked in a cyclical history. Confronted with the "phantasms" of the Algerian past and the intolerance of parties such as the National Front, North African youth are unable to build on past militant experiences because of the "memory holes" within the North African community.

> For example, why didn't the militant experience of beurs serve as a reference for the rioters in Vaulx en Velin and elsewhere? News from the banlieues seems to take place outside the history of immigrant struggles: despite the real achievements of immigrant youth on questions as diverse as the relationship with the media and the problems of expulsions, with each local explosion of violence it is astonishing to see the same return to the starting point with calls for some form of organized reaction. It is as if the history of the banlieues was only a cyclical history. And each immigrant generation was only a generation zero.[76]

Elsewhere IM'média founder and former Rock Against Police organizer Mogniss Abdallah has explained these memory holes in terms of the pattern of immigrant struggles fragmenting than collapsing to the local level. Unable to sustain larger and long-term struggles, it is the retreat to the local level and limited nature of minority actions that accounts for the difficulty of conveying past experiences. "This limitation of perspectives engenders a weakening of the transmission of historical experiences, thus the sentiment of an eternal beginning, each immigrant generation presents itself as a generation zero."[77]

For Farid Aïchoune it is the absence of a collective memory that makes conditions in the banlieues particularly explosive. Pillaging stores and burning cars is a form of revolt by this new "dangerous class" locked out of and marginized by France's consumer society. North African youth are a "new race" like the proletarians of the nineteenth century. "We are witnessing the emergence of a generation without memory, that tries to seek revenge against all." Unmitigated by any kind of collective memory, it is the widespread sense of rage created by a deteriorating urban environment and public schools that fail to provide any promise for the future that result in acts of random violence and destruction such as the urban riots of the early 1990s.[78]

It is important to note that sentiments of failure and betrayal have complicated the transmission of memory. For many North African youth worsening conditions in urban communities serve as evidence of the failure of past struggles to affect real changes. North Africans who came of age during the 1960s and 1970s are the first to acknowledge that growing problems ranging from drugs to the breakdown of the family make it even harder for younger generations to mobilize collectively or to embrace any sense of optimism about the future. Moreover, there is also a widespread and not unfounded cynicism that many associational leaders of the past were more interested in their own social promotion than that of their community. In short, pent-up sentiments of rage and frustration that intermittently erupted across France's urban communities during the 1980s and 1990s were directed both inward and outward. Part of the task of the ongoing memory work must be to forge a sense of trust and confidence across generations within the North African community.

Forging a collective memory does not necessarily imply a strategic retreat into a communitarian past. Mehdi Lallaoui uses posters to recall the history of immigrant struggles in France since the late 1960s. Organized chronologically, *Twenty Years of Anti-Racist Posters*, includes over 300 posters illustrating the wide range of initiatives and organizations engaged in the fight for immigrant rights. Published in conjunction with a traveling exhibition and timed to correspond with the 1989 bicentennial celebrations of the French Revolution, Lallaoui situates the history of immigrant struggles as an integral part of the national story. "During the bicentennial of the French

Revolution, which carried the winds of freedom to the four corners of the world the **struggles for dignity and equality** born of the modern form of slavery that is immigration from the former colonies should not be forgotten." Rather than a rejection of French history Lallaoui positions his own narrative as a natural extension of the French past.[79]

Similarly the authors of *Contribution to the Memory of the Suburbs* evoke the French Revolutionary past when describing efforts by North African activists to promote a new form of citizenship. Here the call for a separation of citizenship from traditional nationality requirements is likened to the demands for equality made by the disenfranchised Third Estate. "One could say that once more in the history of France, those populations that are victims of exclusion initiate the political innovations for which everyone recognizes the need." Rather than contributing to the breakup of the nation, the long-standing call for a new form of citizenship is equated with that same kind of innovative, revolutionary spirit that renewed and restored the nation in the past.[80]

Ethnic minority memory also does not need to be dismissed as inevitably narrow, skewed, or nostalgic. In fact the authors of *Contributions to the Memory of the Suburbs* reject what they see as the mythical rendering of the 1983 March as a spontaneous and homogenous movement. Instead they point out the critical experience gained by associational leaders in past immigrant struggles and the wide range of interests and objectives that made it difficult to sustain the movement. In his own account of the associational movement, Farid Aïchoune is openly critical of the struggles for power and the willingness of many North African leaders to promote their own career interests over that of their community. In *J'y suis J'y reste!* Mogniss Abdallah regrets the failure to maintain a broad-based social movement and the tendency to retreat to localized communitarian actions.

The point of these works is not to present a definitive or exclusive narrative of the past but rather the wealth of militant experiences within the North African community. Testimonial memory is often employed to achieve this objective. Saliha Amara commented she was working on a collaborative project on the memory of the Algerian War through the eyes of immigrant children. "But this is also to show that our parents were militants," Amara explained.

If we are militants today it isn't coincidental, it's only part of larger history. It's important for young people to understand this historical continuity. They've been made to believe that they invented everything, that they were the first. We put this idea in the minds of those who came after us.

You could find the same thing in the press. But this isn't true, it's a continuation.

The nature of militant actions changes over time, Amara added, but it is still part of a larger history that needs to be written.[81] Conveying intergenerational memory is central to IM'média's *The Saga of the Beur Movement*. Through photos, interviews, and short articles, IM'média weaves together the diverse experiences and recollections of younger and older militants from or close to the North African community. *Contribution to the Memory of the Suburbs* is based on nearly two-dozen interviews with former or currently engaged activists. While modest in their claims, the authors of *Contribution* recognize the importance of North Africans writing their own history. "Researching and writing history are also matters of citizenship. It is necessary for us to break with the habit of delegating to 'professionals' a memory which is first and foremost the concern of citizens."[82]

Critical engagements with the past are a means of shattering the amnesia seen as debilitating minority youth in the urban present. Promoting a greater awareness of North African militant experiences is often understood as an integral part and extension of French Revolutionary traditions and an important means of revitalizing French society. Cognizant of the tremendous challenges facing the North African community, learning from the past is regarded as a best way of breaking with the cyclical history that has mired ethnic minority initiatives and building a more effective and sustainable movement in the present and future.

Conclusion

Beginning in the late 1960s North African workers mobilized in response to the failure to recognize their needs and concerns. Operating outside the traditional framework of established political parties and trade unions the immigrant workers' movement represented a new development in French society. From rent and hunger strikes to work stoppages and demonstrations, the mobilization of immigrant workers during the 1970s ultimately caused the French left to become more sensitive to the demands of foreign workers. Forging alliances and collaborative relationships with French supporters, the immigrant workers' movement succeeded in strengthening the rights of foreigner workers.

The children of North African workers who came of age in the 1970s were equally concerned about combating various forms of nonrecognition and disrespect. Born or raised in France they embraced French egalitarian ideals and were deeply offended by the lived experience of school tracking, police harassment, a color sensitive justice system, and discriminatory housing policies. Yet it was physical forms of disrespect that threatened the integrity of North African bodies—such as racial murders or the risk of deportation—that made it difficult to build much-needed alliances with French supporters. Failing to identify with the earlier immigrant workers' movement and lacking trust in their French allies, the North African associational movement was never able to reach any kind of consensus about a future strategy or course of action following the success of the 1983 March.

Given the rise of the National Front during the early 1980s the divisions and doubts within the North African associational movement became even more damaging. While both the left and the right remained eager to seek out ethnic minority intermediaries they preferred to lend their support to more pluriethnic organizations such as SOS-Racisme not rooted in a particular ethnic community and able to tap into a new civically minded generation of French youth. In short, the unraveling of the North African associational movement was both the self-inflicted result of suspicion and distrust and the product of a new political climate around the mid-1980s marked by the rise of the Republican model in which political leaders on the left and right were less inclined to collaborate with ethnically specific political movements.

After the mid-1980s the North African associational movement collapsed and receded to the local level. While North Africans activists continued to engage in a wide range of initiatives their actions tended to be sporadic and dispersed, limited in both duration and scope. Many associational leaders have been absorbed by the political establishment as intermediaries between municipal government and local populations. Both the increased dependency of associations on state subsidies and the formation of a new "beurgeoisie" of local intermediaries attest to the power of the state and French political leaders to harness and control new political forces in French society.

Through their own memory work North African activists and veterans of the associational movement have been trying to pick up the pieces. Recollecting the achievements and failures of past struggles is regarded as a much-needed remedy to the culture of amnesia among ethnic minority youth today. Rather than wallowing in sentiments of victimization or erecting a mythologized past, this is a critical reflection on the history of the immigrant workers' movement and ethnic minority mobilization in France. It is based on the belief that a sober assessment of the past has much to offer those who continue to struggle in the present. In contrast to those who posit the divisiveness of ethnic minority memory, these recollections are often situated within and are cast as an integral part of French history and traditions.

The memory work on North African political struggles has yet to rekindle the kinds of national movements witnessed during the early 1980s. However, the books, exhibitions, documentaries, and other projects completed to date have fostered a greater awareness of the rich history of the North African community and France's larger immigration story. *Le Monde* journalist Sylvia Zappi credits the memory work of documentary film producer Yamina Benguigui and the North African–run association Génériques with Prime Minister Lionel Jospin's decision to move forward with plans to build the country's first immigration history museum. A project likened by one of its advocates to New York's Ellis Island museum, "but with a more dynamic vision showcasing the creativity of immigrants in France through theater, cinema, or trade unions," the realization of a national immigration museum would certainly be a significant step forward in the recognition of France's immigration past and present.[83]

CHAPTER 2

North African Cultural Expression

F oreign workers, refugees, and asylum seekers who arrived in France since the mid-nineteenth century brought with them a rich cultural heritage. This is certainly true for France's North African community. From the earliest stages of North African immigration, singers and musicians offered a source of relief and comfort for a population of male workers in temporary exile. Through the creation of newspapers and magazines, North African militants condemned French rule in the Maghreb (Algeria, Morocco, and Tunisia) and advocated nationalist aspirations. In the postcolonial period, North African novelists, theater companies, musical performers, and a new generation of journalists helped inform the French about the condition of foreign laborers, acted as an extension of a nascent immigrant workers' movement, and provided a wealth of entertainment for a burgeoning foreign population.

Yet most of these productions targeted immigrant audiences and were linked to the problems associated with immigration or the prevailing conditions in the country of origin. North Africans born or raised in France failed to identify with these preexisting forms of cultural expression. The impetus for their cultural initiatives was not nationalism or working-class solidarity. Many rejected identification with the working-class status of their parents and had little affinity for the authoritarian regimes in North Africa. Cultural productions, much like the associational movement, functioned both as a response to the failure of the older generation to address their concerns and as a reaction to a specific set of circumstances in the 1970s and 1980s.

North Africans who came of age in the 1970s faced a serious dilemma. On the one hand, the French government was becoming increasingly hostile to the North African community. French authorities perceived the North

African population as a threat to the nation's cultural and religious composition. The 1970s saw the introduction of a series of initiatives aimed at encouraging or coercing the repatriation of North African residents. On the other hand, North African parents resisted admitting that their stay in France was no longer temporary. Acknowledging that they had settled in France on a permanent basis was tantamount to recognizing the failure of the immigrant-return dream. It was far easier to perpetuate the "myth of repatriation" by extending the anticipated date of return indefinitely.

Caught between the "myth of repatriation" and growing intolerance toward North Africans, some immigrant children turned to collective forms of cultural expression to address intergenerational tensions and to assert their right to inclusion in French society. Theater was one of the first and most popular forms of cultural expression. It was relatively affordable, required little training or technical support, and provided an ideal medium for organizing and presenting individual and group experiences. Theater companies performed primarily for immigrant and local audiences in open-air settings, community centers, residence halls, and festivals.

Because few immigrant children master Arabic or Berber, the two dominant languages in North Africa, most theater performances were in French. In fact, these theater companies, as with later forms of North African cultural expression, often contrasted the ease with which immigrant sons and daughters manipulate or move between regional or colloquial forms of French with immigrant characters who speak with heavy accents, often misuse or misunderstand words, and frequently resort to Arabic or Berber. *Verlan*, a form of slang that works by flipping the first and last syllables of words, popular among Paris-area minority youth during the 1970s and 1980s, became a prominent feature of Paris-area theater companies such as Kahina (1976–1982), Week-end à Nanterre (1977–1980), and Ibn Khaldoun (1978–1980). In recent years, however, *verlan* has been absorbed into mainstream French parlance and has lost much of its prestige as a suburban counter-language.

Theater served as a means of challenging stereotypical representations of immigrant populations and the tendency of older companies to focus on the plight of immigrant workers. Saliha Amara founded the theater company Kahina out of a sense of frustration that the French continued to perceive immigration strictly in terms of single workers.

> When we got on stage for the first time in 1976 we shattered the myth of immigration in the masculine sense of the word. In France immigration was only seen in terms of men with their suitcases who looked for work

and sent their money home to their families. Women and children didn't exist. They were completely erased from consciousness.[1]

For the members of Kahina, a troupe comprised primarily of women and named after a legendary North African warrior queen, theater offered a means of articulating and conveying the concerns and experiences of Algerian mothers and daughters to immigrant and French audiences. Kahina's two plays, "Pour que les larmes de nos mères deviennent une légende" (1976) and "La famille Ben Djelloul en France depuis 25 ans" (1979), addressed the forgotten sacrifices of Algerian women during the war for independence and the tensions experienced by daughters within immigrant families.

According to Aïssa Djabri, founder of Week-end à Nanterre, theater was in fashion in the late 1970s but the tendency was to discuss problems related to the exploitation of foreign workers, not the particular situation of immigrant youth. In contrast to Kahina, the members of Week-end à Nanterre were more interested in exploring the urban, proletarian reality experienced by the sons of immigrant workers.

> We didn't want to do the typical Manichean political play with the management on one side and workers and exploited immigrants on the other. These were things that we knew but weren't really meaningful to us and seemed to bore audiences. Kahina was too caught up in North African culture. We were interested in suburban culture…We wanted to do something different from everyone else. It was suburban culture, verlan, illegal activities, drugs…everything that was going on in the suburbs at the time. This was a proletarian culture but from the perspective of young people.

"Week-end à Nanterre" (the play and company shared the same name), centered on the exploits of three friends during an ordinary weekend in the Paris suburb of Nanterre. In the course of the weekend the friends encounter a variety of people who attempt to influence their thinking. However, for the friends, what really matters is finding money (usually through petty crime) to support their taste for expensive clothes, women, and night clubs.[2]

Some companies saw the collaboration of first- and second-generation actors. This was the case with Ibn Khaldoun, named after a medieval North African intellectual. Troupe founder Hédi Akari had been active in theater during the early 1970s in the immigrant company El-Assifa. But according to Akari, El-Assifa was much more militant and politically oriented than

Ibn Khaldoun. El-Assifa attempted to explain the situation of immigrant workers to their French colleagues at a time of escalating racial tensions following the first oil shock. In contrast, Ibn Khaldoun focused more on the tensions between immigrant parents who came to France for economic reasons and their children who grew up in France and adopted French values and cultural practices.[3]

Ibn Khaldoun's most successful play, "Mohamed Travolta," denounced the controversial government policy of imposing a double punishment (*double peine*) on North African youth. During the 1970s and 1980s hundreds of young North Africans raised in and knowing no other home than France were jailed for misdemeanor offences then deported to Algeria. "At the time there were many young beurs being deported," explained former troupe member Walid Bouazizi.

> If you committed a crime and were sentenced to six months in jail, immediately afterward you were deported. It was tragic for young people born in France, products of French culture and who were only exposed to [North African] culture through their family milieu. They didn't even know how to speak Arabic and found themselves suddenly deported to Algeria, Morocco, or Tunisia without understanding the customs, traditions, or language.[4]

Ibn Khaldoun used humor, a common devise found in many North African cultural productions, to delve into what was a very serious dilemma facing growing numbers of North African youth. Mohamed, the main character and star of the play, is a passionate fan of then popular film *Saturday Night Fever* and makes every effort to emulate its leading man, John Travolta. In the closing scenes tragedy strikes when Mohamed is arrested by French police on trumped-up charges and shipped off to Algeria where he is hopelessly out of place. So popular was the performance among local audiences that Ibn Khaldoun became more commonly known as "Mohamed Travolta."

For the theater company Chakchouka (1981–1988) comedy was a means of creating a shock effect to startle audiences into awareness. Troupe founder Adelkader Khessiba explained that they were inspired by the work of Ibn Khaldoun and hoped to take up the increasingly alarming problem of racially motivated murders in their own performances.

> At one point there were a large number of racist murders. Practically every week there were clashes with the police, French who opened fire on and killed Arabs—young people, 18, 19 and 20 years old. We wanted to

organize a performance about this ... There were maybe forty young people who died because of racist crimes—either in clashes with the police or by *Tonton flinguers*. *Tonton flinguers* are French who open fire when they get fed up with the noise. They get sent to jail for three or four months and that's it. We wanted to create a play about that. We called it "Faits Divers" because the announcements on TV that provided information about those who died were called faits divers.

Khessiba added that "Fait Divers" allowed the theater company to address a range of issues that went far beyond racial violence. From work and drugs to the condition of women in North African families, "all the societal problems related to immigrants were played out." Yet from the start the company was determined to address these difficult issues through comedy. "You laughed for an hour and a half because it was a show that made you laugh. We wanted to convey our message strictly through humor." It is at the end of the play that the audience is shocked into awareness. Watching the evening news the parents of the main character Lakhdar learn that their son's lifeless body has been discovered washed up on the banks of the Seine. It is at this point that the actors suddenly draw the performance to a close by turning to the audience and repeating—"tomorrow it could be you, tomorrow it could be you." "We wanted to shock the audience," explained Khessiba. "You laughed for an hour and a half but that isn't the point, it's that we're being killed, my sister is being forced into a marriage, I don't have work, and I'm being harassed [by the police]."[5]

Testimonial memory, a recurring feature of diverse forms of North African cultural expression during the 1980s and 1990s, was especially pronounced in most theater performances. Troupes frequently based their plays on the memories and experiences of their participants and actors often assumed roles that closely approximated their own lives. This proximity of creative expression and real-life experience gave actors a wide margin of independence to shape each performance. For example, most plays relied heavily on improvisation. In the case of "Mohamed Travolta," for instance, the actors rehearsed specific scenes but almost all of the dialogue was improvised. "The play was never written," remarked Bouazizi. "There was a storyline but within this storyline the actors were completely free to express themselves," Bouazizi added.[6] But even when scripts were produced the content often underwent considerable change and modification with the constant arrival and departure of actors. For this reason, explained Saliha Amara, there were actually three written versions of Kahina's "Pour que les larmes de nos mères deviennent une légende."[7] Similarly, Khessiba remarked that Chakchouka's plays were never static. "If you followed us you would never have seen the same show. There were always changes. Practically the whole play hinged on improvisation."[8]

This fluidity and spontaneity was not the only reason why North African theater companies became so popular among local audiences. It was also their ability to implicate audiences through debates that followed each performance and their willingness to take up a range of sensitive and potentially explosive issues. Jlaïel Hamadi recalled that audiences were always energized by Chakchouka's performances and eager to participate in the ensuing debates. "The show lasted one and a half hours but the debates could go on for two more hours. Each time people always stayed until the very end."[9] This desire to engage with audiences and to encourage debate and discussion is yet another recurring feature of many North African cultural productions.

For the first theater companies music served as a means of drawing audiences, providing entertainment during and after performances, and underscoring central themes. In their early work the actors of Kahina attracted an audience by parading through the immigrant quarter of Barbès (Paris) with traditional costumes and music. "Pour que les larmes de nos mères deviennent une légende," Kahina's first play, concluded with Hamou Cheheb's "Ma Fille" (1977), a song that reinforced the central theme of the play.[10] The theater company Ibn Khaldoun hired professional musicians and composed original music scores for its last and most ambitious play, "Ben Mohammed."[11] In the case of Week-end à Nanterre, militant theater and "second-generation" rock joined forces with the collaboration of Mounsi.

Mounsi was one of the first Algerian youths to use rock music in defense of the immigrant community. He recalled that at the time there were no second-generation North Africans who sang in French about their experiences. "Like Jacques Brel can sing about the Flemish of his [native] Belgium . . . I wanted to sing about my vision of this community in French, in the language of Molière."[12] Mounsi gravitated toward Week-end à Nanterre that corresponded to his own desire to present his personal experiences and views through creative expression. With his band he provided entertainment for the company's long-running play. After Week-end à Nanterre, Mounsi joined another collective initiative on behalf of the immigrant community, Rock Against Police (1980–1982).

Modeled after Rock Against Racism in England, Rock Against Police (RAP) was a loosely knit Paris-area organization that staged some 15 protest concerts during its two-year existence.[13] In contrast to Rock Against Racism, whose concerts took place in central and neutral areas such as Hyde Park, RAP held its concerts in transit cities and HLM housing estates in the suburban periphery—the kinds of urban spaces that were directly implicated in the problems of police injustice, racial violence, and substandard housing that were the chief concerns of the organization.[14] RAP's concerts, which were always free, provided an open and informal forum for debate. At every concert the organizers circulated a newsletter with pertinent information about conditions and events in the cities.[15]

RAP originated in response to the 1980 murder of 15-year-old Abdelkader in Vitry sur Seine and the outrage at the paltry five-year-sentence given to the murderer, the building security guard. RAP leader and longtime activist Mogniss Abdallah describes the initiative as part of a new relationship between urban youths and French society taking shape at the time. "A little everywhere in France, in urban France in any case, young people began to affirm a different kind of relationship with French society, and on the basis of this affirmation, networks were created from which was born 'Rock Against Police.'" According to Abdallah RAP's concerts drew local audiences from Vitry and Nanterre, North African youth were especially prominent. However, the organizers of RAP were themselves multiethnic. "There were Guadelupians, mulattos, French, it became a large, closely knit group which toured for two years and spent much of their time together, a gang."[16]

Through its influence and alliances Abdallah describes RAP as an important experience in the history of ethnic minority mobilization in France. Meeting with young North African women from Lyon, RAP participants inspired the creation of Zaâma d'Banlieue. A precursor to the association Jeunes Arabes de Lyon et banlieue headed by Djida Tazdaït who would go on to become a deputy for the Green Party in the European Union Parliament, Zaâma d'Banlieue launched similar concerts in the Lyon area. An autonomous militant pole within the Paris region, RAP organizers worked in conjunction with former militants of the Arab Workers Movement (MTA) at *Sans Frontière* and Radio Soleil Goutte-d'or. They formed alliances with organizations in England such as Race Today in Brixton as well as the Black Radical & Third World Bookfair.[17]

Far more politically oriented than North African theater companies, RAP and Zaâma d'Banlieue were among the earliest efforts to form autonomous, multiethnic movements among France's urban working-class youth. But neither group was able to provide effective national leadership. Similar to the inability of associational leaders and minority intermediaries to quell or harness urban unrest in the early 1990s, RAP and Zaâma d'Banlieue were powerless in the face of the violence that flared up in the Lyons suburb of Les Minguettes in 1981.[18]

The strength of both organizations was sapped by the arrival of the Socialist government that responded to many of their demands—cracking down on discriminatory practices, introducing new social initiatives, and temporarily relaxing or repealing a number of restrictions on immigrants. More importantly, the decision by the Socialists to abrogate a 1939 decree-law restricting the rights of association for foreigners launched a new phase of North African political action that eclipsed these earlier efforts to mobilize immigrant youth through cultural initiatives.[19] However, the leaders of RAP and Zaâma d'Banlieue remained active in the 1980s associational movement. Their commitment to the creation of an autonomous movement and their serious reservations about forming alliances with French social or political groups functioned as an important current with the associational movement.[20]

Turning Professional

During the 1980s minority political action shifted from neighborhood-based, autonomous associations led by North African youth to the rise of powerful national structures with strong political ties but weak local connections. This professionalization and institutionalization of minority political action is not entirely dissimilar to the evolution of North African cultural expression. After the early 1980s, North African cultural expression moved away from militant collective initiatives by amateur artists rooted in working-class suburban communities to professional forms of creative expression that targeted mainstream French audiences and relied more heavily on mainstream sources of diffusion and institutional support.

Professionalism, a term used repeatedly by minority artists encountered during this study, implies both an advanced degree of expertise and the ability to generate a living from one's work. Turning professional entails an increased degree of dependency on institutional and commercial sources of support. As with the rise of SOS-Racisme and France Plus, North African cultural actors acquired the capacity to take their work to new and ever larger audiences. Yet similar to the realm of ethnic minority politics, commercial and institutional pressures sometimes resulted in a watering down or softening of issues and subjects that might be unsettling or offensive to mainstream audiences. In short, turning professional presented new opportunities and dangers for North African cultural actors in France.

Most of the theater troupes created in the 1970s and early 1980s have either succumbed to internal divisions or attempted to become professional companies. According to Saliha Amara, the time for militant theater is past. While minority artists should be proud of their heritage and attempt to integrate it into their work, they must now establish themselves as professionals.

In Amara's opinion, many minority artists previously exploited their ethnicity, in the absence of real talent, to launch artistic careers. "Today, to be regarded as an artist you have to be a professional," Amara remarked. "Many people used this [beur] label because it was fashionable. But it isn't any more. It no longer pays."[21]

For many theater companies, however, the task of professionalizing was too financially cumbersome. The experience of Ibn Khaldoun illustrates this point. Ibn Khaldoun's last play, "Ben Donald" (1987), featured an elaborate decor, costumes, original music, professional musicians, and a prestigious location in central Paris (Forum des Halles). However, it was the financial investment in "Ben Donald" that ultimately brought about the company's demise. After covering production costs no money was left over to promote the play.

> Ben Donald was somewhat premature. We should have waited and done it as a co-production with a TV station, radio station, association or theater company. We weren't able to manage the promotion, sales, production and staging...This transition ended up ruining us. Renting a theater, technicians, etc...and when you only make 3,000 francs in revenue it doesn't even cover two weeks of overhead.

The company eventually fell into debt and was unable to continue. The remaining 50,000 francs worth of costumes and decor tucked away in a Gennevilliers storage site ended up being vandalized and destroyed by local youths.[22]

Other companies attempted to clear this financial hurdle by restructuring themselves as associations. After making these structural changes, theater companies could negotiate with municipal authorities for a place to meet, practice, and perform. More importantly, they could receive much needed state and local subsidies to undertake more ambitious projects. The institutionalization of minority associations and their increased dependency on government funds was a general trend during the 1980s. The example of the Paris-area company Chakchouka (a kind of smorgasbord in Arabic) is particularly telling.

Like many North African companies Chakchouka grew out of a need to inform the public about the problems confronting immigrant youth. Its long-running play, "Faits Divers," used comedy to address the serious issues of intergenerational tensions, racism, discrimination, and police violence.[23] As they explained in a 1984 interview, troupe members were proud of their independence and had serious reservations about becoming an association.

If we suddenly become an association, everyone will think that we are receiving subsidies and we'll run the risk of ruining everything. Moreover, we'll be obligated to elect a president and a treasurer. But we want to remain independent, to have the same responsibilities, without anyone ordering us around. We don't want to get carried away. We are only trying to talk about our problems, by ourselves, without trying to make any money.[24]

However, after a few years troupe members began to feel that the problems they were treating had become old news. Moreover, some members developed a taste for theater and aspired to become professional actors. They now viewed the institutionalization of Chakchouka as their best chance to make the transition from militant to professional theater.

After deciding to form an association, troupe members took acting lessons, hired a director, and staged an adaptation of Molière's *l'Avare*. Despite their efforts to distance themselves from their militant past, *l'Avare* proved a disappointment. Abdelkader Khessiba and Jlaïel Hamadi, two former members, believed that the company had simply become too associated with the ethnic origins of its actors and the denunciatory content of its charter play "Faits Divers." In Khessiba's opinion, the French were simply not ready to see Arabs performing Molière. By 1988 Chakchouka ceased to function and has since become part of the collective memory of the city of Gennevilliers.

Among the theater companies created in the 1970s, Nedjma was perhaps the only one still in existence by the mid-1990s. But unlike most theater troupes who envisioned their projects as short-term militant initiatives, explained Nejma founder Moussa Lebkiri, he always intended to steer a course toward professionalism. Nevertheless, Nedjma underwent a significant transformation following its creation in 1976. Beginning as a militant company with a little over a dozen actors, the company shrank to just Moussa Lebkiri. With "Histoires du thé à la menthe" (1984), Nedjma shifted from a more traditional format based on multiple actors and roles to a theatrical form of one-man storytelling. In contrast to most North African narratives that take place almost exclusively in France, "Histoires du thé à la menthe" featured a series of lively stories, memories, characters, and events from Lebkiri's childhood in Algeria.[25]

The 1988 publication of "Histoires du thé à la menthe" as *Une Etoile dans l'oeil de mon frère* marked the beginning of Lebkiri's dual career as an actor/author. In 1991 he published *Bouz'louf!...tête de mouton*, a sort of sequel to his first book treating his life after arriving in France. In addition to *Bouz'louf!*, written in the form of a novel, Lebkiri published several of his later performances including *Il parlait à son balai* (1992) and *Prince Troduc en Panach'* (1993). While Lebkiri continued to perform in sociocultural settings out of a sense of personal commitment, he regularly participated in the major French cultural festivals at Avignon, Grenoble, Cannes, and Limoges.[26]

While Lebkiri is by no means a household name in France, he accurately reflects the general evolution of North African theater since the early 1980s. North African theater, once a weapon in defense of the North African community, became a means of survival and a source of social status. This does not mean that amateur theater companies ceased to exist. During the mid-1990s Valence theater troupe La Rose des Sables in southern France, for example, continued to perform its 1980 charter play, "Les enfant d'Aïcha," and added a new performance to its repertoire, "Le Mektoub." However, according to troupe leader Fatiha Mahdaoui, even La Rose des Sables opted for an associational structure in the early 1990s and took part in the prestigious Avignon theater festival.[27]

Professional Constraints

As militant theater troupes struggled to become professional companies and to reach larger audiences, other artists and creators were attempting to launch careers in the French mainstream. Although these artists were all from working-class immigrant families, their professional trajectories were extremely diverse. Some artists received specialized training or attended professional schools. Others benefited from raw talent and the backing of powerful patrons in their chosen fields. Yet others acquired their skills through years of on-the-job training. Regardless of their diverse forms of training, these artists marked a break with the militant, collective projects of the 1970s and early 1980s. While they often drew creative inspiration from personal experiences and evoked many of the same themes found in militant theater, their work was geared more toward French audiences and relied heavily on mainstream sources of cultural diffusion. In their efforts to survive in a highly competitive entertainment business many artists softened potentially offensive aspects of their work or focused on larger themes that would appeal to French audiences. The examples of Mounsi, Mehdi Charef, and Rachid Bouchareb illustrate this point.

After RAP ground to a halt in 1982, Mounsi decided to try his hand at a professional music career. Rejected by several companies, he finally signed a contract with Motor Records. When Mounsi released his debut album in 1984 he intended it to be just as provocative as his previous engagements.

Entitled *Séconde Génération*, the album cover featured a smiling Mounsi with an Algerian flag in his right hand and a French flag hanging from a tooth-pick in his mouth.[28] A checkered, black and white Palestinian scarf is draped over the shoulders of his black leather jacket. In a raspy voice reminiscent of Bernard Lavilliers, Mounsi evoked his North African roots and the condition of immigrant youth in just about every song on the album.

Mounsi's professional debut proved somewhat of a disappointment. While the album sold 30,000 copies, it only covered 50 percent of the invest-ment cost.[29] By the early 1990s Mounsi switched careers from music to lit-erature. His first two novels—*La Noce des fous* (1990) and *La Cendre des villes* (1993)—both featured North African protagonists and take place, at least in part, in suburban settings. However, any similarity with Mounsi's previous work as a singer ends here. While the lyrics in *Séconde Génération* were infused with ethnic and historical consciousness, the characters in his first novels are pure products of a deteriorating suburban universe. Perhaps more than any other North African novelist, Mounsi appears to have detached his characters from the stigma and the historical specificity of their ethnicity.

While Mounsi may represent an extreme example, he is by no means exceptional. In appealing to French audiences many North African artists try to avoid *misérabiliste* depictions of the immigrant community (stereotypical representations of immigrants as passive victims) and soften or gloss over potentially unsettling issues such as racism, discrimination, and ethnic iden-tity. For example, in their first feature-length films Mehdi Charef (*Le thé au harem d'Archimède*, 1985) and Rachid Bouchareb (*Bâton Rouge*, 1985) both focus on a larger suburban universe that immigrant youth share with their working-class French neighbors. Carrie Tarr observes that these films center on friendships between French natives and North Africans whose life condi-tions and outlook are essentially the same.

> Socioeconomic conditions are presented as the principal stumbling block to integration, and cultural differences are marginalized or erased. The films refuse "miserabilism" and minimize or omit references to racism and the legacy of the Algerian War. Even the representatives of oppressive state institutions are shown as relatively benevolent.

Tarr believes that *Le thé au harem d'Archimède* and *Bâton Rouge* attempt to close the gap between North African minorities and the French by "offering French audiences a non-threatening and non-accusatory representation of ethnic difference." Tarr adds that these films also reflected a more optimistic atmosphere toward interethnic relations in the early 1980s.[30]

Ethnic Constraints

The efforts of minority artists to soften their work when addressing French audiences become more understandable in light of the tremendous pressure experienced due to their ethnicity. On the one hand, minority artists who assimilated and practiced Western forms of cultural expression were often interpreted or classified in terms of their ethnicity. On the other hand, artists who attempted to integrate French and North African cultural influences often found themselves marginalized by mainstream sources of cultural diffusion and tracked into sociocultural spheres. The difficulties experienced by minority artists reveal some of the obstacles to multiculturalism in contemporary France.

Like many North African artists, singer Karim Kacel had only a few childhood memories of Algeria from vacations he had taken with his family. He sang in French because it was the only language he knew.[31] At home he listened to some Algerian music but was drawn more to American rock, jazz, and blues, which he discovered at the Kiss Club—a popular club frequented by many Paris-area North African youth during the 1970s. "There I discovered rhythm and blues, the Temptations, etc. Otis Redding was a god to me at the time."[32] These are the sounds that are most audible in his music.

There is nothing unusual about Kacel's music that would distinguish him from mainstream French singers. A number of journalists described his jazz-rock style as part of the "nouvelle chanson française" in the tradition of Brel, Brassens, and Moustaki.[33] Thematically, his music addressed just about everything and anything. The only song that is explicitly connected to his Algerian origins is "La chanson de Kabyle"—a sort of homage to his father.[34] In numerous interviews he reiterated that his only wish was to be accepted as any other French singer without reference to his ethnicity.

Yet like many other *beur* artists during the early 1980s, Kacel's work was overtaken by the excitement about cultural diversity generated by the arrival of the Socialist government. Moreover, the 1983 release of Kacel's first single occurred during the same year as the March for Equality and Against Racism—the pinnacle of the associational movement. Kacel's first single, "Banlieue," was quickly adopted by the press as a theme song for *beurs*, and by immigrant youths as a sort of anthem.[35]

In "Banlieue" Kacel lamented the prevailing social and economic conditions experienced by urban youths in countless cities throughout France. With his melancholy voice he described a desolate universe filled with asphyxiating concrete towers and desperate inhabitants who longed for escape. Yet nowhere in the song did Kacel specify a particular group of residents or offer any ethnic markers. The song was never intended to be about immigration or North Africans. "The public made 'Banlieue' a song about immigration. I never evoked immigration in 'Banlieue.' The song does not say: 'Mohammed, stares at his city,' but: 'He stares at his city.' 'He,' was identified with its author, and because my name is Karim Kacel people immediately thought about the universe of immigration."[36] Kacel commented that most of the media attention he received for "Banlieue" stemmed from his ethnicity, not the quality or character of his music. "Close to a hundred articles were written about 'Banlieue.' Seventy percent because I am an Arab who sings in French and thirty percent uniquely because of my work."[37]

Similarly, sculptor Mohand Amara, a graduate of the prestigious Paris Fine Arts School, rejected being categorized as the exemplar of some sort of minority cultural production. His inspiration came from Renaissance and classical Greek sculpture. The representation of human figures through sculpture, Amara commented, had nothing to do with Muslim North African traditions.[38] In the early 1980s, he recalled, there was much talk of a *beur* cultural movement. But in his opinion there were simply a number of individuals each doing his or her own work. Many, such as himself, had started working years earlier and resented being labeled as members of a "spontaneous" generation. "They talked about a spontaneous generation but I had already spent eight years in school [studying art]. I didn't become a sculptor overnight." Amara explained that journalists who came to interview him often had very little interest in his work.

> Someone would come. He would ask if I'm a sculptor. He would look at my work for two minutes and would then say "let's talk about you." What interested the person was essentially my social context . . . they didn't care about the work. It was always journalists who had nothing to do with the world of art. I got to the point where I was so fed up that I refused all [interviews].

Amara added that Piscasso's work was never understood strictly in terms of his Spanish origins, "he was first an artist and then a Spaniard, but for us it's completely the opposite."[39]

The emergence of several dozen North African novelists since the early 1980s offers perhaps the clearest example of how minority artists, regardless of the character of their work, are constantly interpreted and classified according to their ethnicity. Novels have been the focus of more academic scrutiny and interest than any other genre of creative expression. Scores of articles have been written by French and Anglo-American scholars on the topic as well as at least two monographs, *Voices from the North African Immigrant Community in France* (1991) and *Autour du Roman Beur* (1993).[40] Yet the search to define a *beur* literary genre has proven quite elusive. As author Ahmed Kalouaz points out, the notion of a *beur* literary genre implies a certain connection with or departure from earlier forms of North African literature. But in his case, except for a few writers such as Boudjedra, he knows very little about North African novelists.[41] *Beur* fiction specialist Alec Hargreaves comments that this is typical of other North African writers who are inspired more by African American writers whose condition approximates their own, than any North African literary tradition.[42]

Although North African novelists ascribe to Western literary traditions and influences, most have been marginalized by the French publishing industry. Aside from Mehdi Charef's *Le Thé au harem d'Archi Ahmed* (1983), which appeared at the peak of the *beur* political movement, and Azouz Begag's *Le Gône du Chaâba* (1986), few *beur* novels have been commercially successful. While Charef and Begag have published with two of France's leading publishing houses, Mercure de France and Seuil, most *beur* novelists have contracted with lesser known companies. The Paris publisher L'Harmattan, and its ethnically specific collection "écritures arabes," includes the largest number of North African novelists. Founded in 1975, L'Harmattan specializes in the Third World and North and sub-Saharan Africa in particular. For over 20 years L'Harmattan has functioned as a creative outlet for minority voices "characterized by [their] *'différence'* in comparison to Western culture."[43]

It is precisely this difference, whether it exists or not, which French publishers often attempt to exploit. For example, the Paris publishing house Fixot found Soraya Nini's title "Entre deux ou les enfants du paradis" (Between Two or the Children of Paradise) too literary and suggested *Ils disent que je suis une beurette* (They say I'm a Beurette)—although the author personally rejected the term *beurette* and used it only once in her novel. In addition to the title change Fixot featured a picture of the author on the cover and a definition of the terms *beur* and *beurette*. Nini explained that this is part of the Fixot's traditional format as a publisher specializing in personal accounts.[44] But to many potential buyers the book appears as an autobiography or a sociological account, not a novel. Fixot was clearly more interested in exploiting public interest in the sociological dimension of immigrant youth than seeking out new literary talent.

In some instances *beur* titles can bring favorable publicity to French publishers. Cartoonist Farid Boudjellal admitted this is the case for his work. Boudjellal noted that none of his first books were particularly profitable.

He spent seven years on the trilogy—*L'Oud* (1983), *Le Gourbi* (1985), and *Ramadân* (1988)—which he considers his finest work but was nevertheless a commercial failure. *L'Oud*, which appeared at the same time as Charef's *Le thé au harem*, benefited from the *beur* media boom and quickly sold out the some 1,000 copies run by Futurpolis. *Le Gourbi* sold roughly 5,000 copies and *Ramadân*, 3,000.

While his books may not be profitable, Boudjellal claimed that he has no problem finding publishers. He explained that editors, at least for comics, now publish smaller runs with the hope of building a future following or bringing positive publicity to the publisher. His work is appealing because it generates positive publicity. "I don't make money for my publisher, I help their image. When I come out with a book there are usually reverberations in the press, it interests many journalists, and there are interviews on television." Boudjellal noted that the magazine *L'Événement de Jeudi* devoted a four-page story to his series *Juif-Arab*. "The publisher is happy because they end up talking about him. If the publisher had to use advertising to get people to talk about him it would be more expensive than the book he edited." As the only French cartoonist to feature the theme of immigration Boudjellal pointed out that he has also established his own niche in the market.[45]

Artists who were more rooted in their ethnicity or chose to mix French and North African cultural influences faced similar constraints. Despite their training or professional ambitions these artists were often viewed in terms of their social utility, not their creativity. Sometimes they are excluded from mainstream sources of cultural diffusion and relegated to minority audiences. Other times they met with confusion and were classified as folk artists. Rachid Khimoune, Rachid Taha, and Malik Chibane offer three examples of artists who fit into this category.

Khimoune, a classmate of Mohand Amara at the Paris Fine Arts School, was particularly drawn to the linear designs found in Muslim art—a form of abstract art that predated Western "modern" art by several hundred years.[46] By stamping his work with Arabic calligraphy or imprints of ordinary objects with geometric shapes (manhole covers, brick pavement), Khimoune created elaborate mosaics and sculptures with an orientalized flair. From mosaics of victims of racial murders like Toufik and more ordinary family portraits to statues of right-wing HLM managers, Khimoune used art to convey stories about people and events close to home.

I wanted to tell the story of my community, people like my father who came to this country to dig or fill in holes. That was the story of my community. But I could tell it without *misérabilisme*, with sensitivity and humor. But these were things that were meaningful to me.

Yet despite his training at France's top art school, Khimoune experienced considerable difficulties in attempting to find a place in the mainstream world of art. For several years Khimoune was trapped in sociocultural work and cut off from established centers of cultural expression. He worked all over France with associations and cultural services, but rarely with professional galleries or museums.

I did a great deal of work in France but always in relation with associations and cultural services but very few professional galleries or museums. These were two different things. There was the sociocultural milieu and the artistic milieu. When I wanted to move into the artistic milieu they said no, it's sociocultural [for you]. After a while I had enough, I want to be recognized as a sculptor not as an immigrant youth who works as a sculptor.

Doing everything possible to break out of this track, Khimoune rejected invitations from exhibitions featuring Algerians and choose to display his work alone. "When I was invited to exhibitions on Algeria...I said no, it's not worth it. I'm not Algerian, I'm French and I live here." While Khimoune claimed not to regret his "sociocultural" experience, which allowed him to work closely with ordinary people in countless cities across the country, he was pleased that connoisseurs and art patrons now recognize him simply as a professional sculptor.[47]

Rachid Taha's experiences are similar to that of Khimoune. In 1980 Taha formed a band with two North African coworkers at a Lyons Factory. The name of the band, Carte de Séjour (Residence Card, CDS), evoked the precarious status of many immigrant youth who are rooted in France but retain their parents' nationality. The thematic content of CDS's music paralleled that of an earlier generation of second-generation theater companies. Songs such as "Zoubida" and "La Moda," from the 1983 debut album, denounced the condition of North African women and the scourge of racism in France.[48] "Mirage" and "Ouadou," from the band's second album, offered powerful accounts of the exploitation of North African workers.[49] On a somewhat more humorous note, "Douce France," from CDS's final album, was an orientalized parody of Charles Trenet's French classic.[50]

Unlike most North African groups, CDS's music was primarily in Sabir—a mixture of French, Arabic, and an assortment of other languages spoken by

North African immigrants. While the sound of electric guitars and drums off their first album was reminiscent of the Clash, the band gradually developed its own style. By combining traditional North African instruments with all the paraphernalia of a Western rock band, CDS created an entirely new blend of music. It was the multicultural tonality of CDS, and the more inclusive French society and French culture it represented, that motivated former Minister of Culture Jack Lang to distribute copies of "Douce France" to conservative and extreme-right members of the National Assembly during the 1986 debate over more restrictive French nationality laws.

Despite three albums and eight years of work, CDS remained on the margins of the French music industry. The band was plagued by several problems that continued to hamper Rachid Taha's solo career. First, most radio stations considered CDS's music too "oriental" to appeal to a mainstream French audience. Aside from a few alternative and minority-run stations, the band was unable to gain access to private commercial stations or larger networks.[51] Second, many of the smaller store owners refused to carry CDS's albums, complaining that they would scare away potential French customers or attract the wrong kind of clientele.

> I remember when I lived in Lyon there was a store close to my place that never carried my records or any records with Arab names on them. They said they were afraid the records would be stolen but the truth was that it was pure racism—and it's still the case today. Only the big stores [carry them].[52]

Yet even when record stores sold CDS's albums, they were not always sure how to categorize their music. Interested buyers never knew whether they would find CDS alongside other French rock singers or in the North African folk music section.[53]

Ironically, efforts by government authorities during the 1990s to defend French music against the perceived onslaught of British and American sounds proved an unexpected windfall for ethnic minority artists. In particular, the decision to require radio broadcasters to devote an important percentage of their airtime to French music contributed significantly to the success of French rap groups such as MC Solar, IAM, NTM and a host of more recent performers. Heavily influenced by the body language, performance styles, and physical appearance of African-American groups, with equally confrontational and denunciatory lyrics, rap groups have now become a mainstay of the French music industry.

The success of Malik Chibane's film *Hexagone* (1994) seems to contradict the difficulties experienced by Khimoune and Taha. In contrast to Rachid

Bouchareb, who attended film school and worked in television, or Mehdi Charef, who received the backing of the renowned director Costa-Gavras, Chibane had no formal training and no connections in the entertainment business. Moreover, Chibane's work was far more ethnically specific than the debut films of Bouchareb and Chibane, the first two directors of North African descent to complete feature-length movies. As with Week-end à Nanterre, Chibane wanted to center his film on five days in the lives of five North African friends from the Paris suburb of Goussainville, the director's hometown. Chibane hoped to compensate for what he saw as the absence of cultural works devoted to the stories and experiences of the North Africans in France. For Chibane, gaining legitimacy necessitated an effort to respond to this absence.

> I wanted to pay homage to all the young people I grew up with. It's an homage to the second-generation, not a film on the suburbs. I grew up with guys from Zaire, Normandy and Spain . . . But in this film there are only beurs. This is because I wanted to respond to this invisibility. The fact that we're seen nowhere, that we're culturally invisible . . . I wanted to make a film that would shatter this invisibility and offer an homage to the second-generation . . . Because you don't see beurs anywhere I wanted to put them everywhere. It's a form of compensation by excess, a form of provocation.

Chibane's provocation appears to have been successful. Opening in February 1994 in 140 theaters across France, *Hexagone* drew some 10,000 viewers in the first week and 37,000 by the month of May. Chibane estimated that *Hexagone* would draw a total of roughly 60,000 viewers by the time it finished in July 1994. A remarkable turnout, in Chibane's opinion, for an unknown director with a small-budget film.[54]

While Chibane's film was certainly a Cinderella story, it was by no means an unfettered success. Chibane explained that several production companies rejected his script because it contained too many Arabs.

> I knew this script would not be financed, we're in France . . . I knew who I was dealing with. I am French, I was born in France and I have a very good understanding of French society. I understand its obstructions. It isn't any different than the corner grocer or the people I grew up with. It's the same culture that forged them. I understand the resistance and one of the strongest kinds of resistance that exists is the desire that there shouldn't be any kind of [ethnic] communitarian projects. It's like that in France.

[Ethnic minority] communities aren't wanted. I made a film but they don't see the individuals on the screen, they see a community.

If you make a film with North African characters in France, Chibane explained, it will invariably be seen as an ethnic communitarian project—the French simply do not recognize the individuality of ethnic minorities. Many production companies, Chibane added, are staffed by privileged social groups who are unable to understand the culture of working-class communities. "You're confronted with two problems with Parisian producers. They aren't from working-class communities so they don't understand all that is related to the problems of ordinary people. In addition to this there is the ethnic veneer. So they aren't able to understand the scenario."

Unlike both Charef and Bouchareb, Chibane received no financial support from the National Cinematography Commission, the chief source of subsidies for French filmmakers. It took Chibane six years to scrape together the shoe-string budget for his film. Moreover, Chibane commented that those ministries which did support the film tended to consider it, and their funding, in terms of a social initiative, not a cultural one. In fact, it was Bernard Tapie's Ministère de la Ville, the newly created all-encompassing urban policy ministry, that provided the assistance needed to complete the film.[55]

The tendency to deny the individuality of ethnic minority artists is certainly not unique to France. The commodification of black cultural expression in the United States and Britain, and the willing collaboration of many prominent black artists, does little to reveal the true range of creative influences and perspectives.[56] However, in France there is simply no equivalent to the leveling force of the commercial stakes implicating ethnic minority artists across the Channel and the Atlantic. Moreover, the impulse to identify block categories of African American filmmakers or singers, Asian American writers, or Chicano artists is given even greater force by the institutionalization of ethnic minority politics and cultures. There is nothing in France like the Black Caucus, the Cuban American lobby, or African American and Chicano studies programs in American universities. Whereas ethnic minority artists may become fodder in battles over multiculturalism that rage in the United States, no such culture wars exist in France. Yet it is precisely this proclaimed aversion to American-style multiculturalism and hyphenated identities that masks the common practice of pegging and pigeonholing ethnic minority artists in France. Despite the colorblind and egalitarian rhetoric of French Republicanism, the treatment of ethnic minority artists in France is much closer to what happens in America or Britain than most are willing to admit.

Artists First

Classified and categorized according to their ethnicity, excluded from mainstream venues of cultural diffusion it is not surprising that many minority artists attempted to distance themselves from their ethnicity by emphasizing their professional identity. Whether they were inspired by or ambivalent about their ethnicity, few artists wished to have their creative freedom circumscribed by a potentially stifling minority label. Ironically, while these artists were often critical of French assimilationist traditions and while they benefited from more inclusive conceptions of culture in French society, the constraints imposed on them by their ethnicity often cause them to become staunch advocates of French Republican ideals.

Perhaps the most prominent example of an artist who embraced his North African identity professionally, yet distanced himself from it personally, is Smaïn Fairouze, known simply as Smaïn. One of France's premier comedians, Smaïn acknowledged that his success was partly due to the enthusiasm about *beurs* ushered in by the arrival of the Socialist party. Had he begun his career at another time he might have remained trapped in small, typecast parts such as the drug dealer or delinquent, the "negative Arab," characters that dominated his early film roles.[57] Smaïn's first break came in 1983 when he was selected to appear on Antenne 2's daily comedy show "Petit Théâtre de Bouvard," hosted and named after its creator Philippe Bouvard. But it was a series of one-man shows, beginning with "A Star is Beur," in 1986, that elevated Smaïn to the upper echelons of French show business. In his one-man shows he capitalized on the sudden public interest in suburban ethnic youths, and the tendency of the French to equate all North Africans with these marginalized spaces, by portraying a variety of suburban, *beur* characters. "In the minds of most people, I appear to be a young person from the suburbs. So I exploited this phenomenon while knowing that it didn't correspond at all to my own life" (Smaïn grew up in Paris).[58]

While Smaïn benefited professionally from his ethnic, suburban image, offstage he rejected being cast as a spokesperson for immigrant youth. In numerous interviews Smaïn consciously avoided any overt attachment to the North African community. "Being a leader isn't my goal. Otherwise I would be a politician. My role in the integration process is a solitary one, through what I do. I'm not an activist."[59] For Smaïn and other many other minority artists, their ethnicity represented both a source of creative inspiration and a potential threat to their freedom of expression. The challenge for artists such as Smaïn was to find ways to exploit the creative resources of their ethnicity without becoming submerged within and subsumed by it.

Similarly, while Rachid Khimoune's work is infused with references to his North African heritage, he positioned himself within his profession as an artist. "I want to be recognized as a sculptor, not as a young person from the North African community working as a sculptor." Khimoune believed that art is a universal form of expression capable of appealing to all people. This, however, is not possible without first attaining a high level of professionalism. Above all, Khimoune took great pride in his professionalism achieved through years of training.[60]

Rachid Taha, much like Khimoune, rejected the notion of a *beur* culture. In his opinion, the search for a *beur* cultural elite, was a political ploy to divide North Africans into good and bad immigrants. Moreover, he believed that those who succeeded would be held up to mask the reality of the majority who continue to struggle in France. While Taha believed that it is important to take a militant stand in his work, his reasoning was grounded in his duty as an artist, not his Algerian roots. "An artist, singer, or painter must express him or herself by pointing out certain realities. If they don't, who will?"[61]

Conclusion

Raised in a society that ignored their existence and by parents whose future plans centered on returning to their home country, North African youth turned to cultural expression as a means of speaking out, breaking silences, and asserting their desire to belong. Through diverse cultural initiatives North Africans have long played an active role in challenging stereotypical depictions while articulating their own concerns, anxieties, experiences, memories, hopes and aspirations. As with political forms of mobilization cultural expression is a way of seeking recognition, legitimacy, and acceptance in a country that has yet to fully acknowledge its immigration history or its imperial past.

Yet similar to the North African associational movement, it has proven particularly difficult to sustain voluntary-based militant forms of collective cultural actions. Most of the North African theater companies, the earliest and most predominant form of cultural expression during the late 1970s and early 1980s, succumbed to similar internal divisions or collapsed in their attempts to restructure themselves along professional lines. While Saliha Amara noted that ethnic minorities continued to engage in a variety of cultural initiatives she remarked that the scope of these projects and their relationship to the state have undergone fundamental changes since the time of her theater company Kahina.

> Now it seems like everything is easy. Everything seems possible. And it's true. All you need to do is get three people to create an association, show you're able to manage yourself, and you can get a little money [from the

government] to set up your own little troupe and perform a little in the neighborhood. But for us there weren't fifty troupes at the time. There were only a couple and we toured all around France and even overseas. We were the only troupe with women who addressed these problems, there was no competition. Now you have all kinds of small projects everywhere but which don't ever amount to much because they never go beyond the neighborhood.[62]

In the realm of ethnic minority cultural and political action there seemed to be a parallel failure to build on earlier collective projects that succeeded in transcending local communities. In both cases collective action became more limited to the local level and dependent on state support. This relationship of dependency placed political and cultural actors in a precarious position. Enthusiasm for cultural diversity, or the right to difference, was never particularly strong and gave way by the mid-1980s to a consensus about an invented Republican model of citizenship. In the domain of French cultural policy this new consensus took the form of reduced state support for ethnic minority actions. In her study of French cultural policy during the Mitterrand years Kim Eling notes that the Cultural Development Direction (DDC), the branch of the Ministry of Culture devoted to ethnic minorities and community based projects, always occupied somewhat of a subordinate position. While the establishment of the DDC was of considerable "symbolic importance," Eling explains, "resources allocated to this area of the Ministry's policy have never been on a par with the funding accorded to its traditional 'clients.' "[63] Following the Socialists' fall from power in 1986 the DDC was abolished and never restored upon their return in 1988. The Cultural Intervention Fund (FIC), another agency that played an important role in supporting ethnic minority projects during the 1970s and 1980s lost administrative support even earlier.[64]

Given this increasingly hostile institutional climate it is understandable why many artists tried to establish themselves as professionals with mainstream audiences and commercial sources of support. In light of the tendency in French society to particularize these artists, regardless of the content and character of their work, it is also evident why many cultural actors were reluctant to be too closely associated with their ethnic community. Even those artists who did lay claim to their heritage often cloaked themselves in a professional discourse that closely approximated French Republican ideals.

CHAPTER 3

Radio Beur: Multiculturalism on the French Airwaves

The 1981 decision by the Socialist government to end the state monopoly over radio has been one of the most important but least studied events in the recent cultural history of France. From the establishment of Louis XI's royal postal system in the fifteenth century to the development of the telegraph in the nineteenth century, French governments have historically exercised strict control over all forms of communication. State control over radio began to tighten during the tumultuous years leading up to and following World War II. In September 1939, after the declaration of war against Germany, all private stations were required to relay public broadcasts. At the end of the war, the ordinance of March 23, 1945 revoked the last remaining authorizations held by private stations.[1] From 1945 to 1981 the French government effectively monopolized all radio broadcasts within its own borders. Even the handful of *radios périphériques*—postwar long-wave stations broadcasting to much of France from the border regions of neighboring countries—were controlled by a state-directed holding company (Sofirad) and a state-owned media conglomerate (Havas).[2] As late as 1980, France had only seven legal stations for a population of 50 million—proportionally some 25 times less than the United States.[3]

Since the end of the state monopoly the French airwaves have been inundated with private stations. The number of private stations reached 1,500 by 1985 and 1,800 by 1990.[4] Among the hundreds of *radios locales privées*, an expansive term including everything from national, general entertainment networks to local, specialized broadcasters—are several dozen stations operated by and targeting France's ethnic, racial, and religious minorities, known as *radios communautaires*. According to a 1991 article in *Télérama* there were approximately 30 minority stations in France—a number that has remained more or less the same since 1981.[5]

In actuality, it is impossible to arrive at the precise number of minority stations. The Conseil Supérieur de l'Audiovisuel (CSA), responsible since 1989 for the authorization and policing of broadcasting rights in France, does not officially recognize or keep statistics on minority stations. Just as French law prohibits census takers from recording the national origins of naturalized citizens, a general classification system based on economic, not ethnic, racial, or religious criteria, masks the specificity of minority broadcasters. In practice, however, the CSA and French lawmakers have singled out minority stations in numerous policy initiatives and administrative decisions—yet another example of the glaring divide between the rhetoric and reality of the Republican model.

The First of the Second Generation

The creation of Radio Beur in 1981 was concomitant with the rise of a public discourse that celebrated the merits of cultural pluralism. A segment of the French left that favored the cultivation of regional and minority identities temporarily replaced the term "assimilation," traditionally used when discussing the incorporation of minorities into French society, with "insertion" that suggested the possibility of making citizenship more inclusive by valorizing and protecting cultural, ethnic, or religious differences.[6] Politicians such as centrist Bernard Stasi countered the xenophobic theses of the extreme right by arguing that immigration was an "opportunity for France."[7] Numerous articles in the press featured a young generation of artists and creators from the North African community who were hastily catalogued and categorized as the proponents of a new *beur* cultural movement.[8] In winter 1984, the Centre Georges Pompidou opened its doors to a three-month exhibition, "Les enfants de l'immigration," featuring artists and creators from France's minority communities.

It is important, however, not to exaggerate the political support for multiculturalism. Neither the Socialists nor rival parties have ever embraced the merits of cultural diversity with universal acclaim. Questions about how to incorporate ethnic, racial, or religious minorities were and remain highly contentious and often transgress traditional ideological divisions. Yet during the early 1980s Radio Beur was able to benefit from an unprecedented political willingness to create new possibilities for cultural pluralism. This willingness translated into generous financial support for minority initiatives by various national and local agencies. For example, the Fonds d'Action Sociale (FAS), responsible for the incorporation of immigrants and their families into French society, covered 15 percent of Radio Beur's total operating costs for 1983 and increased its support to 21 percent in 1985.[9] During the 1980s, the FAS was the chief source of subsidies for Radio Beur and hundreds of other minority-run associations throughout France.

In her study of minority-run associations in the Marseille region, Jocelyne Cesari notes that the actions of the FAS were part of a new approach to immigrants and their families. Until the 1980s, social workers and a handful of associations managed and translated the problems and concerns of a North African community still viewed as temporary immigrant workers. As the spread of Islamic places of worship and the growth of ethnic minority associations shattered this homogenous view of the North African community, an elite group of associational leaders gradually displaced social workers and preexisting organizations as the new intermediaries between the state and the North African community.[10]

In many ways, Cesari's description of these intermediaries corresponds to the founders of Radio Beur. Most of the founders were born in the early 1950s and were part of the first generation of North African youth to be raised in France. Their formative years were often heavily influenced by the ideologies of left-wing parties, social workers, and the Amicales (representative bodies of their countries of origin). The founders of Radio Beur were part of a generation that had little in common with the French perception of *beurs* as marginalized urban youth in their teens or early twenties. Most of the founders were closer to 30 than 20 when they set out to create Radio Beur in 1981. They grew up during the 1960s and 1970s and referred to themselves as the "invisible generation." Their presence and that of their families was masked by the French conception of North Africans as transient, single, male laborers. This invisibility offered a variety of advantages. It spared them from the intense public scrutiny and stereotyping suffered by North African youth today and allowed them to benefit from greater economic and educational opportunities. The desire to affirm their existence and to stake out their own place in French society provided the incentive for a wide range of collective actions from theater to journalism.

Almost all of the founders lived through the tumultuous years of the Algerian War. Amar Bennacer, the first president of Radio Beur, recalled that the years following the war were filled with idealism. Raised with the idea that they would one day return to Algeria, the children of Algerian workers in France were swept up in their parents' nationalism. Most took part in activities organized by the Amicale des Algériens.

> You can't understand the history of the second generation without going back to the history of the Amicale des Algériens in the 1960s. At the time the Amicale decided to control the Algerian community for the reconstruction and support of Algeria. Thursdays and Saturdays we got together through activities organized by the Amicale. There were group trips to Algeria and theater companies organized by the Amicale.

Bennacer added that only in the 1970s did Algerian youth in France become disillusioned with the Amicale, seeing it more as a police apparatus bent on controlling the Algerian community rather than a tool for rebuilding a newly independent nation ravaged by years of war.[11]

During the 1970s many Algerian youth turned away from the Amicale and undertook their own cultural initiatives. Amateur theater companies were among the earliest collective initiatives by North African youth. Several of Radio Beur's founding members took part in the elaboration and production of Kahina's two plays, "Pour que les larmes de nos mères deviennent une légende" (1976) and "La Famille Ben Djelloul en France depuis 25 ans" (1979). The militant news magazine *Sans Frontière* provided another important formative experience for future Radio Beur administrators. From 1979 to 1985, *Sans Frontière* defended the rights of immigrant workers, denounced authoritarian regimes abroad, and promoted a budding, civil rights–style movement led by North African associations. Yet many immigrant youth who took part in *Sans Frontière* felt that the magazine was too oriented toward the struggle of immigrant workers and conflicts in the Third World. Moreover, they resented the rigid control maintained by a core group of militants from the Maghreb. Nacer Kettane, who spent two years at *Sans Frontière*, characterized the directors as being too detached from the concerns of his generation.

> We didn't have the same preoccupations. We had always lived here, our concerns were French within the world of immigration. They had other concerns. They were more interested in immigration, immigrants, their country of origin. They were too ghetto oriented . . . A whole group left at the same time at the beginning of 1981.[12]

Ironically, the founders of Radio Beur would later be criticized for many of the same things that caused them to leave *Sans Frontière*—the unwillingness of a core group of founders to relinquish or share power with a younger generation and the failure to define an audience and larger objectives.[13]

A Diversity of Objectives

Although many of the founders had experience in collective projects like Kahina and *Sans Frontière*, none had ever worked at a radio station. During the early months the founders faced a variety of daunting tasks. They had to define their objectives, structure the administration, organize the programs, assure the station's financing, attract an audience, and secure an official frequency on the FM dial. The accomplishments made during these months helped establish Radio Beur as a permanent fixture on the Parisian airwaves for over a decade. Yet the difficulties that arose would trouble the station throughout its existence.

While the founders agreed about the necessity of creating a means of communication for the North African community and immigrant youths in particular, they differed as to what they hoped to accomplish. Many of the founders saw the station in cultural terms while others emphasized a political or social agenda. Some station members joined Radio Beur without any clearly defined goals. They tended to view their participation in terms of a collective adventure, a means of making friends, or a form of pure entertainment.

For Saliha Amara, Radio Beur was an opportunity to counter negative stereotypes about first- and second-generation North Africans by promoting a greater degree of cultural awareness. "Much of the drive in 1981 to create ANGI (Association Nouvelle Génération Immigrée) and Radio Beur was the need to show that Arabs are capable of creating and doing things; they are not dependent people who fit all the stereotypes." Radio Beur was instrumental in breaking down these stereotypes.

> Radio Beur was a means of showing everything that was going on culturally in the immigrant community: music, literature, theater, etc. So people would see that there was a culture behind the term immigration and not just delinquency, prison, dependency—the objective of the station was to break all the clichés of the time.[14]

Nacer Kettane and Amar Driff saw Radio Beur in cultural terms. Kettane described Radio Beur as an instrument for the elaboration of a culture inherited by immigrant youth. He considered the new generation of Algerians raised in France as the "depositories of a cultural, social, and political heritage" that he linked to his parents' generation, the Algerian war, the contributions of immigrants to France since the end of World War II, and the individual experiences of immigrant youth in French cities.[15] Amar Driff joined Radio Beur with the dream of promoting an emerging *beur* culture.

Unfortunately, Driff explained, a flowering of North African artists in the early 1980s failed to establish a larger, self-sustaining cultural movement like jazz or blues.[16]

Driff was correct to point out that despite the surge of creative work from the North African community no new or clearly identifiable form of ethnic minority cultural expression has taken shape. It is possible to identify certain recurring elements and themes such as testimonial memorial or the legacy of the Algerian past. Moreover, many North African artists have been influenced by African American music, writers, and civil rights leaders. It is also not an exaggeration to posit that North Africans share a similar kind of double consciousness, or the sentiment of being participants/insiders and victims/outsiders to Western modernity, that marks black cultural expression in Britain and the United States. Yet these common elements, themes, influences, and sensibilities do not amount to a novel or clearly distinguishable style or mode of creation. In keeping with the nationalist tone of the Ken Burns documentary *Jazz*, it may simply be that the kinds of diasporic influences, traumatic history, and critical mass of consumers that combined to form music such as jazz or the blues represent a uniquely American experience.

In addition to visions of the station as a cultural instrument it was also perceived in social and political terms. According to Kamel Amara, everyone talked about North Africans except themselves. For Kamel the station was a "way of unifying the community and giving them the means to speak out in relation to serious events which could occur."[17] Many of the founders echoed the idea of the station as a mechanism that enabled North Africans to capture the public discourse and to shape their own image and place in French society.

Lastly, some of the founders joined Radio Beur without any particular objectives. Amar Bennacer admitted that he was like a big kid enjoying a great adventure. Though he became the first president of the station, he never imagined the potential that Radio Beur represented.[18] As for Kadour Guebli, he had recently arrived in France and saw Radio Beur as a way of making friends and enjoying himself. He was not a militant but was willing to offer his time and help.[19]

The founders eventually incorporated their objectives into a charter. The thrust of the charter, however, was cultural. It described the station as the receptacle of a rich but still-ignored cultural heritage. The station's mission was not only to establish this culture on an even footing with French culture but also to promote all cultures—regional or foreign—which were seen as sharing in a universal culture. The charter painted the station as the avatar of a cultural revolution in the making.

Radio Beur is the avant garde of a project which bears the name of cultural pluralism. Conscious of our treasure, of our faculties, Radio Beur will modify the French cultural environment. This pluralism, contrary to a digestive assimilation, will be a veritable cultural revolution which will completely change the orientation of French and Maghrebi culture.[20]

Next to these grandiose cultural objectives, the political dimensions of the charter seem somewhat minimal. The charter affirmed the station's intention to maintain its independence and freedom from all political parties and groups. It asserted the right to invite whichever politicians it wanted and proclaimed the need for North Africans to appropriate the discourse about themselves and to start taking an active role in shaping their own lives.

Even less space was given to social objectives. The charter maintained that the station would take up the difficult issues concerning immigrant children such as deportation, violence, delinquency, and unemployment. It stated that Radio Beur would work with local governments and communities to promote artistic creation, reading, and the acquisition of French, Arabic, and Berber. While it mentioned that Radio Beur grew out of the associational movement, it did not address how the station would position itself in relation to that movement. By and large, however, the charter portrayed the station as the pathbreaker of a new multicultural France.

Constructing the Station

After deciding on the name and putting together the charter, the founders began building the station during the winter of 1981–1982. A few members contributed the equivalent of several thousand dollars of their own money to purchase a transmitter and antenna. Kadour Guebli recalled that at the time it was a considerable amount of money—one month's salary for each person.[21] Amar Bennacer, who was working in sales at Darty (an electronics store), helped locate the equipment. To house the station, Hamid Ouchène offered his vacant one-bedroom apartment in Montreuil. Kadour Guebli provided much of the technical expertise and physical labor needed to convert the small apartment into a studio.

Saliha Amara remembered the cold winter day when they fixed the antenna on the roof of the Montreuil apartment building. It was snowing and there was no heat in the apartment so they broke some wooden crates to build a fire.[22] With Abaïd behind the microphone and everything in place they tested the equipment. Miraculously, everything worked. Geubli and Bennacer had driven off in a car and were able to pick up Abaïd's voice on their radio. Soon after this initial test they began airing music and broadcasting the station's phone number.[23]

In Radio Beur's first broadcasts station members called on listeners to support the station by contributing whatever they could. Moa Abaïd had fond memories of the generosity of those who responded with rugs, tables, chairs, and music.[24] In fact, many of those who came to Radio Beur with donations ended up staying on as hosts or administrators. Leïla Amriou was one of the more prominent examples. Surprised to hear Berber music on the radio, she and her mother decided to donate some records to the station that was only a short distance from their house. Amriou eventually joined the administration and replaced Saliha Amara as station treasurer.[25]

Radio Beur's first year was a time of many administrative changes. To comply with official regulations for private, local radio stations, Radio Beur had to structure itself as an association. In accordance with the 1901 law regulating associations, station members replaced the original collective with a general assembly and an administrative council. The general assembly, which consisted of all the members of the association, met once a year to elect the administrative council members (approximately ten) who in turn elected the station's bureau members. The statutes, which Saliha Amara copied from a form she found at the Bobigny prefecture, mandated the creation of several bureau positions—president, secretary, and treasurer—with the possibility of creating an assistant treasurer and secretary. Amar Bennacer became the first president, Saliha Amara treasurer, Nacer Kettane secretary, and Mohand Amara assistant secretary.

Some of the founders emphasized that these positions were needed solely to meet the requirements of the 1901 law and were never intended to be invested with any special status or prestige. Nacer Kettane recalled that titles and positions meant very little in the early going.

We had a collective, we didn't care about power. We created the first bureau the same day that we decided on the name. Saliha asked who wanted to be president. I didn't particularly want to. We didn't know what an association was. I had never seen the statues of an association. It was new for us. It was a new law after the arrival of the Socialist party. Amar Bennacer said he wanted to be president. Saliha said she would be treasurer since she was doing the same thing at ANGI. I took the position of general secretary, but just to fill the position. Mohand Amara became secretary general adjoint, but that was it. It was only to fill out a piece of paper. But everyone had an equal share of power. It was a collective.[26]

Radio Beur was conceived of as a collective project in which no member would be elevated above another. In fact, the founding charter expressly forbid all forms of hierarchies within the station. Nevertheless, these positions would later become a bitter source of conflict and a key factor in the demise of the station.

In addition to administrative changes, the content of the station's programs also had to be addressed. This meant defining the programs and more importantly, making sure there were enough people to keep the station running. Leïla Amriou noted that when Radio Beur began its broadcasts in the winter of 1981–1982 they lacked the people and programs to fill all their air time.[27] In the first months much of the empty time was filled with giant reels of music. Kadour Guebli and Leïla Amriou both recalled how Abedelwaheb Banaïssa, a student at the time, loaded the reels during the day until the staff arrived in the evening.[28] Amriou explained that after the station was up and running they became more aware of the needs of their listeners and organized their programs around them.[29]

Until 1984 the station operated on a shoe-string budget composed of income from concerts, membership dues, and donations. A ban on advertising prohibited Radio Beur, as well as all other radio stations in France, from tapping into its largest potential source of revenue. Station administrators found ways around the ban, such as sponsoring events and selling an assortment of items with the station's logo, but making ends meet was always a challenge.

Finding a permanent home on the FM dial consumed much of the station members' energy in the early years. The years 1982 and 1983 were chaotic in the history of French radio. In January 1982, just as Radio Beur began its broadcasts, the Holleaux Commission was created to process requests for frequencies. By the end of 1983, the Holleaux commission had received some 2,000 applications. In many cities the demand for frequencies far outstripped the supply. In the Paris region (20 km. around the capital) the High Authority decided on authorizing 22 frequencies while retaining some 89 applications. In order to find a place for everyone, the minister of communications asked stations to share frequencies by grouping together and forming alliances. He set an August 25, 1982 deadline for the alliances to be complete. New applications would then be resubmitted to the Holleaux commission by October 1, 1982. The definitive list of authorizations, good for three years, was to be issued on May 6, 1983.[30]

The call for stations to group together initiated a frenzied period of negotiations marked by many failed alliances. Radio Beur was swept up in this frantic search for a permanent home on the FM dial. Representatives from Radio Beur negotiated with a number of stations but were never satisfied with the outcome. Salah Medjani, one of Radio Beur's chief negotiators, recalled that other stations often failed to take Radio Beur seriously. "They all considered us as an insignificant station." Radio Gilda, with whom Radio Beur almost formed an alliance, wanted to absorb Radio Beur into its administrative structure and erase its name.[31]

In September 1982, Radio Beur finally reached an agreement with two stations—Radio Ask and Radio Rencontre—with whom it would ultimately share a frequency. Radio Ask was run by the Armenian Social Aide Association (Association Arménienne d'Aide Sociale); Rencontre represented three stations: Trans Italia, FMR, and Radio Portugaise.[32] On June 7, 1983, the High Authority for Audiovisual Communications, responsible for approving and distributing all frequency requests, authorized the alliance of Radio Beur-Ask-Rencontre to broadcast on 98.5 FM.[33] From 1983 to 1986, the three stations split their air-time and rotated broadcasting hours until Radio Beur secured its own frequency on 98.2 FM in 1987.

Programs

Many former administrators commented that Radio Beur filled a cultural void in France's North African immigrant community. Prior to the end of the state monopoly over radio, North Africans living in the Paris area could tune in to only a few hours of weekly broadcasts. Chérif Chikh, the last president of Radio Beur, argued that North Africans in France had been deprived of their culture for so long that Radio Beur was destined to be a success. "[North Africans] had lived for years in the most complete negation and overnight when they heard their music it was a complete victory. It was as simple as this. Regardless of the quality, the audience came in large numbers to support the station."[34]

For over a decade Radio Beur broadcast a wide range of music from the Maghreb over the Parisian airwaves. It took an active role in promoting scores of native North African singers as well as aspiring ethnic minority artists from France. Many of these performers took part in live programs that gave listeners the chance to call in and ask direct questions. Several stations members commented that Radio Beur was the driving force behind the success of raï music in France.

Yet the diffusion of music extended beyond the framework of station programs. In 1984, Radio Beur released an album featuring a number of previously unrecorded *beur* singers and musical groups. Throughout its 11-year existence Radio Beur claimed to be the largest organizer of concerts in the North African community. Its most successful concert, held at the Zénith

(Paris) in 1985, drew some 7,000 people. With between 1,000 and 2,000 people coming to a typical concert every two weeks, concerts were and remained one the station's principal sources of revenue. Concerts were also the means by which Radio Beur quickly anchored itself in the North African community and acquired a loyal following.

Kadour Jebbouri, who joined Radio Beur in its first months and stayed for the next ten years, commented that the station was the first to organize concerts in the North African community on a regular basis. "Before Radio Beur there were almost never any concerts for young people. No one ever rented out space for people to hear Berber or Maghrebi singers, they weren't performing anywhere else."[35] Malika Ouberzou, who joined the station in its first year, explained that today North Africans in France have much more access to their culture than in the early 1980s. "Now there are concerts at the Palais des Congrès, and the Olympia, but at the time there was nothing. At the time people rushed in to see mediocre singers but are now more selective."[36]

Music was not the only object of cultural promotion at Radio Beur. Scores of North African and French artists and intellectuals from diverse horizons took part in the weekly broadcast "La Tribune de Radio Beur." Shows such as "Triptyque" featured literature, and cinema; "Canoun" and "Tafsut" took up Berber language and culture. "Les Beurs et la Plume" gave listeners the opportunity to compose and present their own poetry.[37] In addition to these programs, the station created its own literary prize for promising North African novelists, published a collection of poems, *Les Beurs et la Plume* (1985) and an account of the 1988 antigovernment demonstrations in Algiers, *Octobre à Alger* (1988).

A great number of Radio Beur's programs depended on listener participation. "Flipper," for example, was a show directed at and run by North African youth. "Juridiquement vôtre," hosted by two lawyers, helped inform listeners about their rights by discussing pertinent topics and allowing callers to ask specific legal questions.[38] Several former station hosts commented that Radio Beur provided a particularly important outlet for women. In 1982 Lila Benbelaïd hosted a show called "Parole de Femmes" in which she invited guests and addressed a host of typically taboo subjects such as marriage, sex, and divorce. It aired in the afternoon when husbands and fathers were away at work and housewives and daughters were free to listen and call in with questions.[39] Aïcha Benmamar, who joined the station in the mid-1980s, added that women lawyers, writers, sociologists, and doctors who took part in many of these programs helped open a discussion and facilitated a dialogue with female listeners. According to Benmamar, the station encouraged women to express themselves and promoted a better understanding between the sexes.[40]

Language

Music occupied much of Radio Beur's air time. Most of the music featured in Radio Beur's diverse programs was by Arabic and North African singers from North Africa. According to Radio Beur's 1991 frequency application, French language music accounted for approximately 20 percent of the music aired by the station.[41] While the music aired by Radio Beur was predominantly Arabic or Berber, most of the speech was in French. As with other minority stations, language tendencies hinged on staff composition, audience, and financial constraints.

Radio Beur claimed a special following among North Africans raised in France. Most sons and daughters of North African workers have only a rudimentary understanding of Arabic or Berber—the two principal languages in the Maghreb. For Radio Beur to appeal to this audience it necessarily had to broadcast in French. Moreover, staff members, most of whom had spent all or most of their lives in France, shared these same language difficulties and were naturally inclined to use French.

Financial concerns also had a bearing on language choices. Stations structured as nonprofit associations, such as Radio Beur, rely heavily on state and local subsidies to cover significant portions of their operating costs. The FAS, responsible for promoting the inclusion of immigrants and their families into French society, is the chief source of subsidies for most minority associations, including radio broadcasters. FAS agent Fernanda da Silva noted that her agency subsidized about 70 stations in 1993—not all of which were minority broadcasters.[42] The chief preoccupation and determining factor for FAS support was the extent to which French or minority stations promoted the integration of immigrants and their families. In making this assessment, the FAS certainly considered French language programming as an important criterion. Thus it is important to distinguish between FAS support targeting ethnic minority communities and policies that foster the perpetuation of ethnic minority cultures.

Audience

There is considerable confusion surrounding audience figures. Minority broadcasters such as Radio Beur often exaggerated their own audience and professional surveys are unreliable. For example, in its 1991 frequency application, Radio Beur claimed to reach 800,000 listeners. Yet in the very same application an IPSOS survey, cited earlier, placed the station's Paris region audience at 121,500 in June 1991.[43] The problem resides in the fact that most nonprofit minority stations do not have the budget to conduct their own surveys and are naturally inclined to overestimate the size of their listening audience. Surveys taken by companies such as IPSOS or Médiametrie draw from disparate geographic samplings that do not reflect the demographic concentration of most minority communities.

In addition to the ambiguity of audience figures, it is difficult to determine exactly who listened to Radio Beur or came to its concerts at any point during its 11-year history. Former station administrators gave highly divergent accounts regarding the composition of Radio Beur's audience. Some claimed that all age groups listened to the station while others maintained that young people had little interest in Radio Beur. At issue is whether or not the station succeeded in attracting the population it claimed to represent.

According to Kadour Guebli and Amar Bennacer, Radio Beur failed to attract young listeners. Because there were few North African musicians from France, Guebli explained, they had to rely primarily on artists from the Maghreb. The preponderance of North African artists caused Radio Beur to be seen more as an immigrant station than one targeting North Africans raised in France. "We wanted to create a station for young people from the immigrant community but ultimately we created a station for the immigrant community." Young people, in Guebli's opinion, had no interest in the traditional music they heard on Radio Beur or at its concerts. Furthermore, the station needed financial support and it was immigrants not their sons and daughters who had the means to make contributions.[44]

Others claimed that the audience was more family oriented. While young people may have listened to mainstream stations by themselves or with friends, they listened to Radio Beur at home with their families. Although Kamel Amara recalled young people coming to the concerts with their parents to listen to Berber music, he believed that most urban North African youths had little interest in the station. "They were not interested at all because it was community oriented, they were more interested in NRJ or other [mainstream music] stations of the kind."[45]

Kamel's sister Saliha Amara argued that all generations listened to Radio Beur. She noted that the concerts were the only occasions when they had direct contact with their audience.

We saw parents and young people who came alone. We saw a mixed public. We knew that young people listened because they also came to the station to visit us. I think we reached all generations.[46]

In Nacer Kettane's opinion everyone listened to Radio Beur, young and old, though the station may have attracted more families.[47]

Divisions and Departure

By the time Radio Beur received its first official frequency on 98.5 FM most of the founding members had long since left the station. The cultural, political, and professional divisions that precipitated their departure would continue to trouble the station throughout its existence. Culturally, many resented what they considered to be the preferential treatment given to Berber culture. Politically, positions created to fulfill administrative requirements became the object of unending conflict and internal division. Professionally, Radio Beur was a disappointment to those who hoped to create a streamlined media modeled after a business.

Some station members denied the existence of any form of cultural or linguistic discrimination at Radio Beur. They argued that the frequent accusation that Radio Beur favored Berber culture and music, was understandable given the historical tensions between Berber and Arabic speakers in Algeria. During the period of conquest and colonization French authorities tended to conflate all Berber minorities with Kabyles, Algeria's largest Berber population. Kabyles came to be seen as culturally, religiously, and even racially closer to the French and consequently easier to assimilate and a more promising source of labor than the Arab majority. It was above all the reading of Kabyles as less influenced by Islam and more inclined toward French secular thinking that underpinned the "Kabyle myth."[48]

While never formalized into an official policy, the construction of schools and the creation of language, history, and cultural programs were among the many French actions that favored minority Berbers, especially those concentrated in the mountainous eastern regions of Kabylia and consequently known as Kabyles. By the late nineteenth century Kabyles were disproportionately represented in teacher-training schools in Algeria. "89% of the students of rural origin were also of Kabyle origin."[49] While Berber speakers represent some 25–30 percent of Algeria's total population, they were the first to arrive in France during the interwar years and remained the dominant segment of the Algerian immigrant population well into the 1950s.[50] Although more recent migrations have modified the composition of France's North African community, Berbers still predominate in the Paris region. Those who rejected accusations of cultural discrimination at Radio Beur claimed that Arabic-speaking minorities in the Paris region inevitably exaggerated the importance of Berber culture and music at Radio Beur.

Yet the Berber/Arabic issue troubled many of the founders who were themselves of Berber origin. It bothered Youcef Boussaa so much that he stayed for only a few months before leaving the station.

When people started to say there are too many Berbers not enough Arabs the conflict is important and moreover these problems were even more important because they were formulated by people who couldn't even correctly speak Arabic or Berber. I speak Arabic, Kabyle and French. I felt that I had no part in this conflict. When the French kill an Arab they don't ask if he is an Arab or Kabyle. I wasn't going to chose sides.[51]

Kamel Amara stayed for over a year but felt that he was becoming increasing isolated as new members arrived and most of the original group departed. He was angered by what he described as the Berberization of the station.

Most of the programs were in Kabyle which the Arabic speaking listeners would not necessarily be able to understand. I wanted to play a little of everything: Arabic, Kabyle, and Anglo-Saxon music and sometimes, by impulse, I only played Arabic [language] music just to make the point that while I'm a Kabyle I also listen to music in Arabic . . . It was at Radio Beur that I discovered that even within our own community there could be an anti-Arab racism, I didn't know this when I was a child so it shocked me a little.[52]

Moa Abaïd, one of the few Arabic-speaking founders, added that while there was a willingness to promote cultural diversity at Radio Beur, each host tended to do whatever he or she wanted. "It was very ambiguous, it wasn't a desire to Berberize the station."[53]

Disagreements that surfaced about how to balance North Africa's cultural diversity highlight the migration of cultural divisions across time and space. Sentiments of distrust and suspicion associated with cultural identities articulated by French authorities in the colonial past continue to function as a source of division and discord in the postcolonial present. As Anne McClintock has argued, these kinds of cultural continuities demonstrate the weakness of the term postcolonial that suggests a definitive break with the colonial era.[54]

If cultural issues were particularly sensitive and divisive at Radio Beur it was also because they remained a source of discord in Algeria. Radio Beur began broadcasting only a year after protests erupted in Kabylia in 1980 against the official policy of Arabization and for a greater degree of political and cultural recognition of Algeria's Berber minority. Through their broadcasts and concerts Radio Beur was instrumental in promoting the work of prominent Berber singers such as Idir, Aït Manguellet, and Ferhat who left for Paris in the 1970s and often used their music to promote democracy and recognition of Berber history in Algeria. The timing of Radio Beur's creation, its support for Berber performers, and the long history of ethnic tensions in Algeria were all factors that had the potential to contribute to cultural strains within the station and the perception of Radio Beur as being biased toward Berber speakers.

In addition to the issue of cultural diversity, endless personal and political conflicts drove many of the founders away from the station. For Amar Bennacer the problem became one of power.

> People became very conscious of the instrument they had in their hands. There began a power struggle. The power was in the hands of the administrative council and the presidency. Some people took advantage of the station as a means of creating a name or a political base.

Disillusioned and frustrated by the infighting, Bennacer finally decided to leave the station in which he had served as the first president.[55]

Many of the founders commented that positions which had been created to fulfill administrative requirements acquired a certain prestige and became the object of bitter internal struggles. They complained that those who worked for these positions were interested solely in their own personal or professional advancement and cared little about the North African community. Early on, Radio Beur became the locus for the creation of rival clans and competing ambitions—forces that would ultimately destroy the station.

Some of the founders envisioned the station as a professional instrument or business and decided to leave after becoming dissatisfied with its amateurism. Amar Driff imagined a station "with reporters not one in which they read the headlines of *Le Monde*. The idea was to create a powerful, professional instrument which would capture the creative energy of the community." Despite the ambitions of station members to intervene in a number of different areas—social, political, cultural, historical—it was impossible, according to Driff, because they lacked capable people.[56]

Kadour Guebli explained that he came from a business background and saw the station in terms of profit and losses. His thinking, however, did not mesh with the reality of a volunteer-based association.

> At the time I called for a definition of each person's responsibilities. I didn't think we all had to meet each time a decision had to be made. We needed to set it up and direct it like a business. But each time we needed a consensus. But to make the station work we absolutely had to have money. You couldn't make it work with all volunteers.

He eventually grew tired of the endless meetings and decided to devote himself to his job and family.[57]

The 1980s seemed to mark a series of successes for Radio Beur. Radio Beur secured a place on the FM dial, played a key support role in the rise of the associational movement, and became a recognized intermediary between the state and the North African community in the Paris region. In 1985, after a brief transitional stay in Bagnolet, Radio Beur moved into a new expanded studio in St. Ouen. When it came time to renew its frequency in 1986, station administrators were ready to request the right to broadcast around the clock on their own frequency.

Yet many of the internal problems that surfaced in the early years worsened in the course of the 1980s. The success of the first civil rights–style march on Paris in 1983, led by North African–run associations, precipitated a debate within the station about its dual role as a militant association and a professional media. Despite efforts to improve the quality of its programs and personnel, Radio Beur was forced to rely on scores of volunteers to keep it on the air. Many of these volunteers saw the station as a means of attaining a more valorized social status—a desire that was readily exploited by administrators seeking personal or professional gain. The tension between Arabic and Berber cultures continued to trouble the station. Radio Beur was unable to arrive at a cultural balance in its programming and was still regarded as a Berber station. As for the Radio Beur's audience, it remains unclear whether or not young people took any interest in the station.

Media or Militant Association

The year in which Radio Beur received its first frequency also marked the rise of a civil rights–style movement initiated by associations run by North African youth. According to Adil Jazouli, author of the most widely recognized account of the "beur" movement, Radio Beur was a key player in the 1983 March and one of several influential North African associations that hoped to convert the movement into a national federation or ethnic lobby.[58] Yet former Radio Beur administrators give highly divergent accounts of the station's role in the March for Equality and Against Racism.

Saliha Amara described Radio Beur as one of the three pillars behind the preparations for the arrival of the marchers in Paris. "In 1983 with ANGI, *Sans Frontière*, and Radio Beur we created the Paris collective which was an attempt to organize all the groups in the Paris region in relation to the marchers."[59] Samia Messaoudi, secretary general of Radio Beur at the time of the March, concurs with Amara. According to Messaoudi, Radio Beur informed its listeners about the progress of the March, encouraged listener participation, and invited the demonstrators to voice their ideas over the air.[60]

Yet, Kaïssa Titous, president of Radio Beur at the time of the March and the only woman ever to hold that position, charged that station officials were reluctant to support the movement.

> We were hoping that the station would become the instrument of what would become a much larger movement. But there were some at the station who felt that it belonged to them, they had created it... While they agreed that the station could act as a vector for the movement it was not to become an instrument for that same movement.

Titous believed that she was ultimately forced to resign because her political aspirations for Radio Beur conflicted with those of the other administrators.[61]

Titous's rivals rejected her charges and pointed out that Radio Beur opened its doors to hundreds of associations throughout its 11-year history. It even created a permanent time slot in which associations were invited to come and explain their work. They noted that it was often difficult to balance the station's dual role as a professional media and a militant association. As a media the station had to maintain a certain degree of independence and freedom of action. But being a militant association meant taking a stand in defense of the North African community. Titous, they charged, was willing to sacrifice the station's autonomy by locking it into a political movement.

Titous willingly admitted that her interests lay more in politics than the administration of a radio station. After her brief presidency at Radio Beur she joined SOS-Racisme and then went on to become the director of the 1988 presidential campaign of Pierre Juquin, candidate of a reformist wing of the Communist party.[62] However, it is also true that early on in the station's history, Radio Beur became a battle zone for the control of influential administrative positions, particularly the presidency. Given the ferocity of the individual rivalries that ultimately destroyed Radio Beur, it seems more likely that Titous's short-lived presidency was the result of long-standing internal divisions and competing ambitions within the station.

Amateurism versus Professionalism

Professionalizing the station became an even more important issue after Radio Beur received its first official frequency in 1983. The task, however, remained an imposing one. Radio Beur never possessed the resources to offer all the services it wanted. For example, it was never able to create its own news show because this meant purchasing a telex and hiring and training reporters—luxuries that it could not afford. Throughout its history Radio Beur relied primarily on scores of volunteers to keep it on the air. People were constantly coming and going and few hosts put in the time and effort needed to produce professional caliber programs.

When Achour Fernane came to Radio Beur in 1985 he was surprised by the shortage of personnel. Fernane had spent three years as a programs producer with the Algerian national radio RTA before arriving in France in 1982 and was one of the few trained professionals at Radio Beur.

> I came from a large station. When I did my program there were 10 people who worked with me. When I had to travel on assignment I had a technician, a chauffeur, and for the production I had someone who handled the montage, the mixing... When I discovered [Radio Beur] I wondered how you could work under these conditions. I mean, to find yourself suddenly responsible for an entire program. When I did a program [at Radio Beur] I put everything together, I did the mixing, and I chose the records. In Algeria I had a producer who handled all this.[63]

Mohand Dehmous, president of Radio Beur in 1988 and 1990, commented that professionalizing the station was one of his highest priorities and most disappointing failures. Originally joining Radio Beur as a host in connection with his journal and association Nous Autres, he stressed that the time and energy he put into his own show were exceptional. "In terms of the content, most of the programs were not elaborated or well structured. This was always my criticism of minority-run stations, that in terms of their content they were rather mediocre." The station, according to Dehmous, was not a professional one but rather a mechanism that allowed for spontaneous expression. Though he wanted to professionalize the station he felt that it was impossible to find the right people. "What can you do. If you fire someone you don't have anyone to replace him."[64] Chérif Chikh recalled that it was often difficult to convince those at the station that they needed training. "Some didn't even realize the need to professionalize and felt that they were already professionals after working at the station for a few years."[65]

One important obstacle to the professionalization of Radio Beur was the entrenched nature of its rank and file members. Several station members commented that Radio Beur became a refuge for marginalized youth from the North African community. The difficulties of "insertion" into French society created a population eager to latch on to any organization that promised some form of social standing and economic opportunity. Chérif Chikh recalled that some members began to think of themselves in terms of their work at the association, forgetting that associations were not intended to serve individuals as their primary social activity.[66]

A number of former administrators commented that because they had good jobs and a solid professional identity they were more free than others to act with the true interests of the association and North African community in mind. They did not need to look to Radio Beur to fill any kind of professional void. Nacer Kettane noted that his work at Radio Beur was strictly personal. He was professionally secure when he joined Radio Beur and had no interest in power politics. "I was a medical student at the time. For me the station was a militant action. I knew that I would be a doctor. My professional situation was already determined. The station was something extra in relation to my culture."[67]

The socioeconomic dimension of Radio Beur underscores the importance of recognizing that multicultural projects should not be thought of exclusively in terms of culture. The dissemination of news, music, and specialized programs for the benefit of the North African community was only one aspect of Radio Beur. It was also a highly contested space where marginalized immigrant youths sought out economic opportunities or a more valorized individual identity and ambitious administrators vied for control of a station that represented an important power base in the North African community.

Balancing Arabic and Berber Culture

In addition to the difficult task of professionalization, Radio Beur struggled to achieve some sort of ethnic balance in its programming. The charter clearly states that Radio Beur would treat all cultures and languages equally. There was to be no discrimination. The station would become a model of multiculturalism. Yet even after the first few months of operations many of the founders left because they felt that the station tended to privilege Berber culture.

Working on a study of Radio Beur in 1988, Fattah Allah found that Berber (or Kabyle) music was given a disproportionate place at the station. "The particularity of the music broadcast by Radio Beur resides in the central place reserved for Kabyle music." He noted that the breakdown of music according to the three cultural guidelines was not followed. "Arabic music is almost completely absent, and the music time is practically split between Occidental and Kabyle music with the later predominating." Fattah Allah explained that this was partly due to the predominance of Berber hosts at Radio Beur.[68] Hamid Ouchène, former station director, commented that the cultural breakdown was a guideline that was not always respected by individual hosts. "Theoretically the station played 33 per cent Arabic, Berber and French music but this was not what happened in reality."[69]

In his short study of Radio Beur in 1989, Michel Anglade discussed the efforts made by Radio Beur to diversify its personnel and programs.

> Moroccan and Tunisian hosts were recruited. Pied-noir Jews have been given a music show. Radio Beur has even tried to go beyond the boundaries of the Maghreb and has opened itself to Sub-Saharan Africa and to the Antillies through a "black" show hosted by a Martiniquan.[70]

While president of Radio Beur in 1989 and 1990, Mohand Dehmous tried to expand the number of shows in Arabic.

> Most of Radio Beur's audience were Berber speakers in the Paris area. But I don't think that you can say it was a Berberist station. When I was in the administrative council I looked everywhere for Arabic speaking people to do programs strictly in Arabic. We had programs in Kabyle, French, Chaoui. In our charter it stipulated that we expressed ourselves in the three languages but objectively it was difficult to find people to broadcast shows in Arabic all the time.[71]

Others continued to reject the accusation that Radio Beur was too Kabyle oriented. For Nacer Kettane this accusation was a reflection of the cultural racism in Algeria that had been transplanted to France. He noted that before Radio Beur there was very little Berber music on the French airwaves. This should not be surprising, he said, because immigration is a reflection of what goes on in the country of origin except that immigrants are usually even more radical. He asserted that Radio Beur, however, did not practice any kind of cultural or linguistic discrimination. "We were a tolerant, not a closed station."[72]

Audience

In addition to the Berber/Arabic question, the audience composition of Radio Beur remains a mystery. Though the station targeted the entire North African community, it staked a special claim to second-generation listeners. The 1991 frequency application describes Radio Beur as "the number one community station. Its field of intervention is constituted by the Maghrebian community living in France and more particularly by the young people from this community: the Beurs."[73] Yet when asked to define Radio Beur's audience the mixed nature of responses given by its former administrators raises questions about whether or not the station interested the generation it claimed to represent.

According to Kader Jebbouri, longtime Radio Beur administrator and technician, the station started off with a mainly first-generation audience but gradually drew more young people. Jebbouri explained that this was due to the preponderance of traditional music aired by the station in its first months. As Radio Beur diversified its music and programs larger numbers of young people began to tune in. He added that the key role Radio Beur played in spreading *raï* music in France did much to attract younger listeners.[74]

Nadia Hadjeli, who joined Radio Beur in the mid-1980s, made exactly the opposite argument. She claimed that in the early years Radio Beur succeeded in attracting a younger audience because of the nature of its shows and music, which appealed to a younger generation. In the latter part of the 1980s the station lost this segment of its audience because of a tendency to air more traditional music and programs with no connection to the interests or concerns of young people. "Toward the end of the 1980s, 1988 or 1989, it was more the immigrants who called for music. They no longer had shows on the banlieues or other topics which could interest young beurs." In Hadjeli's opinion, the airing of what she described as poor quality raï music did more to scare away than attract a younger audience.[75]

Achour Fernane, who joined Radio Beur in 1985 and stayed on for the next five years, was convinced that most young people took little or no interest in Radio Beur. Fernane, vice president of Radio Beur in 1990, claimed that the station was followed primarily by first-generation immigrants, families, and perhaps some older sons and daughters of immigrant workers who were curious about their roots.

> We failed to attract young people. Up to a certain age they listened to Radio Beur because their mothers and fathers listened. But once they were outside, in high school, they listened to other things, NRJ, Voltage FM, Radio Nova.

Fernane explained that younger members of the North African community wanted to be like their French friends and listened to the same mainstream stations. Only as they grew older did they come to appreciate stations like Radio Beur.

> If you go into a high school and ask a young [North African] you'll see that he listens to the same thing as Françoise and Pierre, he has roughly the same values, watches the same TV shows. Only after going to college

will some Maghrebians listen to Radio Beur because the setting determines their choice. In college they meet more people in unions from different cities and it is at this time that they begin to ask questions about their own identity and culture.[76]

Mohand Dehmous agreed that a large part of Radio Beur's audience was composed of immigrants.

It was fundamentally a station for immigrants. It was immigrants who gave it its consistency, who identified with it and most of those who directed it were immigrants. There were no beurs within it.[77]

Samia Messaoudi, longtime administrator and general secretary, added that the station was more successful with families then young people. If young people listened it was because their mothers had the station turned on at home. "We would have liked to have had more young people who felt concerned about the station by themselves without it being the mother or family listening to Radio Beur in the kitchen and the son who goes into the kitchen and listens to the station."[78]

Generational Divisions

While it is uncertain how many North African youths listened to Radio Beur, it is clear that there were few young people in the station's administration. Most of the administrative council and bureau positions were held by an older generation born in the early 1950s. Despite yearly elections, the composition of the administrative council and bureau positions remained fairly stable throughout the 1980s. For most of the decade, three people occupied the presidency of Radio Beur: Nacer Kettane, Mohand Dehmous, and Mouloud Chalah.

Many younger members of Radio Beur commented that the older generation refused to relinquish power. Nadia Kessaci was 20 when she joined Radio Beur in 1986.

Many young people took part in the station without ever becoming part of the administrative council . . . They could have done interesting things. I said at the time that the older people should make room for the younger ones who had something to say to people like them. I think they should have left the station to young people between twenty and thirty and allowed them to direct the station.[79]

Kessaci's husband, Mohand Dehmous, regretted that Radio Beur failed to transfer its administrative positions to a younger generation.

> I felt that we needed new people in the administrative council. If we wanted it to be a beur radio we needed beurs in the administrative council not old people like us but young people with a different mentality who react differently and have different references and concepts, but this never happened. People hung on to their positions while they earned nothing from it; that was what was so incredible. But for some of them it was very important to say that they were members of the administrative council of Radio Beur.[80]

The growing prominence of Radio Beur within the North African community partly explains this reluctance to give way to a younger generation. Presidents of Radio Beur came to command the respect and loyalty of rank and file members who often saw the station as a way out of a devalorized identity. Moreover, broadcasting in the Paris region to the largest concentration of North Africans in France, it is understandable why older administrators would be hesitant to transfer the reigns of power. Beyond the influence offered by administrative positions, Radio Beur eventually generated advertising revue, which may have proved too much of a temptation for some station members.

Faced with the reality of an administration that did not conform to the *beur* image several of the younger administrators commented that they had been used to project a more appropriate facade. Kamel Amara was some ten years younger than the other founding members.

> I think that they used me at the time because I was the beur element. Because I was the youngest they certainly wanted me to talk with it being understood [that I represented] the beur youth, those who were 17, 18, or 19 years old. The others were 27 or 28 and sometimes 30 years old.[81]

Leïla Amriou was 20 when she joined Radio Beur in 1982. Like Kamel, she was frequently chosen as a spokesperson for Radio Beur. She noted that the other station members were aware of the shortage of young people at Radio Beur and tried to correct the problem. "At a certain point those in the station realized that they were not very representative of the younger generation and that's when they tried to interest other younger people to do shows on the music they liked."[82]

Yet many of the young people who joined the station's administrative council felt that Radio Beur and the majority of its administrators had little to do with their generation. Leïla's younger sister Linda and her friend Wahiba joined Radio Beur in the early 1980s and hosted a show called Multirythm featuring jazz, funk, and rock. "As far as *real beurs* we played music for young people." Linda explained that most of the shows featured more traditional music that tended to scare away listeners from her generation. She remembered that other station members were not pleased with her show because she and Wahiba used the language of young people on the air.

> We spoke on the air like we did in real life; some didn't like this and in the administrative council we argued....Others wanted us to speak more politely, not like young people.

According to Linda the station aired too many shows in Arabic and Kabyle, which young people could not understand. She thought the programs should have been divided 50/50 into traditional and young people's music. She felt that most of those at Radio Beur, including the hosts, were products of North African culture and had little to do with immigrant youth raised in France. "There weren't many people born in France—me, my sister Leïla, Wahiba, maybe Kamel and that's it—the others came young or later but there weren't many who were born in France."[83]

When Kamel Amriou's (no relation to Linda and Leïla Amriou) mother told him about Radio Beur, he was furious about what he heard.

> If they hadn't called themselves Radio Beur I never would have listened to them. I felt that they had insidiously taken a name which didn't correspond to us. They couldn't call themselves beur because they weren't. They were all closer to forty than thirty. Beurs are people today who are closer to thirty.

Kamel joined Radio Beur because he felt that his generation needed real representation. However, he did not believe that Radio Beur ever had much to do with his generation. "It was a total failure because the true beurs were never represented." Young people, like himself, knew of the station through their families. "They [families] listened to folklore but beurs don't." He believed that the station limited itself largely to families.[84]

While many of those interviewed agreed that Radio Beur administrators did not qualify as *beurs* there was no consensus on the precise meaning of the term. Are *beurs* only teenagers or people in their twenties? Did one stop being a *beur* at a certain age? Should *beur* be understood in cultural terms rather than age? Are *beurs* only those born in France and attuned to Western forms of popular culture? Is it possible to be a *beur* if you were born in North Africa but came to France at an early age? The difficulty of establishing who qualifies as a *beur* may be just as complex and uncertain as determining who deserves to be regarded as French.

The Decline and Fall of Radio Beur

Despite a host of internal divisions, Radio Beur continued to prosper. According to an independent 1990 IPSOS survey the station's audience in Paris and its immediate suburbs grew from 59,928 in 1989 to 89,892 in 1990. In the Paris region (Ile-de-France), during the same period, the audience increased from 76,536 to 127,560.[85] But shortly after Radio Beur reached its zenith, it began a rapid downward spiral culminating in the station's disappearance from the FM dial in 1992. The collapse of Radio Beur was caused by a new political and economic context that took shape in the late 1980s. First, a growing hostility toward ethnic minorities in France shifted political support away from multicultural initiatives such as Radio Beur. Second, in 1987, the station acquired the right to broadcast around the clock on its own frequency. Third, in the same year, station administrators decided to begin airing commercials. Fourth, the brutal repression of antigovernment protests in Algiers in October 1988 enhanced the political significance of Radio Beur as an intermediary between the North African immigrant community and both the French and Algerian governments. This new context intensified and unleashed centrifugal forces long present within the station.

By the late 1980s almost all traces of a public discourse in favor of multiculturalism had vanished. North African youth, who a few years before represented an "opportunity for France," now became the new "dangerous classes" who populated France's demonized suburbs (*banlieues*). The rise of public sentiment against immigration and the electoral success of the extreme right caused the Socialists to abandon their earlier liberal positions toward immigrants and minorities.[86] Finding solutions to the problems of unemployment, drugs, and urban violence took precedence over the promotion of cultural diversity. "Integration" became the new term used to discuss the incorporation of minorities into French society. It was a much broader and more ambiguous term than "insertion" and applied to all those who were excluded from the mainstream for cultural, social, or economic reasons. Integration became the all-encompassing solution to the complex problems of insiders and outsiders in a polarized, postindustrial French society.

The diminished support for cultural pluralism in the course of the 1980s is also reflected in the policies of the FAS. Michel Yahiel, director of the FAS from 1986 to 1991, commented that during the Chirac interregnum (1986–1988) his agency faced strong pressure to cut off subsidies to private local radio stations, which were seen as having too much influence. He personally tried to shift FAS support away from cultural projects that targeted specific communities to ones that encompassed larger, more diverse audiences.[87] He also responded to widespread concerns over abuse of state subsidies by associations throughout France. In the late 1980s, the FAS introduced new control measures to monitor how associations used state subsidies. A surprise audit of Radio Beur by the FAS in 1989 reflected the growing government suspicion of minority cultural projects.

This changing climate was worsened by internal divisions within the station. Though former administrators claim that Radio Beur was always financially strapped, the influx of money from commercials combined with the new 24-hour format exposed the station to the danger of appropriation by individual interests and to increased problems of corruption. Archour Fernane, vice president of Radio Beur in 1990, resigned when he became aware that people were taking kickbacks from advertising. According to Fernane, a small circle of people controlled and profited from the station's resources. Those outside that circle, regardless of their position, had no access to the station's accounting books.[88] Karim Sadi-Haddad, a longtime DJ at Radio Beur who joined the administrative council in 1987, recalled that everyone was fighting over control of the sales department because that was where all the money came in.[89]

Infighting, which was nothing new at Radio Beur, became more pronounced after 1988. It was in October 1988 that protests exploded in Algeria in response to the country's economic crisis and perceived political bankruptcy. In an effort to restore order Algerian security forces killed hundreds of protestors and took thousands into custody.[90] That same year three factions formed within the station and each leader—Mohand Dehmous, Nacer Kettane, and Mouloud Chalah—accused the others of selling out Radio Beur to foreign or French political interests. The most serious accusations were that Mouloud Chalah, president of Radio Beur at the time, was collaborating with the Amicale des Algériens, the most important arm of the Algerian government in France. Many believed that the Amicale wanted to use the station to police the Algerian community in France and to bolster its sagging image. Kettane and his supporters were in turn accused of working with the Socialist party. At a later date, Mohand Dehmous was charged with collaborating with the Algerian government. While castigating their rivals, all three leaders portrayed themselves as the true defenders of the principles of autonomy and independence enshrined in the founding charter.

Until the 1980s, the Amicale des Algériens had played a preponderant role in the political and cultural life of France's Algerian community. However, immigrant youth, who had become increasingly rooted in France and disenchanted with the absence of democracy in Algeria, participated in fewer and fewer numbers. By 1984, while the Amicale enjoyed the support of 60 percent of the Algerian community, immigrant youth accounted for only 15 percent of the membership. The Amicale did take steps to strengthen its appeal to younger members of the Algerian community. In 1988 the Amicale created a youth organization, Recherches-Perspectives-Expression-Société (REPERES). REPERES, which encouraged second-generation Algerians to exercise their civic rights as French citizens, demonstrated a more flexible attitude toward the special status of immigrant youth (despite the fact that the Algerian government still refused to recognize dual citizenship).[91] However, even this measure failed to redress the declining membership of immigrant youth. By the early 1990s the Amicale was "virtually defunct."[92]

The proliferation of minority-run association certainly contributed to the break between immigrant youth and the Amicale. The creation of autonomous associations challenged the ascendancy of the Amicale and empowered North African youth to define their own relationship with France and Algeria. This newly acquired autonomy sometimes translated into overt criticisms of Algerian policies, such as Radio Beur's coverage of the suppression of the 1988 antigovernment protests. The Amicale responded with outrage in its official publication, *Actualité de l'émigration*, to the tendency of many immigrant youth to side with the protesters.[93]

It is impossible to discern what role, if any, the Algerian government played in the final years of Radio Beur. Evidence of political intervention is limited to hearsay. What is more important is how widespread these accusations became after the events of 1988 and how they played on and accentuated older factional divisions. Nacer Kettane admitted that factional conflict took over the station after 1987. "The group exploded into several clans, the station lost its dynamism. I should have left in 1987 but many urged me to stay arguing that others would destroy the station."[94] Many other former administrators echoed Kettane's comments. While they had more to lose by staying on at Radio Beur, they argued, someone had to defend the integrity of the station against those who would stop at nothing to corrupt and destroy it.

Mohand Dehmous described the turmoil at Radio Beur in terms of three currents that took shape in the late 1980s. The first was the Amicale des Algériens, which wanted to infiltrate the station to prove to the Algerian government that it was effectively controlling the Algerian community in France. The second was French political forces sensitive to the behavior of North African youths in the cities and who were slowly becoming aware of the potential of the *beur* electorate. Dehmous naturally placed himself in the third current.

> A third current wanted to preserve the free and independent station charter. These were people who believed that the station was meant to serve the community and shouldn't be allied with the Algerian government through the Amicale or with the French government through the Socialists or others. This was the original idea.[95]

Throughout his personal history of the events at Radio Beur from 1989 to 1991, Mouloud Chalah castigated his principal rivals for betraying the station and the North African community. He portrayed himself as the faithful defender of Radio Beur fighting for the well-being of the station and the community that it served. He called on the minister of the interior, the minister of justice, and even the prime minister to resolve the conflict.

> I call with all of my heart on all the associations, those which believe in what we do. For democracy, to organize their efforts to condemn those who would assassinate this community media. My efforts in these last years and those of my team have enabled Radio Beur to be a leader of its kind in France. It remains loyal to its engagements which work for liberty, democracy, and a better understanding in French society.[96]

Whether or not any of these charges hold any truth, it is certain that accusations of political treachery were an effective means of discrediting rivals. Most former administrators continued to believe that after 1988 Radio Beur became the victim of larger political forces.

The increased political and economic significance of Radio Beur led its factional leaders to exploit the station's two principal structural weaknesses—ambiguous membership lists and proxy voting. Throughout its history the administrators of Radio Beur never established an official membership list. Every year the station submitted the names of the administrative council members to the local prefecture but never a list of everyone in the association. In principle, only the general assembly, which consisted of all the members of the association, could admit new members. In practice, administrators brought in whomever they wanted. Nacer Kettane noted, "anyone could claim to be a member of the station. Only the original collective papers and the first bureau were legal papers, the rest are not clear."[97] Without any officially recognized membership list, the authority of station officials always lacked legitimacy.

To complicate matters, voting practices were equally ambiguous. The statutes failed to set limits on proxy voting. From the mid-1980s, certain administrators arrived at general assemblies with large numbers of proxy votes from absentee station members. These votes were inevitably used to secure the positions of those who possessed them. After spending several years in the administrative council as treasurer, Malika Ouberzou left in 1985 when Mouloud Chalah became president and his supporters took control of the station. She was angered by the methods she claimed Chalah used to secure his election.

> The vote wasn't exactly democratic, he arrived with seventeen proxy votes. To come with seventeen proxy votes when there were twenty-five at the meeting was somewhat grotesque. No one dared to say no. There were no regulations at the time determining at what time someone could join the administrative council or not. Chalah was there all the time and could bring whomever he wanted.

Finding herself in the minority Ouberzou decided to resign.[98] By the end of the 1980s the introduction of new members into the association and the problem of proxy voting reached unparalleled levels of abuse.

In 1989 Radio Beur was crippled by a series of general assemblies in which all three factional leaders declared themselves to be the legitimately elected presidents of the association. Conflict paralyzed the station; bills went unpaid; the banks no longer knew whose signature was valid for the station's accounts; and the post office sent the mail to a mediator. Radio Beur actually went off the air for several days after the electricity company cut the power.[99] Ultimately, the court was left to decide which membership list and election was legitimate. In an effort to resolve the conflict the court appointed several provisional administrators to oversee the station's operations and to organize new elections. None of these measures proved effective.

Eventually, one of the factional leaders, Nacer Kettane, founded a network of stations in the south of France under the name Beur FM. In 1992, after resigning from his position as copresident of Radio Beur, he presented his own application for a Paris frequency. Kettane's plans for Beur FM in Paris rejected the associational model in favor of a privatized, commercial station. During the winter and into the summer of 1992, Radio Beur and Beur FM locked horns in a struggle over the Paris frequency. In June 1992, the Conseil supérieur de l'audiovisuel decided in favor of Beur FM granting it 12 hours of broadcasting time on 106.7 FM from which it continues to operate.[100] Radio Beur's application was rejected and the station disappeared from the airwaves in September 1992. Shortly afterward, Mouloud Chalah, whose lifework had become closely connected to the station, committed suicide.

Conclusion

Radio Beur represents a landmark experience in the history of ethnic minority struggles for recognition in France. For over a decade Radio Beur functioned as a vector of entertainment and information for a community that had long been relegated to the margins of French society. Through its broadcasts and concerts Radio Beur helped promote aspiring and veteran performers from the Maghreb and France's North African community. From its programs to its concerts Radio Beur became an important site of exchange and interaction within the North African community. As former President Kaissa Titous remarked, "it was a place for informing people, for socializing and meeting people. Radio Beur was a house built collectively. Everyone had his or her own stone."[101]

Yet the trials and tribulations of Radio Beur ultimately paralleled those of the associational movement. Launched during a period of unprecedented optimism about the prospects for ethnic diversity and ethnic minority actors in France, the managers of Radio Beur were never able to reach a consensus on the future objectives for the station. Should they be a militant or professional station? Was it possible to be both at the same time? As with the associational movement, defining objectives was so difficult precisely because staff members and management lacked trust and confidence in each other and were constantly worried about being manipulated by outside political forces. Riven by fears of political intrigue and foul play, caught up in a welter of mutual accusations and recriminations, what had begun as an adventure by a handful of friends ended up degenerating into a bitter struggle in the courts over the control of the station.

In the case of Radio Beur we learn that divisions within the station were present from a very early date. In fact some of these divisions, such as the charges that Radio Beur favored Berber culture and music, were rooted in the colonial past and mirror ongoing tensions in the Algerian present. While rejected by many former station members, the conviction that Radio Beur was biased toward Paris's majority Berber population was enough to precipitate the departure of some of the station's founding members. Just as Algeria continues to be torn by divisions between the Arabic-speaking majority and the Berber minority, Radio Beur was long plagued by the challenge of striking a cultural balance that would satisfy all of its members.

However, Radio Beur's undoing appears to have been largely caused by its own success. Just as the station reached its largest audience, acquired the right to broadcast around the clock and to collect new sources of revenue it became caught in internal conflicts that finally caused its demise. Amidst the political backdrop of mass protests and violence in Algeria, Radio Beur factionalized and charges began to circulate that rival leaders were in bed with either French or Algerian authorities. Given the station's claim to autonomy, accusations of political manipulation were the surest way of discrediting rivals. My contention is that the new sources of commercial revenue and the prestige gained by the station within the North African community became a magnet for ambitious individuals that overwhelmed larger concerns for the well-being of the station. Moreover, because so many rank and file members of Radio Beur lacked a stable and secure professional identity the station offered a powerful substitute that could be exploited by individuals seeking to promote their own leadership roles. As with the associational movement, just as the political climate was hardening toward ethnic minority projects Radio Beur failed to maintain the kind of solidarity that was paramount for its survival.

CHAPTER 4

Exhibiting Minorities: The Politics of Recognition at Beaubourg

On January 18, 1984 the Centre Nationale d'Art et de Culture Georges Pompidou, commonly known as Beaubourg, opened its doors to an unprecedented three-month exhibition. Entitled, *Les enfants de l'immigration* (immigrant children), the exhibition showcased the creative work of young artists and creators from France's diverse ethnic minority communities. Set in one of the capital's premiere cultural institutions, then drawing over seven million visitors a year, and offering a prominent place to North African youth, *Les enfants de l'immigration* seemed to offer exactly the kind of institutional recognition and public forum long sought by cultural and political actors from France's North African immigrant community. Attracting some 4,800 visitors daily—one-fifth of Beaubourg's daily average—and over 400,000 in total, *Les enfants de l'immigration* appeared to be an unparalleled success.[1]

Landmark Event

Conceived as a "living exhibition" (*spectacle vivant*), *Les enfants de l'immigration* was built around a stage used for plays, concerts, and dance. In the course of the exhibition some 29 theater troupes, 22 singers and musical groups, and 10 dance companies performed on stage at Beaubourg. Moreover, a series of scheduled debates and a number of live broadcasts by minority-run radio stations transformed Beaubourg into a place for lively and often passionate discussion. According to José Chapelle, commissary for the exhibition, Beaubourg had never before experienced anything like

Les enfants de l'immigration. With stands for people to sit and watch the daily performances, *Les enfants de l'immigration* was an unparalleled event in the history of the Centre.[2] Véronique Hahn, Chapelle's colleague and co-organizer of the exhibition, added that *Les enfants de l'immigration* drew people who had never ventured inside of Beaubourg—especially members of France's immigrant communities.[3]

The exhibition consisted of three sections, which fanned out from the stage and contained a variety of more conventional exhibits—movies, pictures, sculptures, reports, poems, and frescos. Each section represented a segment of France's immigration history. The first section, *l'arrachement* (the tearing away), evoked over a hundred years of immigration to France through documents and audiovisual reports on the history of Italian and North African workers in the Longwy-Villerupt mining region. The second section, *le creuset* (the melting pot), focused on the present. By far the richest section in terms of exhibits, *le creuset* contained some nine cubicles or mini-sections each representing different aspects of the lives of immigrant youth. For example, the mini-section *dedans et dehors* (inside and out) used photographs to contrast the family life of North African, Senegalese, and Portuguese immigrant children with their experiences outside the home. The *espace d'intégration* (integration space) featured a variety of initiatives by immigrant youth from the founding of a fast-food restaurant (California Burg) and jazz ballet company (Ballet Jazz Art) to the creation of a moving company (Transit Service) and a Portuguese language rock band (Diferencas). *Le Patrimoine Common* (Common Patrimony) took up a range of political and social issues from the rise of an autonomous associational movement led by immigrant youth to efforts to transform the image of Les Minguettes (Lyon), one of France's more ethnically volatile urban centers. Finally, the third section, *la construction*, represented the future of France's foreign population. Within this section four towers illustrated the efforts of immigrant youth to shape their future through associations, news magazines, publishing companies, and entertainment initiatives. Video reports offered insights into what "interculturality" could bring to schools and urban renewal projects. A fresco, composed of photographs, invited visitors to consider how immigrant children enrich French society. In short, the exhibition became a kind of journey through a certain vision of the past, present, and future of immigration in France.

Central to *Les enfants de l'immigration* was the autonomy of its participants who played an instrumental role in shaping the character of the exhibition. For this reason, Chapelle explained, the organizers tried to find intermediaries who were as close as possible to the participants and avoided large associations and government agencies charged with the issue of immigration. While a number of ministries and agencies provided funding, they did not take part in the actual design and conceptualization process. With support from Beaubourg staff, a variety of projects were put together locally then transported to the Centre.[4] Inter-Service Migrants (ISM), which catalogues and acts as a promotional intermediary for minority artists, offered vital technical and logistical support in selecting and coordinating the work of performing artists.

Unlike most Beaubourg exhibitions, *Les enfants de l'immigration* contained a wide range of amateur and semiprofessional productions. There were drawings by schoolchildren and prisoners as well as sculptures by graduates of Paris' elite École des Beaux Arts and music by accomplished performers. It was this mixture of professional and amateur productions combined with a vast array of live performances and debates that made *Les enfants de l'immigration* so unique and drew unprecedented numbers of ethnic minority visitors.

In his survey of some 800 visitors, Philippe Coulaud observed that an unusually high number of people came exclusively for the exhibition. According to Coulaud, four out of ten visitors came with the intention of seeing the exhibition. Moreover, 25 percent of those who visited *Les enfants de l'immigration* came more than five times and 10 percent of the visitors frequented the exhibition more than 25 times—an exceptionally high percentage of repeat visitors in Coulaud's opinion. "While Beaubourg's library (Bibliothèque Public de l'Information) has built a loyal following, (one out of two [visitors] has come more than twenty times), this phenomenon has never occurred at a temporary exhibit, at least not on this scale."[5]

Les enfants de l'immigration seemed to be perfectly in keeping with the spirit of Beaubourg. Envisioned as a pluri-disciplinary institution that would help democratize and promote a broader more inclusive conception of culture, Beaubourg was the inheritor of both the democratizing impulses of the Popular Front and the antielitist, antistatist spirit of 1968. Even the setting and architecture of Beaubourg underscored its mission to break with the ivory tower tradition of France's cultural institutions.[6] Located in a historically working-class neighborhood, Beaubourg's design, "which displays the inner-workings on the outside," was a deliberate effort to demystify the Centre by visually exposing it to the public.[7]

Yet until *Les enfants de l'immigration*, Beaubourg had never before addressed the theme of immigration. The Musée National d'Art Moderne (MNAM), responsible for the largest number of exhibitions at Beaubourg, focuses on various works, topics, and personalities in the realm of modern art. The Centre de Création Industrielle (CCI), which ultimately took charge of the exhibition, specializes in subjects related to urban space such as architecture, foreign cities, and urban youth. Although the MNAM and the CCI had organized hundreds of exhibition since the creation of Beaubourg in 1977, no time or space had ever been accorded to immigration or France's ethnic minority communities.

Not surprisingly, prior to *Les enfants de l'immigration*, Beaubourg had failed to attract visitors from ethnic minority communities of Paris. While the courtyard outside Beaubourg had long been a popular gathering place for people of all stripes and colors, rarely did ethnic minorities venture inside the museum. "As for me and my friends," writes Omar from Châtenay-Malabry, "all that we knew about this prestigious international cultural center was the square, and we went there quite often. We only went inside to get out of the cold or rain." For Omar and his friends Beaubourg remained an ivory tower institution. "To us the Center seemed so oppressive, its culture so inaccessible, so dry, only students and tourists seemed to set foot inside. The culture outside, on the square, was so different from that on the inside."[8]

By extending recognition to ethnic minorities *Les enfants de l'immigration* made it possible to bridge the divide between outsiders and insiders at Beaubourg. Coulaud notes that some 64 percent of the exhibition visitors were foreigners—79 percent of whom resided in France. North Africans were by far the largest group, accounting for over half of the total number of nonnationals who came to Beaubourg. Among the North Africans Algerians were more than twice as numerous as Moroccans and Tunisians. Aged between 25 and 39, these visitors were not only the most numerous but also the most active and enthusiastic at the exhibition. "Nothing escapes them," comments Coulaud, "neither the videos and projections, nor the traditional museological supports (paintings, sculptures...). They see everything and they participate in everything as well. In fact, they make up the majority of the audience at the debates, performances, and shows."[9]

The response to *Les enfants de l'immigration* by North African visitors attests to the powerful need for positive forms institutional recognition. Long relegated to the margins of French society, criminalized in the press and official discourse, subjected police controls and the threat of expulsion, Beaubourg offered North Africans, and Algerians in particular, the opportunity to speak for themselves and to make themselves heard in the very heart of the nation's capital from within one of its most renowned cultural institutions. "This 17 January," writes Omar from Châtenay-Malabry, "for the first time we will come to the Centre, we will climb the stars, we will express ourselves, but our thoughts and eyes will be turned to the square, to this culture, to our popular cultures, so close to the Beaubourg giant yet so completely ignored."[10]

Limits of Recognition

The affirmation of ethnic minority communities and cultural expression has little to do with the history of museum practices in France or elsewhere. Museums have more often been characterized as ceremonial monuments, secular temples, or ritual sites exploited by and for the benefit of the state and its ruling elites. With the founding of the Louvre as a public museum in 1793 the French pioneered the art of organizing and displaying culture as a means of bolstering the image of the state. In the years after the Revolution most countries followed the French example. "Every major state, monarchial or Republican, understood the usefulness of having a public art museum. Such public institutions made (and still make) the state look good: progressive, concerned about the spiritual life of its citizens, a preserver of past achievements and a provider for the common good."[11]

Modern art museums, such as Beaubourg, supposedly represent a departure from traditional museum practices. "The concept of the public and the reverence for the classical Western past that informed the older museum do not operate in the modern ones," writes Carol Duncan. This same cultural shift is now apparent in many older museums that have been revamped in ways which decenter Western collections making them less Eurocentric.[12] Yet critics of modern art museums point out that the selection and display of non-Western art is often predicated on the extent to which such objects correspond to and affirm the styles and forms of modern art in the West. We typically appreciate non-Western art not on its own terms, argues James Clifford, but only as a mirror for the perceived universal qualities we see in Western forms.[13]

Was *Les enfants de l'immigration* just another way of making the state look good? Did the exhibition demonstrate much of an effort to understand ethnic minorities on their own terms? According to Véronique Hahn, responsible for conceptualization and realization of the exhibition, the idea that immigrant children could become part of French society while maintaining their parent's culture was integral to *Les enfants de l'immigration*. The exhibition was part of a context, during the early 1980s, in which the right to difference was seen as being an essential component of the integration process.[14] *Les enfants de l'immigration* featured members of France's diverse minority communities and demonstrated how their cultural initiatives, among others, enriched French society. Moreover, the participants were cast as the avatars of "a cultural movement born out of their history and the events which touched their generation."[15]

The CCI was itself concerned with the cultural implications of France as a modern industrial society. In existence since the founding of Beaubourg in

1977, the CCI "treats the daily environment of an industrial society: urbanism, architecture, objects, visual communications, collective equipment, etc." Through publications and exhibitions the CCI's mission is to "contribute to the formation in France of a cultural movement concerning the environment produced by the industrial system."[16]

According to Paul Blanquart, CCI director from 1982 to 1984, *Les enfants de l'immigration* grew out of his interest in the globalization of labor markets and the mixing of peoples—a central element of modern industrial societies.[17] The children of immigrant workers, Blanquart noted, were situated at the crossroads of modernity and the North–South axis, or relations between industrialized and developing nations.[18] The North–South axis and immigration as its by-product were subjects of considerable interest to Blanquart and themes that he featured in the CCI's program for 1983 and 1984. For example, two volumes of the CCI publication, *Culture au Quotidien* (Everyday Culture), released in January 1983 and January 1984, treated the subject of immigration. The first, *Des immigrés et des villes* (Immigrants and Cities), looked at immigration as a source of innovation within French cities. The second, *Enfants d'immigrés maghrébins* (Children of Maghrebi Immigrants), detailed a range of cultural and social initiatives by immigrant youth in France. Reporting on *Les enfants de l'immigration* for the Council of Europe, Antonio Perotti described the exhibition as an extension of the publication *Enfants d'immigrés maghrebins*. By featuring the cultural and social projects of immigrant youth, the exhibition underscored the diverse processes of integration into French society.[19]

Blanquart added that *Les enfants de l'immigration* also responded to his personal criticism of the CCI for treating the environment as an object designed and controlled by specialists and engineers—an optic that reduced the role of residents to that of consumers or products of an elite class of technicians. Through projects such as *Les enfants de l'immigration* Blanquart hoped to reintegrate urban residents into the "intelligence of the environment."[20] "[Culture] is also a relation, full of resonance, between people and their surroundings: it is thus impossible to treat places, objects, and signs independently from individuals who shape and are shaped by them."[21] *Les enfants de l'immigration* was thus a project that intended to show not only how the environment of an industrial society generated cultural productions but also the role in which the children of immigrant workers played in this process.

Yet if the exhibition fit within the overall logic of the CCI and that of its director, questionable political support for the right to difference may help account for the weak institutional reaction. Immigration became a political football in the early 1980s. By the time of the exhibition the Socialist government was already beginning to harden its stance toward immigration, adopting ever more rigid security and control policies. In a context where being soft on immigration was increasingly viewed as a political liability, it is not surprising that French officials and government agencies, even Beaubourg itself, were reluctant to support the exhibition. *Les enfants de l'immigration* was simply an event of questionable value in making the state look good.

On several occasions, Blanquart recalled, he almost had to call off the exhibition because of a shortage of funds. Without the last-minute support of the Caisse des dépôts et des consignations, Blanquart emphasized, the exhibition would not have taken place.[22] Excluding Beaubourg, which covered approximately half the 1,835,000 franc cost, the Caisse des dépôts was in fact the largest contributor with a 300,000 franc grant.[23]

Yet the Caisse des dépôts, whose primary mission was to "manage the saving of [French] households, notably tax-exempted savings, transforming them in to public interest investments," evinced more of an interest in the social than the cultural dimension of the exhibition. Responsible for the construction and management of low-income housing, urban revitalization projects, and job training, the Caisse des dépôts saw the exhibition as a means of strengthening social relations by supporting the "comprehension of cultures and the acceptance of difference."[24]

It was at this time that the social implications of immigration had reached a crescendo. Blanquart recalled that in 1983, the year in which his staff began organizing the exhibition, the anti-immigrant National Front party scored its first electoral victories, notably with the triumph of Jean-Pierre Stirbois in the former Socialist municipality of Dreux. Just weeks before the opening of *Les enfants de l'immigration*, a national protest movement spearheaded by North African youth, completed a highly successful march on Paris. According to Blanquart, many within the Socialist government had not yet taken a firm position toward these events. He pointed out that while Minister of Culture Jack Lang and Secretary of State for Family, Population, and Immigrant Workers Georgina Dufoix both attended the inaugural ceremonies and voiced their support for the exhibition, neither made any kind of official speech.[25] Lang had in fact scheduled a speech but declined at the last minute without explanation.[26] Véronique Hahn felt that neither Lang nor Dufoix had supported the exhibition with much enthusiasm. While official personalities did not always make speeches at inaugural ceremonies, the novelty of *Les enfants de l'immigration* made the absence of such a speech somewhat surprising.[27]

Sylvie Bessenay, former ISM representative and responsible for selecting and coordinating live performances at *Les enfants de l'immigration*, disagreed that French ministries were reluctant to support the exhibition. Bessenay, who subsequently worked at the Ministry of Culture, argued that Beaubourg did not assume enough of the responsibility for the exhibition. The Ministry of Culture, Bessenay pointed out, gives Beaubourg and other institutions block grants for programs covering a given year—not on a project-by-project basis. This is not the case for other agencies such as the Caisse des dépôts, which fund specific events. Bessenay believed that CCI organizers behaved somewhat opportunistically by trying to capitalize on the immigration theme through requests for subsidies from agencies such as the Fonds d'Intervention Culturelle (FIC) and the FAS, which work in connection with France's foreign populations and threatening to cancel the exhibition without their support. Bessenay wondered why Beaubourg did not pick up more of the expenses.[28]

The reticence of Beaubourg staff and administration to support the exhibition may explain why Blanquart felt that *Les enfants de l'immigration* merited additional funds from the Ministry of Culture or other immigration-related agencies such as the FIC and the FAS. According to Véronique Hahn, the exhibition failed to generate much interest at Beaubourg. While *Les enfants de l'immigration* drew people who had never before come to Beaubourg, it was in her opinion "a kind of curiosity" that left the institution unmoved. The fact that only a small portion of the exhibition was recorded and preserved for posterity demonstrated and resulted from this disinterest on the part of Beaubourg. Moreover, the organizers received very little logistical support from Beaubourg. Hahn added that the novelty of *Les enfants de l'immigration* may have overwhelmed Beaubourg.

> One day there was dancing, the next theater, the next a radio show, then theater again. We had never seen this before. Usually we are very organized and professional here. I think this went beyond everyone. It was too much out of the norm. When we defined the exhibition as a permanent show (*spectacle permanent*) people told us that we were crazy, we'd never succeed.

She commented that the exhibition did not create any kind of opening or specific interest at Beaubourg. Once it was over there was no follow-up or anything that came afterward.[29]

The decision to select José Chapelle and Véronique Hahn to manage the exhibition may also have reflected the disinterest on the part of Beaubourg. While both organizers were generally commended for their work on *Les enfants de l'immigration*, neither had ever been responsible for an exhibition. Both were employed in the publishing section of the CCI and were not specialized or trained in running exhibitions. Hahn argued that because she and Chapelle had treated "socially" related issues, it was appropriate that they take charge of the exhibition. She added that there was no one else to take job.[30]

While Beaubourg frequently covered the entire cost of many of its exhibitions, it only paid for about half of *Les enfants de l'immigration*. Blanquart admitted encountering significant resistance toward the exhibition on the part of Beaubourg's administration. Jean Maheu, president of Beaubourg, discouraged Blanquart from moving ahead with the project. According to Blanquart, Maheu was concerned that the content of the exhibition might provide an excuse for the National Front to intervene and create a disturbance. Completely out of line, in Blanquart's opinion, was the refusal of Beaubourg's financial director to give his accord to Rachid Khimoune's work, which addressed the problem of racially motivated murders. Fearful that such work might provoke viewers, the financial director addressed his concerns to the president of Beaubourg who ultimately sided with Blanquart.[31]

While neither Blanquart, Chapelle, nor Hahn acknowledged any form of censorship, certain works were excluded from or marginalized by the exhibition. In a special issue of the immigration magazine *IM'média*, devoted entirely to *Les enfants de l'immigration*, Paulo Moreira commented that the organizers discouraged works that portrayed police brutality and injustice. "The limits of the institution became visible when some of the drawings and photos, a little too critical vis à vis the police or a UDF (centrist) deputy from Marseilles, posed problems." While recognizing that not all police were racists and agreeing that racism was not a problem limited to conservatives, Moreira doubted that the best solution was to ignore these issues that represented such an important daily reality in the lives of immigrant youth. "History is full of aberrations which germinated because of an all too prudent silence. Immigrant youths are fed up and French society has everything to gain from hearing them out—until the end."[32]

Colonial Legacies

French officials and organs of the state were not alone in their reticence to fully support and acknowledge *Les enfants de l'immigration*. Perhaps the most glaring failure of the exhibition was its inability to attract French visitors. The goal of the exhibition was to inform the largest audience possible about the various initiatives and contributions of France's ethnic and racial minority groups. According to José Chapelle, Beaubourg had an obligation to reach a nonimmigrant French audience but failed in this regard. "It wasn't a mainstream

French audience which came most often to the exhibition." She noted that most of the visitors were members of the North African immigrant community.[33]

Philippe Coulaud observed that more than a few people who came to Beaubourg wondered if "there were any French at the exhibition." On certain days, Coulaud commented, it was easy to conclude that immigrants monopolized the event—"sort of an exhibition animated by immigrants for immigrants." While his survey refuted this claim, it did confirm that "foreigners" (a murky term used by Coulaud that refers primarily to immigrants but can also include their children) accounted for a disproportionate percentage of the total number of visitors.[34]

Most of the French visitors were members of the middle class—the French working class was largely underrepresented. French visitors frequently learned about the exhibition from posters, did not plan a trip exclusively for *Les enfants de l'immigration*, and were not likely to attend a show or debate. Lastly, French viewers were among the lowest number of repeat visitors. In short, those French who came to *Les enfants de l'immigration* fit the more passive profile of the chance visitors who attend most CCI exhibitions. On average, Coulaud noted, only 8 percent of Beaubourg's visitors come expressly for CCI exhibitions.[35]

Given the visibility of North Africans at the exhibition, and Algerians in particular, one way of accounting for the absence of French visitors, and perhaps even the institutional response, is to point to the legacy of the colonial past. Involving nearly an entire generation of French servicemen the Algerian war toppled the Fourth Republic, unleashed a rebellion within the French military, and concluded with the exodus of nearly one million European settlers. While it is inaccurate to describe the war as a repressed memory, by no means has the conflict been fully integrated into public consciousness. Up to 1983, just one year before the Beaubourg exhibition, French secondary schools ended their history curriculum with World War II. Nearly a decade after the exhibition, in 1992, at the time of the thirtieth anniversary of the Evian Accords that ended war, opinion polls revealed little support for delving into the Algerian past—a conflict that still "brings back painful memories."[36] It was not until 1999 that the French government finally recognized the conflict as a war and there is still no officially designated commemoration date.

Both the forgetting and the remembering of the Algerian past have been used to account for the virulence of racist sentiments and popular hostility toward North Africans in France today. Adopting a Freudian framework Anne Donadey argues when we fail to work through difficult experiences we run the risk that they will resurface with a vengeance at some turbulent point in the future. "The current anti-Maghrebian racism in France, with its violent rhetoric and actions, is an 'aftermath of memory,' 'a replay of the rift,' caused by the Algerian war."[37] For Naomi Greene it is the persistence of bitter memories about France's loss of Algeria that helped fuel the meteoric rise of Jean-Marie Le Pen and the far-right National Front in the 1980s. "Playing on the memory of France's humiliating defeat in that country, Le Pen is prone to warlike rhetoric suggesting that France is now being 'invaded' by the forces of Islam."[38]

Given the tensions still associated with the Algerian past it is not surprising that a mainstream French public was less inclined to visit or return to an exhibition featuring North Africans and Algerians in particular. Opening its doors only a month after the March for Equality and Against Racism, *Les enfants de l'immigration* was among the first large-scale initiatives to bring ethnic minority experiences and voices to the general public. Still mired in the past, the French public may simply not have been ready to listen.

Yet when we look at structure of the exhibition we find no traces of the imperial past. Divided into three sections—the tearing away, the melting pot, and construction—the organization of the exhibition reflected a monolithic understanding of French immigration history. In fact, in the first section, the only one devoted to the immigration history of France, Algerians are indiscriminately lumped together with Italian immigrants. The connotation was that Algerian immigrants were following the same kind of trajectory as their Italian predecessors. Moving through the exhibition visitors could be reassured that whatever their difficulties Algerians were part of a larger immigration history that inevitably led to integration and inclusion in French society.

Such a narrative, however, ignores the very particular colonial context and power relations that shaped the course of Algerian immigration and French attitudes toward North Africans in the present. In contrast to earlier waves of European immigrants Algerians were subjected to a long history of surveillance and control policies brought about by an influential colonial lobby fearful of losing control over a pliant labor force. Early on this same colonial lobby was responsible for circulating negative stereotypes about North Africans that persist into the present. Without the protection of a national government, Algerian workers almost invariably found themselves assigned to the dirtiest, most hazardous, and most poorly paid occupations.[39] Cultural productions by the children of Algerian workers demonstrate an acute awareness of the connections between racism in France and the Algerian past. Beaubourg's failure to address the particularities of the Algerian past and its bearings on the present is an indication of the reluctance to delve into the colonial era and the period of decolonization.

The bulk of the exhibition centered on the present, or the section entitled the melting pot. Here we are introduced to the various dimensions of the integration process from family life and the experiences of immigrant daughters to living conditions in the working-class suburbs and various cultural and economic projects launched by ethnic minority youth. In short, while the exhibition failed to contend with the colonial past it ended up reproducing the sociocultural perspective that dominated much of the scholarship on immigration in the 1980s and 1990s. As Alec Hargreaves observes, most of the work on immigration is really about integration. Integration is an expansive term that can imply race relations or all that is at issue regarding the inclusion and acceptance of ethnic minorities in France today. "Integration," Hargreaves notes, is the "conceptual framework within which the social consequences of immigration are most commonly articulated by academics as well as policy makers in France."[40] Rather than attempting to understand the children of immigrant workers on their own terms, *Les enfants de l'immigration* offered a prepackaged product adopted wholesale from the dominant academic discourse.

However, even for younger generations unaffected or unconcerned about the Algerian past it is also possible to argue that ignorance of the nation's immigration history did little to promote interest in the exhibition. Although the purpose of the exhibition was to foster awareness and understanding of France's immigrant communities, this mission was certainly complicated by the sheer neglect of the topic for so many years by state authorities, public schools, and French intellectuals. As late as 1997, writes Gérard Noiriel, immigration was still largely absent from many primary school textbooks. "It is also remarkable that the term immigrant is only used when talking about the United States. France remains, for the authors of these textbooks, a country of *immigrés*; that is to say foreigners destined to return one day to 'their' country of origin."[41]

A Sociocultural Event

The sociocultural slant of the exhibition was one of the most frequently aired criticisms of *Les enfants de l'immigration* by both its organizers and participants. The rationale behind the selection of artists and performers at *Les enfants de l'immigration* reflected a common problem faced by many minority artists in France—social criteria took precedence over cultural concerns. This problem, however, is somewhat more complicated in the case of the CCI whose mission is to connect cultural forms of expression to their social context. Cultural objects, writes Blanquart, must always be understood within the "totality of their context, without ever disassociating the social, technical, and symbolic."[42] But in the case of *Les enfants de l'immigration* the emphasis placed on the social context seems to have far outweighed cultural concerns. Véronique Hahn explained that in selecting works for the exhibitions the priority was given to artists who had something to say about their relationship with French society—although some traditional forms of cultural expression as well as works detached from the theme of immigration were also included. But artistic quality, she commented, was not their first concern. More important was selecting works based on what they said or expressed.[43]

Some participants rejected the sociocultural character of the exhibition. For example, sculptor Mohand Amara regretted having taken part in the exhibition as the "son of an immigrant" and not as a "plastic arts specialist." He would rather have exhibited his work in another part of the museum, "more connected to his profession as an artist."[44] Mogniss Abdallah, founder of the press company *IM'média*, which also took part in the exhibition, argued that true recognition implied "an appreciation of the value of the cultural products." He did not think that this was ever the case because cultural products were lumped together with personal accounts, social work, and sociocultural initiatives. "Are these not the limits of a discourse on social innovation locked into the yoke of a sum of social handicaps among others?" Had the participants been appreciated as artists, he concluded, they would have been paid.[45]

Sylvie Bessenay agreed that while *Les enfants de l'immigration* attempted to explore the juncture of art and its social context, not enough attention was given to issues of artistic merit. Beaubourg, in her opinion, was too permissive in choosing its artists and should have established strict standards for all participants. "Beaubourg is an important cultural center for contemporary art—not for amateur theater, painting, sculpture. All of this was admitted." Bessenay described the exhibition as a bizarre mixture of amateur and sophisticated works of art. She believed that the willingness to admit much poor quality work undoubtedly caused attendance to suffer. She felt that if the exhibition had ever been handled by professional organizers within Beaubourg it may never have taken place.[46]

Mixed Results

As *Les enfants de l'immigration* drew to a close at the end of April 1984, the results were mixed. While the exhibition brought a new audience to Beaubourg, it failed to attract French visitors. The exhibition challenged negative images of immigrant youth and reaffirmed the notion that France's ethnic minorities were not only integral members of French society but were also instrumental in the process of cultural renewal and enrichment. However, the celebration of cultural pluralism only went so far. In most cases the exhibition supported and showed an interest in personal accounts linked to larger urban social and economic conditions shared by French natives. By featuring amateurs and semiprofessionals lumped together in an assortment of social and cultural productions, the exhibition created false hopes and expectations for some while leaving others with the feeling that they had been recognized only as immigrant children, not artists.

The reluctance of French institutions, including Beaubourg, to support the exhibition revealed the political sensitivity of immigration during the early 1980s. It was at this very moment that the National Front was helping to transform immigration into an issue of national concern. While initially coming to power on a pro-immigration platform and adopting a number of measures favorable to France's ethnic minority communities, by the time of the Beaubourg exhibition the ruling Socialist party was already adopting a tougher stand toward immigration. If the function of museums has long been to help make the state look good it was precisely because immigration became such a volatile issue that Socialist leaders shied away from associating too closely with the exhibition.

The reticence of the state to support the exhibition was only matched by that of the French public. French visitors were among the most infrequent and most passive visitors to *Les enfants de l'immigration*. Exhibition organizers admitted that their inability to reach a French public was perhaps the greatest disappointment of the exhibition. Yet given the difficult and still unresolved history of the Algerian War it seems reasonable to wonder whether the prominent place of North African within *Les enfants de l'immigration* was simply too much and too early for French visitors. Long relegated to the margins of French society and French history, Beaubourg offered an unprecedented form of recognition to North Africans in France. Well aware of the meaning of this unique event North Africans, especially Algerians, were among the most numerous and most enthusiastic visitors at the exhibition. Sadly, this desire for recognition was not reciprocated by the French public.

The sensitivity of the Algerian past manifested itself in the organization of the exhibition. Although Algerians occupied the most prominent place within *Les enfants de l'immigration*, the exhibition failed to shed light on the particularities of the Algerian past. Instead of helping visitors to understand the roots of present-day anxieties about North Africans, the exhibition simply buried the Algerian experience indiscriminately within the larger history of immigration to France. In the end, however, the present took far greater precedence over the past as the exhibition prioritized the theme of integration and inclusion into French society. The emphasis on integration mirrored the sociocultural focus of the bulk of French immigration scholarship raising questions about whether the exhibition was only reproducing the dominant academic discourse rather than trying to understand the immigrant experience on its own terms.

After Beaubourg

Les enfants de l'immigration did not end at Beaubourg. The demand generated by the event resulted in two projects, both under the supervision of the FIC—an interministerial agency under the aegis of the Ministry of Culture. The first was a sort of "vast mural recounting the memory of the entire event" in the form of twenty 80 × 120 cm panels created by a plastic arts specialist in conjunction with the CCI and entrusted with the agency ISM. In addition to the mural, the three copies of the Beaubourg package included pictures, posters, and videos from the exhibition.[47] In its reduced form, *Les enfants de l'immigration* appeared in hundreds of municipalities throughout France and continued to circulate well over a decade after the exhibition.

Far more ambitious, the second project included plans to organize a certain number of regional exhibitions modeled after Beaubourg but adapted to local conditions. The first two took place in Strasbourg and Toulouse during spring and early summer 1985. However, both exhibitions were undercut by a number of problems. In the case of *Strasbourg, Ville en Couleurs* (Strasbourg, city of colors), as the event was labeled, the difficulties were qualitative. Much like Beaubourg, the Strasbourg organizers failed to establish strict artistic requirements for participation in the exhibition. Sylvie Bessenay, who helped put together both the Strasbourg and Toulouse exhibitions, likened *Strasbourg, Ville en Couleurs* to an intercultural festival, not an important event showcasing the creative output of ethnic and racial minorities in northeastern France. Held in a kind of exhibition hall, not a museum or cultural center, *Strasbourg, Ville en Couleurs* became, in Bessenay's words, a "sociocultural" event. Having planned to stay for all ten days of the exhibition, Bessenay decided to leave after the opening day.[48]

Toulouse Multiple (Multiple Toulouse) was a far more polished event. The exhibition took place at the Espace Bonnefoi, a recently inaugurated cultural center operated by the city of Toulouse. With two stages for shows, a library, rooms for videos and meetings, and a park for open-air events, the Espace Bonnefoi offered a high-quality setting for the exhibition. In addition, a number of sites within Toulouse served as the setting for debates and diverse performances. The exhibition featured paintings, sculpture, photographs, scores of musical groups, dance and theater companies. An estimated 10,000 people attended the ten-day exhibition. Although no surveys were taken, Bessenay estimated that visitors were not limited to the Toulouse region. However, she added that the brevity of the exhibition, the lack of preparation time, the absence of a public relations team or strategy, together with a number of additional promotional and organizational problems did not allow the exhibition to reach a larger, general public.[49]

Bessenay credited the achievements of *Toulouse Multiple* to superior organization and more rigid artistic requirements. An association, created specifically for the exhibition and comprising local cultural associations and regional representatives from the Ministry of Culture, took responsibility for organizational details and the selection of exhibitors. Unlike Beaubourg or Strasbourg, artists exhibiting at *Toulouse Multiple* had to present an original creation.[50] However, as Bessenay highlighted in her report, *Toulouse Multiple* was undercut by serious financial difficulties. These difficulties were largely due to the decision of the Ministry of Culture to dissolve the FIC, responsible for coordinating institutional support for the exhibition.[51]

In addition to its financial difficulties, *Toulouse Multiple*, as with Beaubourg, was criticized for giving too much space to members of the North African community. Bessenay explained that this was because North African associations responded more enthusiastically and in larger numbers to the Toulouse initiative while associations representing more established immigrant groups showed less interest in the exhibition. Support for and participation in the exhibition, in Bessenay's opinion, was inversely proportional to the degree to which each community had been integrated into French society. But the organizational committee, she maintained, "made real efforts to represent the totality of minority cultures in the region."[52]

Conclusion

Toulouse was the last of the Beaubourg successors. Plans to organize exhibitions in other cities never materialized. Never again did the CCI or the MNAM address the theme of immigration and only once, in a 1987 exhibition *Immigration d'en France*, did the topic appear at Beaubourg. CCI director Paul Blanquart, dissatisfied with his inability or the inability of Beaubourg to carry out his larger agenda, resigned from his position prior to the end of the exhibition. The FIC and its successor the Mission pour les Echanges Interculturels (Mission for Intercultural Exchanges—MEIC), key organizers and coordinators of the Strasbourg and Toulouse exhibitions, were definitively dismantled by the Ministry of Culture.

André Videau, former FIC and MEIC representative for Beaubourg, Strasbourg, and Toulouse, recalled that in the early 1980s there was a certain consensus that making France work better meant allowing ethnic or regional minorities to cultivate their cultural differences. This earlier interest in minority cultures, he believed, gave way to a new discourse about the suburbs and suburban culture. While infused with elements of ethnic and racial consciousness, suburban culture refers to a shared space, not any particular minority group, and is consequently more commensurate with Republican ideals. It is part of what Videau saw as a preference to focus on what people have in common, not what makes them different—a preference which Videau agreed was a more productive means of reinforcing social ties. Similarly, Véronique Hahn remarked that the French have rightly become wary of the call for the "right to difference" which she now regarded as a potential threat to core Republican values such as equality in education.

Videau and Hahn attest to the Republican backlash to the earlier celebration of cultural diversity. By the late 1980s key funding agencies such as the FAS were shying away from projects targeting specific ethnic minority communities and favoring those that encompassed broader, more diverse audiences. Agencies such as the FIC and the DDC which had been important sources of state funding for ethnic minority initiatives were dismantled. In her position at the Délégation Développement Formations, a division of the Ministry of Culture that seeks to broaden access to culture to new segments of French society, Sylvie Bessenay continued to work with ethnic minority cultural actors. But according to Bessenay, by the mid-1990s the tendency was no longer to support artists as ethnic minorities but rather as "young people from the suburbs." The approach was now more territorial, targeting low-income or disadvantaged areas that often included but were not limited to ethnic minority populations. Culture still mattered but it was now harnessed to redress larger socioeconomic inequities rather than favoring the creative expression and self-awareness of particular ethnic or racial groups.[53]

CHAPTER 5

French Television in the Age of Multiculturalism

A 1990 poll conducted for FR 3, "La Marche du siècle," and *Le Nouvel Observateur*, ranked immigration as one of France's greatest problems, second only to unemployment. Nearly two-thirds of those polled felt that there were too many immigrants in France.[1] The French media have undoubtedly played a central role in shaping widely held negative views of immigrants and diverse minority groups. Yet much of the research on the treatment of immigrants and minorities in the media has centered on the press. The role of television remains largely unexplored.[2]

According to Marie-Françoise Lévy, immigration began receiving expanded coverage on French television after 1975. Lévy finds that programs featuring immigrants or minorities on France's three principal stations—TF 1, France 2, and France 3—have been dominated by documentaries and magazine news shows. Her study, which examines the years from 1975 to 1991, is divided into three periods. First, from 1975 to 1980, immigration became an established theme on French television within the framework of documentaries. These shows focused almost exclusively on recent waves of immigrant workers and North Africans in particular. During the second period, from 1980 to 1986, documentaries remained the principal form of coverage while the thematic emphasis shifted from immigrant workers to their families and children. In the final period, from 1986 to 1991, magazine news shows gradually displaced documentaries. These shows usually focused on particular events and used brief field reports to set up pertinent debates or discussions. More polemical and more sensationalist than documentaries, magazine news shows, Lévy contends, gave immigration its current stature as one of the most controversial subjects in contemporary France.[3]

According to Lévy, this last period, from 1986 to 1991, marked what she describes as the timid emergence of fictional programs featuring immigrants or minority characters. While French producers began to treat the theme of immigration or cast minority characters in shows such as the adaptation of François Cavanna's autobiographical novel *Les Ritals* and police series including *Navarro, David Lansky*, and *Le Lyonnais*, this same period also saw some of the first programs written and produced by members of the North African community. In 1990, France 3 aired *Sixième Gauche* featuring an Algerian and French family sharing the same floor of a suburban apartment building. The series was cowritten by Akli Tadjer, a second-generation Algerian, and Henri de Turenne. The same year, M6 broadcast *La Famille Ramdam*, based on the daily life of an Algerian immigrant family in Paris. *La Famille Ramdam* was created and coproduced by Vertigo Productions, France's First television production company owned and operated by two sons of North African immigrants. In 1992, Vertigo collaborated with Flach Film to create *Seconde B*. Unprecedented in its realism, *Seconde B* featured a multiethnic cast of suburban high school students and addressed a range of social issue from drugs to AIDS.

Journalist Timour Muhidine points out that some of the new programs run counter to the more conventional negative representations of North Africans in French movies and television. For the first time shows such as *Le Lyonnais, Sixième Gauche*, and *La Famille Ramdam* cast North Africans in positive roles. In *Le Lyonnais*, Kader Boukhanef plays the uncorruptible and cool-headed police detective Selim Rey.[4] In *Sixième Gauche*, the Ben Amars peacefully coexist on the same floor of their suburban apartment building with the Villiers. *La Famille Ramdam* showcases the exploits of a well-adjusted North African family living in a middle-class Parisian neighborhood. Did shows such as these help to soften some of the racial stereotypes often seen on French television, opening up new spaces of recognition and understanding?

Introduction: La Famille Ramdam

In the early months of 1989 Aïssa Djabri and Farid Lahouassa began developing their first television series, *La Famille Ramdam.* Unprecedented in French fiction, the project focused exclusively on the life of a North African immigrant family. As children of Algerian immigrants and graduates of the IDHEC film school, Djabri and Lahoussa drew much of their inspiration and creative energy from personal and professional experiences.[5] With the help of Françoise Verney, an influential figure in the French entertainment world, they refined the project and completed a few sample episodes. To promote the show they created a company, Vertigo Productions, named after their favorite Alfred Hitchcock film.

Djabri and Lahouassa were confident that *La Famille Ramdam*, a mixture of generational conflict and humor, would appeal to a wide range of French viewers. While the primary objective of the series was to entertain, the show was also designed to inform viewers about the particular social codes and personal relations that structure the existence of immigrant families. For this reason the cocreators felt that the *La Famille Ramdam* was most appropriate for one of the nationally owned stations such as France 2 or France 3 with more of a public service mission.[6] However, none of these stations expressed any interest in the series. Moreover, just about every major French broadcaster, including TF 1, France 2, La Sept, and Canal Plus, turned down the series. "Only Canal Plus offered a reasonable explanation: French television viewers were accustomed to 'middle-class' sitcoms and may not identify with the popular milieu of the Ramdams."[7]

Despondent, but not ready to accept defeat, Djabri and Lahouassa sent their proposal to M6, a private station created in 1987. The proposal arrived at an opportune time when M6, which had established a reputation for rebroadcasting American series, was considering the possibility of producing its own show. It is difficult to say whether M6's status as a commercial station, the result of the 1981 decision by the Socialist government to end the state monopoly over television, had any bearing on its interest in the series. Other private stations, such as Canal Plus and La Sept, rejected the series. However, M6 was certainly more inclined to model itself after American broadcasters whose multiethnic programs, such as the *Cosby Show*, had achieved a considerable success among French viewers. Thierry de Navacelle, director of fiction at M6, recalled that the station was attracted by the originality of *La Famille Ramdam*.

> We liked the idea of *La Famille Ramdam* because it was something different, original. A Maghrebi family but it wasn't something social or cultural, it was a true comedy. It didn't discuss problems with immigrants. It was an immigrant family which lived like French families and had the same problems as French families such as school, money, work, education, the relationship between parents and children. That was always our objective.[8]

De Navacelle was ready to move ahead with the project but made his decision contingent upon two concessions from Vertigo Productions. First, he asked Vertigo to coproduce the series with a more experienced company—IMA

Productions. Second, he wanted to gear the show more toward M6's audience. This meant strengthening the connection between the Ramdams and French families, de-emphasizing anything that was too ethnically specific, and elevating the family's social status. IMA's Martine Leheureux recalled that M6 and the series' coproducers spent a considerable time modifying the original scenario.

> The objective was to create a sitcom like the *Cosby Show* which was the reference point for M6 and IMA. We didn't want to present Arab characters which would unsettle French viewers...We put together all the necessary elements so the French public would not be unsettled, so they would like the family and wouldn't say at the beginning, they are Arabs. It was for once a chance to present immigrants as people like you and me.[9]

Djabri and Lahouassa regretted revising the series but felt that they had few options. It was either make the changes or abandon the project.

Yet even with these concessions M6 had serious reservations about proceeding with the series. De Navacelle explained that given France's colonial history and tenuous relationship with Algeria, station executives feared that viewers might not be receptive to the show.

> France is very different from the United States because it was a colonizing country. Racism toward North Africans is very strong, you can't deny it, it exists. There is more racism toward North Africans than toward black Africans. We were afraid that the show would be rejected so we made a pilot and tests.[10]

In some respects the test audiences confirmed the worst fears of station executives. Initial reactions to the series title and concept were extremely negative. Test viewers suggested masking the Arabic connotations of the series title which, for them, evoked unsavory images of racism. Some viewers responded negatively to M6's description of the Ramdams as a "beur family." For adult viewers too many stereotypes encumbered the word *beur*. However, the actual test episodes dispelled most of these reactions and reassured the audience that the Ramdams were just like any other French family.[11]

To what extent did the Ramdam family lose its specificity in order to accommodate French viewers? The following section responds to this question by considering several categories—social status, racism and discrimination, and the French colonial legacy. In addition, it examines the particular role of minority writers in shaping more authentic characters and conflictual situations. The conclusion provides some explanations for the ultimate cancellation of the series after its 40-episode run.

Social Status

In the original scenario the Ramdams live on the twelfth floor of a government subsidized high-rise referred to as a "tower of Babel" for the ethnic diversity of its inhabitants. The father, Driss, age 50, is an illiterate factory worker who uses a moped to commute between the family's apartment and place of work. Faced with a society that he often finds bewildering, Driss does his best to maintain a sense of tradition in his family. The challenge of adjusting to French life, however, often proves overwhelming. "Driss is not adapted to the modern world which he sees as threatening. For him, taking the metro is an adventure. He still looks for a lighter to turn on the microwave which his wife bought on credit payable in 24 monthly installments." His wife Nedjma, age 48, embodies a mixture of tradition and modernity. She is superstitious but dreams of receiving an education that she attempts through a correspondence class. Her predilection for Western culture is a source of constant anxiety for her husband.

The Ramdams have four children—Mehdi, Nadia, Momo, and Alilou. Mehdi, age 28, the eldest son, is a neighborhood practitioner. Although he no longer lives at home, his office adjoins the family apartment and is the setting for numerous scenes. Mehdi's middle brother Momo, age 20, dropped out of high school and lives off of a variety of part-time jobs and get-rich-quick schemes. Momo and his friend Pierrot, age 21, "dream of making a fortune to prove to the others that studying is not the only way to succeed in life." Nadia, age 16, the only daughter, is an idealist who hopes to make the world a better place. She staunchly defends her North African girl-friends against their traditional families but is herself torn between her own desire for independence and her attachment to her family. Alilou, age 8, the baby in the family, is constantly getting into trouble—cutting the cable TV lines in the building before a big soccer game or getting a free pass to the movies by claiming that he is an orphan.

In addition to the parents and children the original scenario features several secondary characters—the grandfather and two French friends, Suzanne, and Jean-Noël.[12] The grandfather, age 70, comes from Algeria on occasion to spend time with his son Driss. Each visit invariably sets the stage for a clash between Algerian traditions and compromises the Ramdams have made in adapting to life in France. Suzanne, age 48, is a neighbor and friend of the family. A taxi driver who works the night shift, she is a solid working-class character. Jean-Noël, age 45, another friend of the family, is a bass player with the Radio France philharmonic orchestra. Divorced, with a five-year-old girl Julie (who is Alilou's best friend), he dreams of finding the perfect wife and building a family as strong as the Ramdam's.

In the televised version the Ramdams live in a middle-class Parisian neighborhood. Their Vietnamese and African neighbors, along with an assortment of working-class French characters, are nowhere to be seen. Suzanne and Jean-Noël are replaced by Patricia and Serge—two younger, more attractive, and more economically prosperous characters. Patricia, age 37, works for a fashion magazine and Serge, age 37, is a successful advertising executive.

While Driss remains the force of tradition and his wife Nedjma continues to lean toward European culture, both characters attain a dramatically new level of refinement. Driss and Nedjma are now perfectly fluent in both written and oral forms of French and Arabic. Rarely do their children intervene to correct their parents for errors of word choice or pronunciation. Driss's new job is that of a Parisian taxi driver with 20 years of experience behind the wheel. As for Nedjma, she appears even more adjusted to French culture than her husband. In various episodes we discover that not only is she completely at ease behind the keyboard of a French minitel but she is also a connoisseur of opera music.[13]

The focus of the televised version shifts away from the parents to the eldest son Mehdi. Alec Hargreaves notes that the recentering of the show on Mehdi, the success story in the family, further distanced the series from its working-class origins. Moreover, the actor who played Mehdi (Mehdi El Glaoui), well known to French viewers for his lead role in the 1960s children's series *Belle et Sébastien*, lent a certain "pre-Frenchification" (cultural assimilation) to the character.[14] Many of the episodes begin with Mehdi's visits to a mysterious female psychiatrist whose body, except for her legs, remains hidden from view. Mehdi's conversations with the psychiatrist about his personal problems and the events in the life of his family serve as a vehicle for introducing individual episodes. Through black and white flashbacks, voice-offs, and Rod Serling-like apparitions, Mehdi guides the viewers through his own complex past as well as that of his parents and siblings. M6's introduction to the series describes Mehdi's psychoanalysis, absent from the original scenario, as the "common thread" that ties the show together.

Ironically, the efforts on the part of M6 and the coproducers to assimilate the Ramdams into French culture actually made it more difficult for some viewers to identify with the family. For example, Nedjma struck certain viewers as more of a *pied-noir* mother than an Algerian one.[15] Others noted that Nedjma seemed so perfectly integrated that they found it unconvincing when she failed to understand or respect French professional practices—such as her habit of barging in on her son Mehdi while he is examining a patient.[16] The test episodes demonstrated the difficulty of balancing both the French and Algerian dimensions of the Ramdams. If the Ramdams were too Algerian, they might alienate French viewers. If the characters were too French, they risked losing their credibility as an immigrant family. Throughout the series it was the latter that posed more of a problem.

Racism and Discrimination

Perhaps the most glaring absence in *La Famille Ramdam* is racism and discrimination. At work or school neither the children nor their parents ever suffer from racial slurs or discrimination. Mehdi's patients, who are predominantly European French natives from all points on the social spectrum, never show any surprise or reluctance because of his ethnicity. Similarly, his father Driss encounters no hostility during his daily rounds as a taxi driver. France is cast as an idealistic society where people of all colors live together harmoniously.

Scenes from school portray a world that is equally colorblind. In fact, through flashbacks we learn that Mehdi was always a standout student and teacher's pet. Encouraged and assisted throughout his school years he ultimately attained the highest echelons of the educational system. Even the status of his brother Momo, a high school dropout, is never seen as the result of institutional discrimination but rather that of personal choice. Endlessly embroiled in new money-making schemes, Momo and his friend Pierrot show no interest in pursuing their studies. However, when Momo has a sudden change of heart in "Momo bachelier" and tries to make up for three years of lost work, he misses a passing grade by only a few points. His results echo the show's meritocratic message that hard work and determination are all that one needs to succeed in school as in other ventures—even if the motive is an attractive woman.

Physical traits that distinguish North Africans from European French natives have no stigmatizing force in *La Famille Ramdam*. In only one episode, "Nadia de Bergerac," do characters express a desire to change their looks. In this episode Nadia sinks into a state of depression after becoming convinced that her nose is too big. She organizes a support group, "On est tous beaux" (We're all beautiful), for others who share similar anxieties. In the same episode we learn through flashbacks that Mehdi was also self-conscious about his appearance during his teenage years. Embarrassed about being short, he hesitated to reveal his true height in front of women.

Nadia and Mehdi's worries are examples of universal anxieties, not the particular concerns of ethnic minorities. Never do any of the Ramdams find themselves at the receiving end of familiar glances from anonymous faces reminding them that they do not fit in. As a result, the audience is left with the false impression that discrimination and racism fall by the wayside as minorites attain higher degrees of cultural and social assimilation.

Colonial Legacy

In addition to glossing over the reality of institutional and individual forms of racism and discrimination, *La Famille Ramdam* disregards the legacy of French colonialism and the Algerian War (1954–1962). While the eight-year war cost the lives of several hundred thousand Algerians, displaced countless others, and sparked the first wave of family immigration from North Africa, we never learn what impact it had on the Ramdam family. The parents never speak about it to their children and it never comes up in any conversations. Prominently featured in cultural productions by North African youth, the Algerian War remains an invisible issue that is never addressed and never questioned.

In many scenes the failure to recognize the importance of the colonial past is startling. For example, in "La prémière fois" Mehdi is all nerves before his first day at work. When he finally makes it out the door his parents envision him in military fatigues with a duffel bag heading off to begin his military service. At first glance this picture may seem humorous and innocent, especially given the proximity of Mehdi's office to the family's apartment. After reconsidering the scene, however, it becomes apparent that M6 and the series' producers envisioned Mehdi as an ethnically neutral character and ignored or intentionally avoided addressing the complex and potentially explosive image that a second-generation Algerian in military fatigues could evoke for both French and Algerian viewers. The show presents Mehdi simply as any other French citizen fulfilling his obligation to the nation.

This same oversight occurs in "Homo Momo." In this episode, Nedjma invites a young North African woman to dinner in an attempt to play the matchmaker for her son Momo. In the course of the dinner conversation the guest learns that Momo succeeded in avoiding his military service by being deemed physically unfit. Surprised that Momo fails to see the gravity of his offense, the young woman warns him that his record will not fair well with future employers. Once again, the issue of military service is treated as a simple formality concerning all citizens. No thought is given to the fact that many Algerian parents consider service in the French military or the acquisition of French citizenship as a form of treason. In this case, matters are made worse because it is a North African character who blatantly ignores the multiple ramifications of military service for Momo and his family.[17]

Family Relations

The vitality and strength of traditional roles and relations within the Ramdam family is just as surprising as the absence of all references to the colonial legacy and the Algerian War. Semiautobiographical novels by writers of North African descent reveal the tremendous strains that immigrant families experience in adapting to life in France. Fathers see their prestige and authority undermined by years of low-status physical labor and their inability to master written and spoken French. Mothers, who never chose to come to France, often find themselves saddled with the dual burden of raising and providing for their families. As traditional parental roles break down new, power relationships take shape. In some cases mothers team up with older brothers to impose their authority on daughters. In other situations daughters acquire an increased margin of independence when parents realize that it is they, not their brothers, who have the best chance of prospering in France.[18]

The Ramdam family experiences none of these pressures. Driss holds down a steady job as a taxi driver while his wife Nedjma cares for the three younger children. While Nedjma's predilection for Western culture often puts her at odds with Driss's conservative inclinations, they are on the whole a balanced team who care deeply about each other and their children. As for the Ramdam children, they sometimes quarrel among themselves and with their parents but are never rude or disrespectful and their disagreements are always resolved. Nadia, the only daughter, is subject to some extra supervision from her father, but she still enjoys a considerable degree of independence. All of the Ramdams are generally understanding and supportive of each other. When there is a problem they all pitch in to help out.

The compassion and concern that Driss and Nedjma show for their children is the comic element in numerous episodes. When Driss and Nedjma believe that Momo has become a drug dealer in "Momo dealer" they go to great lengths to protect their son. As each new customer exits from Momo's room with a mysterious bag of white powder, they buy back and hide the goods. In an attempt to understand his son's motivation, Driss tries smoking some of the powder. The episode ends in a moment of laughter when Mehdi enters the room and explains to his father that he has just made himself sick smoking contraband henna.

Most episodes of *La Famille Ramdam* stress universal problems familiar to any family. In "Je suis là Billy!" Nedjma feels devalued as a mother whose children are quickly growing up and no longer require her care. Looking for a new sense of purpose and meaning in her life she decides to create a telephone line for people who feel alone and despondent. The burden of answering calls and resolving problems quickly ends up exhausting the entire family. In "Le depart en vacances" Driss and Nedjma are saddened when their children no longer want to spend summer vacations together as a family. After each of the children leaves home a series of freak incidents causes them all to return after only a few days. Much to the parents' surprise and joy the entire family is reunited for the holidays.

While these shows may be heartwarming and humorous they say little about the particular relations and tensions that structure the lives of immigrant families. The sentiments that Driss and Nedjma express for their children are shared by most French viewers. However, these shows provide no information about North African lifestyles and family relations, which might be unfamiliar to a French audience. As Alec Hargreaves correctly observes, only by stepping into and walking around in the shoes of the other can we arrive at a new and deeper understanding.[19] Through its emphasis on commonalities, this is precisely where *La Famille Ramdam* falls short.

North African Perspectives

To a large extent the failure of *La Famille Ramdam* to present a more authentic North African family was the result of French writers who knew little about the immigrant milieu. In fact, Farid Boudjellal and Azouz Begag were the only two writers of North African descent involved in the series. Boudjellal, an established cartoonist with over nine books to his name, wrote five of the forty episodes; Begag wrote one episode. While the other writers dealt with problems that could happen to any family, Boudjellal preferred to address issues of identity and culture specific to North African families. Most of the episodes, according to Boudjellal, were not very realistic or coherent because the producers wanted to make the series accessible to as large an audience as possible. He described this tendency as the "Dances with Wolves" syndrome in which the main character encounters an Indian tribe and falls in love with a captured white woman. French producers, like their American counterparts, imagine that viewers are incapable of identifying with anything that is different from themselves. Consequently, while the other writers did everything to assimilate the Ramdams, he wanted to explore their identity by creating confrontational situations.[20]

The ethnic and religious dimensions of the Ramdams, absent throughout most of the series, are central to the episodes written by Boudjellal. In "Ramadan," for example, the family confronts the difficulty of maintaining Muslim traditions in France. One by one each of the Ramdams fails to respect Islam's most sacred holiday, which requires one month of daytime fasting. Mehdi stops fasting when it begins to create problems for his professional life. During a routine examination he confuses the internal sounds of his patient's body with the grumbling of his own stomach. Alarmed by the unusual noise and failing to notice that the stethoscope is resting on his own stomach, he prescribes a strict diet for his patient. When Mehdi realizes what he has done he decides to find some food. In the next scene, Driss walks into the living room and catches Mehdi snacking from a box of cookies. Angered by his son's impertinence, he accuses him of being a bad Muslim.

Mehdi: I'd rather be a bad Muslim than a bad doctor.
Driss: The Arabs invented medicine but they never used it as an excuse for not observing the Ramadan.
Mehdi: Of course, because they never had to live in a country filled with food. When I see a patient I can imagine everything he ate since breakfast.

This humorous exchange evokes not only the challenge of upholding Islamic practices in a Western society but also the many compromises necessitated by life in France. The episode ends in a moment of reconciliation between the father and son. This occurs when Driss, the last of the Ramdams still observing the Ramadan, comes down with the flu and is unable to continue fasting. Now in need of Mehdi's professional attention, Driss realizes that his son cannot properly care for him or other patients without eating.

In "La famille idéale" Boudjellal pokes fun at French conceptions of North Africans and the complex nature of individual identity. The episode begins when Serge asks the Ramdams if they will become the centerpiece of an advertising campaign for a new canned food product, Hallal. Hallal, Serge explains, is a revolutionary food substitute that tastes and smells like pork. As the "ideal North African family," the Ramdams will help introduce the product to millions of Muslims living in France. While Serge's sales pitch wins the Ramdams' enthusiastic support, it quickly becomes clear that there is no consensus on what it means to be the "ideal family." When Serge arrives for the photo session he is stunned to find Driss in a tuxedo, Nedjma with a blond wig and glittering dress, Momo in a leather outfit, and Alilou dressed like Michael Jackson. The episode becomes even more comical when Serge's boss has a flash of creative genius and decides to dress the Ramdams in traditional North African clothes. Embarrassed about the situation in which he has placed his friends, Serge refuses to go along with the idea and quits his job.

The humor in this episode stems from the divergent conceptions and misconceptions of individual identity. For the Ramdams, being the ideal family means dressing up in style and looking their best. But even within the family we see a diversity of ideals. Nedjma dreams of becoming the North African version of Catherine Deneuve while her youngest son Alilou idolizes Michael Jackson. The episode brings home the message that individual identity is personal and often unpredictable. When outsiders try to impose their own preconceptions on the Ramdams, they inevitably end up far from the mark.

Conclusion: La Famille Ramdam

The failure of *La Famille Ramdam* to incorporate more insightful and provocative perspectives such as Boudjellal's was partly due to a growing conflict between the coproducers. In the course of the series tensions mounted between Vertigo and IMA over the financial management of the show and the writing of individual episodes. Djabri admitted that Vertigo was gradually dispossessed of its project and had little to do with the last 20 episodes.[21] As Vertigo lost control of the series, it was taken over by the French writers of IMA, a mainstream production company.

While the conflictual relationship of the coproducers contributed to the cancellation of the series, *La Famille Ramdam* never succeeded in drawing a large audience. After 12 episodes the show peaked at a 5.8 percent audience share—far below the 7 percent that M6 averaged for all of its programs during the same time period.[22] Hervé Nougier, responsible for marketing at M6, noted that any series that scores below the station's overall average is generally considered a failure. Station executives tried to juggle the hours and number of episodes broadcast per week but the series continued to perform poorly during the more competitive evening hours. According to de Navacelle, the disappointing audience share and disagreements between the coproducers made it impossible for M6 to continue with the series. He acknowledged that M6 could have done a better job scheduling the series. Programs like *La Famille Ramdam* are usually broadcast on a daily basis, not once a week. In de Navacelle's opinion, starting with only one episode a week and switching time slots after the first three months were scheduling errors that hurt the series.[23]

Amaya Urtizverea, IMA's top producer for *La Famille Ramdam*, believed that the series never had the solid backing of M6 executives. She attributes the changes in broadcasting times to a lack of commitment on the part of M6. Moreover, given the growing tensions between the coproducers, M6 resented finding itself in the middle and was unwilling to continue with the series. She added that the climate of the Gulf War and the difficulty of maintaining the show's originality after 40 episodes also contributed to its demise.[24]

As for Djabri and Lahouassa, they felt that it may have been too early for a show like *La Famille Ramdam*. The French are still reluctant to valorize the merits of diversity and the tradition of assimilation remains strong. Yet even with a highly assimilated family such as the Ramdams, they believed, the French were still reluctant to embrace the series. The absence of sponsors, in their opinion, proved this point. It was the failure of *La Famille Ramdam* to draw more sponsors, they argued, that ultimately led M6 to cancel the series. According to Djabri, there may still be too much at stake between the French and North Africans for a show like *La Famille Ramdam*. The history of colonialism, the Algerian War, and the role of Islam in France remain highly contentious issues. French viewers, they contended, are not prepared to look at North Africans dispassionately. "When people see the *Cosby Show* they like it but when they see *La Famille Ramdam* they see an Arab family." While they were satisfied with having completed the show they regretted the changes made to the series.

> We realized that the TV station was wrong. The series was not meant to reassure [French viewers]. The TV station felt that if we presented a nice immigrant family, a well integrated family with successful children that it would reassure the French public. But it didn't reassure them. The proof is that the sponsors didn't come.

Nevertheless, Djabri and Lahouassa were convinced that a segment of the North African community appreciated the show because it was how they wanted to imagine the future for their children. "We allowed a part of the immigrant population to dream. Because for them it was a show, not their daily experience. But for the French the show was an anomaly."[25]

Introduction: Seconde B

In March 1993, almost two years after *La Famille Ramdam*, the public television station France 2 began airing its new series, *Seconde B*.[26] *Seconde B* was part of a trend in French television toward programs targeting younger viewers—a market then dominated by TF 1 with hit shows such as *Hélène et les garçons* (4 million viewers) and *Le miel et les abeilles* (2.7 million viewers).[27] In contrast to TF 1's powerhouse shows and French sitcoms in general, *Seconde B* did not feature affluent French characters of European ancestry detached from the pressing social issues of the day. Instead, it presented a multiracial group of friends in a working-class, suburban high school. In the course of the series the main characters—Michael, Pauline, Nadia, Kader, and Jimmy—encounter and must come to terms with a host of social issues from AIDS to lesbianism.

In contrast to *La Famille Ramdam*, which was restricted to a middle-class universe, *Seconde B* brought viewers directly into the politically charged suburbs or *banlieues*. As such it had the potential to offer new perspectives not only on ethnic minorities but on what have become France's most demonized social spaces precisely because of their close association with postcolonial immigrant populations.

Realism or Republicanism

In 1992 executives at France 2 decided to initiate a bid for a new youth series. Ideally, the new series would help boost the ratings of France 2's youth time slot, entitled Giga—weekdays from 5:10 to 7:20 PM—comprised exclusively of American programs such as *Happy Days* and *Major Dad*. The French production company Flach Film, noted for such blockbuster movies as *Trois hommes et un couffin* and *Le Grand Chemin*, was interested in the project but had never produced a television series. Executives at Flach contacted Vertigo Productions, which had only recently completed *La Famille Ramdam*, to coproduce the series. For six months the two companies worked together to elaborate a project that became *Seconde B* and was ultimately accepted by France 2.[28] Although Vertigo withdrew from the show early on due to disagreements with Flach Film, the content of the program remained faithful to the original project.

Seconde B features a group of five friends in the Arthur Rimbaud High School—a fictitious school in the Paris conurbation.[29] Aside from M. Jamin, the idealized French literature teacher who acts as a mediator and intermediary, adults occupy only secondary roles.[30] Unlike most French youth series, the action in *Seconde B* is not confined to a few indoor locations. Scenes take place in the classroom, school hallway, Michael's apartment, a neighboring café, outside the school, and at the foot of the surrounding apartment buildings. Moreover, each 26-minute episode, which consists of a primary and secondary plot, treats two related or completely different stories.

Central to the show is Cosmic Radio, the school radio station founded and operated by the five friends. Cosmic Radio serves a variety of functions. It is a meeting place, a locus of sociability, a weapon for combating wrongdoers, an informational tool, an instrument for promoting political awareness, and a means of connecting the high school to the neighboring communities. Though the introduction to the series stresses that Cosmic Radio is in no way the key to the show, it serves as the subject of several episodes and acts as a focal point around which the central characters gravitate.

What sets *Seconde B* apart from its rival series is its apparent realism. The comfortably middle-class French characters of European descent in series such as *Hélène et les garçons*, live in impenetrable, tranquil worlds where romance and innocent mischief are their only preoccupation. Simone Girard, responsible for *Seconde B* at Flach Films, noted that while shows like *Hélène et les garçons* draw large audiences they seldom deal with problems concerning young people. When they do address these issues they are in a somewhat diluted form. In contrast, the stars of *Seconde B* tackle a wide range of problems. In each episode they move from ignorance to understanding as they come to terms with the issue at hand. For example, in "Amitié volée" (Stolen Friendship) Michael feels betrayed when he realizes that his friend David is gay. By the end of the episode, however, Michael comes to understand that David's sexual orientation should not undermine their friendship. This episode echoes what Simone Girard referred to as the show's central message—tolerance and respect for the differences of others.[31] By promoting compassion and understanding when dealing with issues of difference the series does much to enlighten its viewers.

Seconde B's tolerance and respect for the difference of others does not mean that the series advocates multiculturalism. While the series addresses problems such as racism and discrimination, absent in *La Famille Ramdam*, its characters are just as ethnically and religiously neutral as the Ramdam family—despite the fact that three out of the five characters come from different minority groups. When the series does explore the ethnic or religious aspects of individual identity, it is either devoid of all substance or summarily condemned.

In "Tag mon coeur Jimmy" (Spray paint my heart Jimmy), Jimmy, of Senegalese descent, perplexes his friends when he suddenly joins a group of black taggers and tries to spray paint their slogan on the walls of the Rimbaud school. However, Jimmy's friends soon realize that he is really interested in an attractive female member of the group. When Jimmy discovers that she is already dating the ever-mischievous Julien, he abandons his efforts to join the group. Similarly, in "Publications Mensongières" (Deceitful Publications), Kader's sudden interest in his Algerian heritage is driven by his affection for Anais, a young Vietnamese girl who hopes to learn Arabic. To improve the odds of winning her favor, he tries to convince her that he is her ideal teacher. The plan eventually falls through in a moment of laughter when both Kader and Anais realize that neither can speak their ancestral language.

Both episodes underscore how detached Jimmy and Kader are from their cultural, racial, and linguistic roots. When the characters suddenly take an interest in their heritage their motivation is purely superficial. Kader explains to Jimmy that in order to win Anais's affection he must "pretend to be interested in what she's interested in." While it is true that minority youth have assimilated French values and cultural practices, this does not mean that they have become completely detached from a sense of ethnic identity. The persistence of racism and discrimination have served as catalysts for minority political and cultural expression based on the creation of a negative ethnic identity. Although *Seconde B* addresses the problems of racism and discrimination, it ignores how the stigma of rejection can lead to the crystallization of ethnic identities. In scenes such as those mentioned earlier, ethnic or racial identity is reduced to a costume of convenience, devoid of all meaning.

On numerous occasions *Seconde B* echoes what had by then become the dominant model of citizenship, that particularist forms of identity had no place within a Republican French culture. "Embrouille au beur noir" (Black and beur confusion) and "Bon Anniversaire" (Happy Birthday) offer perhaps the clearest illustrations. In "Embrouille au beur noir" Jimmy joins a popular break dance group, Zap Africa, whose black members reject Kader because he is North African. The two friends eventually find themselves in opposing groups—the black supporters of Zap Africa and the North African Oulah Bledman. Tensions mount between the two groups until a fight breaks out in the local café. While wrestling with each other on the floor of the café, Jimmy and Kader realize how ridiculous they have both become. After laughing off their differences and renewing their friendship, they get together at Cosmic Radio to rap against racial intolerance.

> Black, blanc, beur c'est un couleur
> Black, blanc, gris, t'as pas choisit
> Qu'on voit des races, c'est dégeulasse
> Le mec qui est mon pot, c'est ca qui me botte
>
> En equipe il faut jouer collectif
> Si non on va tous finir par arracher les tiffs
> Si tu veux faire couler le sang rester
> sur le banc des remplacants
>
> Black, white, beur is a color
> Black, white, beur you didn't choose
> Seeing races is disgusting
> Friendship is what turns me on
>
> Being a team means pulling together
> Otherwise we'll all end up at each others throats
> If you want to fight stay on the sidelines with the bench warmers

While the song underscores the capacity of friendship to transcend all forms of diversity, a message heard throughout the series, it also reproduces the dominant Republican discourse by implying that "playing as a team" means putting aside ethnic or racial differences that act only as a source of division.

In "Bon Anniversaire" Malika provokes a mini headscarves affair when she arrives at the Rimbaud school in a *tchador*.[32] Seeing her outfit, M. Portal becomes enraged and threatens to expel her from his establishment. Jamin, who normally sides with his students, supports Portal's position and advises Malika to either find a Koranic school or discard the tchador. The students respond by dressing up as Orthodox Jews, priests, nuns, and so on. Jamin is at first taken aback thinking that his students are showing their solidarity for their classmate's religious rights. However, he quickly learns that the real objective was to show Malika how chaotic things would be if everyone decided to display their religious beliefs. As in the real headscarves affair, the episode concludes in a somewhat ambiguous fashion. While advocating tolerance for diversity, the show reaffirms that outward signs of ethnic or religious difference are better off left at home.

The support that *Seconde B* lends to French Republican ideals frequently results in a complete disregard for or surprising ignorance of the importance of ethnic or religious differences. This is most visibly the case with Nadia. There is absolutely nothing that distinguishes Nadia from her French friend Pauline. Nadia enjoys a wide margin of independence with few visible constraints. She appears with at least five or six boyfriends in various episodes, frequents a café with her friends, embraces her dates in public, dresses however she pleases, and comes and goes at whatever hours she chooses. One episode, "Le choix de Nadia" (Nadia's Choice) centers on her possible pregnancy. There is no indication that Nadia, as a member of a Tunisian immigrant family, might not share the same lifestyle as her French friends.

The Frenchification of Nadia's character is partly the result of middle-class French writers who apparently know little about the suburbs and even less about minorities. In novels by women of North African descent, for example, daughters are often subject to intense family pressures. Saddled with the burden of upholding the family honor, immigrant daughters are surveyed by their family members and neighbors, deprived of all social relations with men, and restricted to the home and school. When the pressure proves too great many women resort to running away, prostitution, drugs, or even suicide. Nadia experiences none of these pressures. Her reactions are purely French. When she believes she is pregnant, her only concern is how she will raise the baby, not what impact it will have on her relationship with her family. This is undoubtedly because Nadia's family, like the families of the other characters, has no bearing on the story.

Claude Chauvat, France 2's head of the series, admitted that there were no minorities among the writers. Moreover, he noted that the writers tended to model their characters after their own experiences. In his opinion this was most evident in terms of sexual relations. Sexual relations, Chauvat explained, were treated from the viewpoint of middle-age French adults. Students switched partners regularly and engaged in sex on a casual basis. According to Chauvat, this depiction does not accurately reflect the reality of French youth today. As a Volunteer in a high school outside Paris he was able to see the toll that AIDS has taken on young people. Students do not switch partners frequently and sex is not a casual affair. Those who break these norms are in the minority. Nevertheless, he added that the writers took time to understand the suburbs and their inhabitants. Aside from a few shortcomings, he felt that they created reasonably credible characters.[33]

Simone Girard agreed that the writers did their homework. Moreover she argued that whites are perfectly capable of writing about minorities. "You don't need to be a beur to know about beurs." She added that *Seconde B* is fiction, not a documentary, and was never intended to speak to the problems of minorities or multiculturalism in France. The strength of *Seconde B*, according to Girard, is the range of social issues it addresses and the message of tolerance it conveys.

While it would be unfair to judge the show by standards it was not intended to uphold, the introduction to the series specifically states that *Seconde B* will tell the story of the "complexity of lifestyles" in the suburbs. In the case of Nadia, the show falls far from the mark. In many ways Nadia represents the strength of French Republican ideals. She is an outstanding student recognized by her peers and teachers alike. She is usually responsible, coolheaded, and never drawn into the fray. When Jimmy and Kader are at odds in "Embrouille au beur noir" she refuses to side with either the black or *beur* gangs. She condemns them all for their stupidity and reminds them that they no longer live in the "time of tribes." "We're all in this same hole and you find ways to fight against each other." Nadia is the voice of universal reason struggling against the divisive forces of ethnic and racial diversity. She is the future transmitter of French culture and the hope that her community will find a place in French society.

However, the status of Jimmy and Kader, who are exceptionally poor students, raises some doubts about the prospects for assimilation. Although their European French friend Michael is two years older, because he has repeated twice, his competence in class is not as subject to criticism as that of his friends. When called upon by their teachers, Jimmy and Kader repeatedly reveal their complete ignorance and total disinterest in the material at hand. Jimmy, more than any other character, is corrected for problems of word choice, usage, and pronunciation. Claude Chauvat pointed out that he considered Jimmy to be excessively violent in the first episodes and encouraged the writers to make the character more amiable. Despite these changes, Jimmy and Kader remain academic underachievers and problem students.

Suburban Culture

It is perhaps more accurate to consider *Seconde B* not as a multicultural series but rather as a celebration of suburban culture. Through their clothes, street slang, and rap music, Jimmy and Kader evoke many of the outward signs of this murky suburban culture whose essential appeal and exoticism lies in the impossibility of locating it within any specific culture. Suburban culture, even when charged with violence or social deviance, is tolerable within a French Republican framework because it is not ethnically, racially, or religiously specific. It is simply a new form of low culture that can be appropriated and reinterpreted by mainstream society. The presentation of the series objectives echoes this colorful allure of the suburbs.

> Rap, tag, verlan and its derivatives, are the realities of the suburbs which have become part of the daily environment of adolescents from the ages of 15–18.
>
> Today, *the suburbs set the trends* and create models of behavior for all young people. Its influence through the media is considerable. As for the violence which it contains, it reveals larger tensions and problems which perturb all of society and raise questions about traditional values.
>
> We will tell the story of the expressive and emotional wealth of the suburbs and the complexity of lifestyles they contain through *the adventures of a group of five adolescents in the second grade of the Rimbaud High School.*[34]

The suburbs are an exciting place on the cutting edge of "new trends" and "models of behavior." It is precisely this exotic dimension of the suburbs, not the "complexity of lifestyles" that *Seconde B* transmits to its viewers. In part, Vertigo Productions withdrew from *Seconde B* because they felt that Flach Film and France 2 were not interested in presenting a serious picture of the suburbs. Aïssa Djabri, codirector of Vertigo, argued that *Seconde B* was more about marketing an image than pursuing any form of realism.

We never felt very engaged in the project which had to center on a certain kind of suburb, a softer one which speaks to everyone and sends images of rap and graffiti, things which are not very real in the suburbs. These things don't really exist in the suburbs. People don't listen to rap or spend their time doing graffiti. There is another ethnic reality which is much stronger. But they didn't want this reality, they just wanted the imagery of Smaïn—the good, clever beur wearing hightops. They wanted a consumer product. We pulled out very quickly.[35]

However, it is possible to regard suburban culture as a mechanism capable of reinforcing the integration process while offering an expanded form of participation in French society. By bridging or synthesizing ethnic, racial, or religious identities, suburban culture precludes the crystallization of group identities and promotes the notion of a unified culture rooted in a shared environment and shared experiences. This does not imply a digestive form of assimilation where minorities discard their differences and enter into a French mold, but rather the ability to continue including individuals, not groups, while recognizing their particular heritage.

Suburban Images

While *Seconde B* fell far from the mark in its depiction of ethnic minorities it tended to reinforce negative images of the already much-demonized *banlieues*. By restricting much of the focus of *Seconde B* to the confines of the Rimbaud High School, the series offers a very limited picture of the suburbs. In most instances the world beyond the walls of the school appears threatening and chaotic. Perhaps the best example is the *Chacals Vicieux* (Vicious Jackals). As their name suggests, these are not amiable characters. Delinquents who take great pleasure in random violence, the Chacals are a constant threat to the main characters and their classmates. In one episode the Chacals terrorize Henri, a secondary character, by spray painting his hair green. In another show they break into the school, steal a television and VCR, and send a security guard to the hospital in a coma. Though they appear on a number of occasions we almost never see them or learn what motivates their actions. The only connection between the school and the Chacals is Julien. But like Jimmy's brother Dom, Julien is a thoroughly negative secondary character who precludes the possibility of establishing any dialogue.

The disorder in the surrounding communities, typified by the Chacals, frequently breaks loose within the school. In the hallways students roller skate, listen to music, and sell a variety of merchandise from shirts to pornography.

In class fights break out, school property is destroyed, and teachers become the target of derision and ridicule. Claude Chauvat noted that the math teacher, Madame Mallot, received so much abuse from students that the station's youngest viewers had trouble watching the show. Chauvat asked the writers to tone down the criticisms in later episodes.[36]

In sharp contrast to the absence of discipline among the students are the characters of M. Jamin and M. Portal, the two principal adults in the series. M. Jamin, the literature teacher, is a model of compassion and understanding who does everything he can to instill a love of learning in his students. When any of them has a problem they can always count on his help and advice. M. Portal, the principal, is strict but fair. Despite the difficult environment in which he must work, he is committed to maintaining the integrity of his establishment. This dual image of the suburbs and public schools reflects popular beliefs that the suburbs are unruly places that require the intervention of skilled teachers and administrators. Within this chaotic universe the public school retains its conventional image as the most powerful instrument in the Republican arsenal for incorporating new citizens into the nation.

As the exclusive operators of Cosmic Radio the main characters possess a formidable communications tool for bridging the gulf between the school and its neighboring communities. In most cases, however, Cosmic Radio functions strictly as a one-way transmitter of accusations and denunciations. It is the voice of reason whose existence is perpetually threatened by the forces of chaos and mayhem at work both inside and outside the school. In "Liason Dangereuse," a group of neo-Nazis try to put Cosmic Radio out of commission by breaking into the station and vandalizing the studio. In "Tag mon coeur Jimmy," Julien and his friend almost succeed in ousting the main characters from the station. While serving as a powerful weapon in the fight against wrongdoers, Cosmic Radio fails to unveil the shroud of mystery that hangs over the world beyond the school. When outsiders such as the Chacals try to voice their opinions over the air they are denounced and cut off.

Conclusion: Seconde B

Much like *La Famille Ramdam*, *Seconde B* struggled to build an audience. After reaching an average market share of 23.96 percent during the first ten episodes, the series sunk to 19.8 percent with its last 16 shows.[37] Claude Chauvat blamed these results on the overly serious and pedagogical character of the early episodes, which failed to correspond to the audience's expectations.[38] A test study performed for France 2 confirmed a generally negative reaction to episodes in which both the primary and secondary plot treated serious topics. Moreover, the test revealed how some shows, such as "Les années plastoc," which addressed the issue of AIDs, were seen as too didactic. This particular episode came across as part of an AIDS prevention and awareness campaign.[39]

One of the difficulties faced by the series was its failure to draw viewers under the age of 15. Most of the audience fell into the 15–24 age group with the youngest viewers remaining loyal to other programs, especially those on TF 1. Chauvat commented that it was difficult to appeal to all viewers. Older viewers appreciated the show's realism but younger viewers felt that the issues addressed by the series did not apply to their age group. When Chauvat took over the series he tried to respond to this problem by toning down the series while at the same time attempting to maintain its integrity and original objectives. "All of my work on the second part of the series . . . was to see how we could make things more gay, lively, so that life in the 'banlieue' will not be systematically connected to drugs, AIDS, rape, prostitution, unemployment, etc. . . ."[40]

Despite its difficulties, *Seconde B* proved more successful than *La Famille Ramdam*. While *La Famille Ramdam* was canceled after 46 episodes, *Seconde B* completed 52 with orders for an additional 52 episodes. The rating for the series increased from an average market share of 21.42 percent after the first 26 episodes to 23.67 percent following the last 26 shows. Even the rebroadcasting of the first episodes outperformed their original numbers.[41] Despite its success among French viewers, the impact of *Seconde B* on the issue of diversity in French society was somewhat mixed. While the series advocated tolerance for all kinds of diversity and condemned racism and discrimination, the audience was heavily prompted to view ethnic, racial, and religious differences as destabilizing forces that are better restricted to the private sphere. In the end, diversity gained another foothold on French television, but it was seen through the optic of French Republicanism.

Conclusion

La Famille Ramdam and *Seconde B* were both innovative attempts to portray previously untreated dimensions of French society. Each series marked a departure from the negative portrayal of minorities in the media. However, the demands of targeting large audiences, French Republicanism, and the predominant role of French writers deprived the two series of a more authentic and provocative presentation of their respective worlds.

Mainstream television works in terms of ratings. While *Seconde B* survived longer than *La Famille Ramdam*, neither series was a smashing success.

In both cases television executives urged their producers and writers to make their characters, plots, and themes as accessible to as many viewers as possible. For *Seconde B* this meant toning down characters or forms of conduct which risked offending the sensibilities of younger viewers. Secondary plots were made more humorous to offset the gravity of the primary intrigue. All of these changes, initiated by Claude Chauvat, helped *Seconde B* climb in the ratings. They also took some of the edge off the original shows. In *La Famille Ramdam*, the concessions made for French viewers were even more dramatic. The working-class Ramdams saw their social status elevated to the middle class. Ironically, in some cases they became so assimilated into French culture that test viewers had trouble identifying with the characters as immigrants.

The preoccupation with ratings was not the only force shaping the two series. In many cases French Republican ideals also contributed to a rejection of ethnic and racial identities. When *Seconde B's* Nadia condemns ethnic and racial gangs as a form of "primitive, tribal behavior" she is echoing French Republican ideals. When her friends Jimmy and Kader rap against racial intolerance they are singing to the same tune. Both *Seconde B* and *La Famille Ramdam*, presented characters who had largely been assimilated into French culture. As with American sit-coms such as the *Cosby Show*, which served as a model of *La Famille Ramdam*, there was certainly a deliberate effort to make the series acceptable to mainstream, middle-class viewers. Yet without recognizing the predominance of the Republican model by the late 1980s, typically defined against American multiculturalism, we cannot fully understand the French tendency to reject, reduce, or efface ethnic differences.

As the creation of individual writers, both series were shaped largely by professionals from mainstream production companies. Only in the case of *La Famille Ramdam* did minority writers take part in crafting the series. As one of the two minority individuals involved in the series, Farid Boudjellal offered a fresh and provocative approach that was lacking in most of the other episodes. While the other writers attempted to assimilate the Ramdams into French culture, Boudjellal prioritized situations of conflict and confrontation in which issues of identity and culture came to the forefront. This minority perspective was totally absent in *Seconde B*. As a result, the series tended to disregard or de-emphasize the importance of ethnic or racial identity. Nadia's character, devoid of any and all ethnic markers, is a case in point.

Instead of offering alternative or more nuanced depictions of the suburbs *Seconde B* exploited and reinforced prevailing images of the urban periphery. Tapping into the allure of ethnic exoticism and deviance *Seconde B* billed itself as a window onto the "realities of the suburb." What we find, however, are the familiar images of a chaotic universe riven by crime and ethnic strife. It is only through the presence of beleaguered institutions, such as French public schools and their dedicated staff, that hope endures for a better future. If the idea of the civilizing mission lives on in the postcolonial present it manifests itself in connection with the *banlieues*.

CHAPTER 6

Les Banlieues: Suburban Space and National Identity

nxieties about North Africans in the present operate in conjunction with powerful sites of memory. One of the most prominent sites is the *banlieues*. Inadequately translated as suburbs in English but closer to inner city in American parlance, *banlieues* in French typically conjures up frightening images of failed urban communities torn apart by violence, drugs, delinquency, unemployment, and above all North African youth. Exclusionary spaces or neighborhoods of exile, the *banlieues* are perceived as repositories for all France's social ills and unwanted populations.[1] If there is much talk in France today about the crisis of the nation, that crisis is most frequently located in the *banlieues*.

French Recollections

Urban space has long played a central role in the imagining of collective forms of identity in France. From the early nineteenth century the East/West division of Paris reflected and helped reinforce the left/right, working-class/elite divide in the capital. Street names, monuments, and various political processions were the symbolic markers and commemorative acts that reified this divide and anchored it in the collective consciousness of the left and the right. As with many of the sites in *Realms of Memory*, Maurice Agulhon argues that Paris has fallen victim to the ravages of time. In particular, it was the bourgeoisification of the capital during the postwar years that spelled the end of this once-powerful site of collective memory.[2]

If the East/West divide in Paris has lost its ability to harness collective imaginations, this is certainly not the case for the equally, if not even more powerful, symbolic division of the capital and its environs into urban center and suburban periphery. However, it is true that much of the historical memory of this divide has been forgotten. For Henri Boyer and Guy Lochard, the current depiction of the crisis of the suburbs as a "recent development" is clear evidence of the forgetting of a space long characterized by a "state of chronic instability."[3] It is the "fragmentary knowledge of the history of the Parisian suburbs," stresses Annie Fourcaut, that compounds the general confusion about this space.[4] To prevent the memory of the suburbs from slipping into oblivion, or being reduced to what Nora describes as "a thin film of current events," it is paramount to show historically how the urban periphery has been represented over time.[5]

The principal categories in which the *banlieues* have been imagined since the nineteenth century are those of the *banlieues noires, rouges,* and *roses.* The *banlieues noires,* the older and predominant representation of the suburbs, is grounded in a long history of defining urban space in terms of insiders and outsiders, civilized and uncivilized that can be traced back to ancient Greek and Roman times.[6] Yet it was not until the nineteenth century that the image of the *banlieues* began to loom large in the collective imagination. As the forces of industrialization triggered the massive growth of the urban fringe during the first half of the nineteenth century anxious Parisian elites began to formulate an enduring dark image of the suburbs. It was the perceived lack of fixity of these so-called strangers and floating populations that led Parisians to associate them with disease, immorality, and political sedition— a collective stigmatization and absolute otherness that Louis Chevalier encapsulates in the term, "the dangerous classes."[7]

Just as a botanical vocabulary of soil, roots, and land is employed to define notions of national belonging today the discourse and imagery used to characterize marginal spaces and their populations in early nineteenth-century France relied heavily on an environmental lexicon.[8] Medical professionals and urban specialists played a central role in articulating a visually charged, environmental language that shaped how government officials and popular writers discussed and deciphered working-class neighborhoods. Urban specialists like Parent-Duchâtelet, Louis-René Villermé, and Eugène Buret helped cast working-class neighborhoods as frightening spaces littered with decaying buildings, polluted streets, and overcrowded dwellings that seemed to breed crime, disease, poverty, misery, and political sedition. This same imaginary and rational that invited and justified government intervention was picked up and given wider circulations in the serialized novels (*roman-feuilleton*) of the early nineteenth-century popular press. Some of France's best-known writers of the period, such as Sand, Dumas, Balzac, and Sue, used their literary skills in the pages of the press to offer sensationalized accounts of working-class neighborhoods.[9]

While the image of the *banlieues noires* as an environmentally determined *lieu de perdition* (site of immorality, disorder, and sickness) remains a constant from the early nineteenth to the present, the center of gravity shifts over time. Following Haussmann's sterilization of the capital and absorption of the near suburbs, it was *la zone* that captivated the imaginations of those who depicted the suburbs.[10] The zone referred to the slums and shantytowns that sprung up illegally in the military zone adjacent to the fortifications built around Paris by the July Monarchy in the early 1840s. If the general public amalgamated the zone with the suburbs from the Belle Epoque well into the interwar period, French cinema seems to have played an important part in the process.[11] Flamboyant gangsters known as the apaches, whom Michelle Perrot describes as "young marauders of the faubourgs . . . who saw themselves in this Indian image, which they claimed as a symbol of their defiant mobility and their brawling spirit," figured prominently in France's early cinematic productions. With their own "frontier territory," style of clothing, language, and hierarchy the apaches were an irresistibly attractive subject for French directors anxious to attract first-time movie goers.[12]

It was the victory of the Communist party in Paris's working-class municipalities during the 1920s that helped give rise to the new image of the *banlieues rouges*, which temporarily displaced or overlapped with that of the *banlieues noires*. On the silver screen the *banlieues* might still be a place of "solitude and despair," writes Jean-Paul Dollé, but during the years of the Popular Front, it became a "privileged territory for learning about working-class solidarity." During the 1930s cinema helped sharpen the image of what was a previously "vague and undefined space." In interwar films the *banlieues* became a space where a new popular culture was taking shape, where difficult social struggles were being waged, a space that now had a face, "that of the Parisian proletarian, which will be forever remembered in the face and allure of Jean Gabin."[13]

By the late 1950s the old image of the *banlieues noires* was once again returning but with a new standard bearer—the *blousons noirs*. The *blousons noirs* were emblematic of the emerging cultural and generational tensions within the working class produced by the forces of postwar modernization and the rise of an international youth culture.[14] These French rebels without a cause were generally cast as ruffians and hoodlums by the press—"Marlon Brandos of the suburbs," who struck fear into the hearts of "honest people barricaded in their apartments without a police station to run for help."[15] The *blousons noirs* were part of a representational shift in accounts of the suburbs now cast not only as a space dominated by youth and generational conflict but also as a physical space in transition. It was during the 1950s and 1960s that the *banlieues* became enormous construction sites as government planners responded to the long-standing shortage of housing in the urban periphery by undertaking massive public housing projects. Most typical of these projects were the *grands ensembles*—a mixture of towers and five- or six-story apartment blocks intermeshed with parks, schools, and shopping centers. Derided for their uniformity and inhuman scale, these geometrical complexes were often lambasted as "dormitory cities," "barracks," "concentration camps," and "rabbit cages." Lamented in nostalgia-riddled films like Jacques Tati's *Mon Oncle* (1958) or Pierre Granier-Deffere's *Le Chat* (1971), the rise of the *grands ensembles* was even cast by journalists as the source of a new illness called "Sarcellite." A derivative of Sarcelles, one of the largest and most controversial of the *grands ensembles*, the symptoms associated with Sarcellite were "total disenchantment, indifference to social life, insurmountable boredom, ending in nervous depression in benign cases, and suicide in acute cases."[16]

Today *la galère* is the new term used to designate the sickness that afflicts youths in the *banlieues*. *La galère* is a highly volatile sense of detachment and frustration among suburban youths produced by an environment that excludes, alienates, and stigmatizes. *La galère* is always at risk of degenerating into *la rage*, a destructive form of explosive anger associated with the urban riots that have periodically erupted across France's suburban landscape since the early 1980s.[17] Powerfully conveyed in films such as *La Haine* (1996) the *banlieues* are cast as ethnically saturated spaces seething with a rage that threatens to spill over into the urban center. In a long tradition of French borrowings from American territoralized images of otherness beginning with James Fennimore Cooper's "savages" in the early nineteenth century, the new term used to stigmatize the suburbs is ghetto.[18] Refuted in countless studies, ghetto has nevertheless become common currency over the past two decades.[19]

It is important to note, however, that the media have singled out North African youths as the new terrors of today's suburbs.[20] North African youth have been integrated into scenarios that Marie-Claude Taranger argues have become as archetypal as the American Western. With an unchanging décor, familiar cast of characters and typical scenario, the coverage of the *banlieues* typically features a backdrop of "towers, concrete, and apartment slabs," with "young immigrants on one side and the police and French natives on the other." A confrontation is then triggered by "the theft of a car, a beer, a croissant, or a police check in which an immigrant is wounded by a police officer, a merchant, or an angry racist neighbor." This in turn unleashes "a violent explosion—clashes with the police, cars set alight, stores looted and vandalized and official declarations." Such is the suburban crisis as portrayed on French television.[21]

Yet if North Africans are now at the center of representations of the suburbs that remain firmly anchored in the tradition of the *banlieues noires*, they have also been cast in ways that renew with the tradition of the *banlieues roses*. The image of the *banlieues* as a space of leisure and recreation, associated with impressionists like Monet, literary works including Maupassant's *Une partie de campaigne* (1881) and Zola's *Thérèse Raquin* (1867), and certain interwar films such as *Prix de beauté* (1930), *Fric-Frac* (1939), and *Partie de Campagne* (1936) seem to have given way to the physical reality of urbanization.[22] Yet the *banlieues roses* is not restricted to simple depictions of an idealized bucolic space of recreation. It also entails and is based on an understanding of the suburbs as a site of creative inspiration. Whether artists like Monet celebrated the rosier image of the suburbs or poets such as Baudelaire in *Le spleen de Paris* revealed the wretchedness and misery of the urban periphery, the urban margins have long been regarded as a site of change, heterogeneity, and ambiguity that has captivated, challenged, and fueled the creative imaginations of French artists and intellectuals.[23]

It is squarely within this dimension of the creative vitality of the *banlieues* that North African cultural actors were singled out in the early 1980s. Within a context in which the newly elected Socialist government threw its weight behind modern culture, the press identified a number of artists and creators from the North African immigrant community cast as emissaries of a *beur* culture in the making.[24] Since the 1990s suburban culture is less associated with a specific ethnic community and cast more as the product of a hybrid urban space. Rap, tag, and graffiti are the sounds and images that now define this hybrid space of creativity where a shared urban environment seems to override ethnic differences. "Rap, tag, verlan and its derivatives, are the realities of the suburbs which have become part of the daily environment of adolescents from the ages of 15–18," reads the introduction to *Seconde B*. But much like the image of musical performers such as La Mano Négra, Les Negresses Verte, and rap artists like I'AM, MC Solar, and NTM, *Seconde B* projects an image of "an amorphous suburban culture whose essential appeal and exoticism lies in the impossibility of locating it within any specific group or culture."[25]

Ethnic Minority Memories

The familiar universe of the *banlieues noires* is certainly in evidence in the diverse forms of cultural expression by the sons and daughters of

North African workers. Karim Kacel's song "Banlieue" describes the suburbs as an "asphyxiating horizon of towers . . . a boredom filled universe . . . where the greyness (*grisaille*) only inspires one to leave."[26] The narrator in Mehdi Charef's novel *Le thé au harem d'archi Ahmed* (1983) mocks the name of the city where the main character Madjid lives. There are no flowers in the "City of Flowers" only "buildings without souls" and concrete walls covered with "graffiti, slogans, and distress signals."[27] In the lyrics of Mounsi's "Mister Chester Himes" there is no difference between the ghettos of America and the suburbs of France. "If Christopher Columbus had sailed up the Seine and crossed over the pont de Puteaux or the pont de Suresnes, he would have discovered . . . my Harlem."[28]

Similar to French accounts, the *banlieues* appear as an environmentally determined space of illicit activities. Violence, crime, delinquency, drugs, and prostitution are cast as almost natural by-products of a landscape of misery and despair. "When I was a kid," begins the narrator in Malik Chibane's film *Hexagone* (1993):

> this city was the best. It was a place filled with adventures, buildings and friends. But when you get older it shrinks, starts to suffocate you and the *galère* begins. You drop out of school, you begin to lose track of the days, you forget your way and now it's the months you can't remember.[29]

Just about all of the characters in Mounsi's novels seem to be caught up in the suburban *galère*. In *La Cendres des villes* (1993), Marina, the girlfriend of the main character Najim, sinks into a life of drugs and prostitution after fleeing the physical abuse of her father.[30] Karim Kacel's "Banlieue" implores listeners to understand that if a young person turns to crime or alcohol it is because he has little chance of holding out against the prevailing conditions in the suburbs.[31]

Representations of the suburbs by the progeny of North African workers demonstrate a shared memory of the *banlieues noires*. In numerous creative works the *banlieues* are cast as a space of misery and despair that seems to generate its own array of immoral and illicit forms of behavior. Often borrowing from the same popularized lexicon of terms such as ghetto and *galère*, the *banlieues* are described as a space dominated by young people and their daily struggle to cope with an oppressive urban environment.

Yet while these works may conform to certain aspects of the *banlieues noires*, they also attempt to offer a broader panorama of the urban periphery. Several of the founders of the first theater companies in the 1970s remarked that they took up theater in response to their frustration that prevailing depictions of suburban North African immigrant families were often skewed and excessively narrow. "At the time, no one talked about immigrant youth... only the problems experienced by their parents," recalled Aïssa Djabri, founder of Week-end à Nanterre (1977–1980). "We thought it would be a good idea to do something on young people, the kind of people we knew."[32] Echoing these remarks, Saliha Amara, founder of the theater company Kahina (1976–1982) commented:

Nothing was being done on immigration. Immigration was understood only in terms of the single worker with nothing about their wives or families. The immigrant was a man with a suitcase living in a hotel or dorm who looks for work or spends his time working, that was it—no wife, children or family. And we were supposed to identify with this. Even in the movies on immigration it wasn't us. We had to speak up.[33]

Filling a void and anticipating much of the work taken up by sociologists and social workers in the 1980s, theater companies like Week-end à Nanterre and Kahina drew from the shared experiences of their members to recount the challenge of surviving in the *banlieues* and the tensions that often surfaced within immigrant families.

The diversity of life experiences offered by second-generation North African cultural productions marks an important departure from what Taranger describes as the archetypal media depiction of the *banlieues*. For example, in "Week-end à Nanterre" it is true that three delinquent friends are at the heart of the play. Yet in the course of the weekend in question these friends encounter a variety of suburban characters who attempt, albeit unsuccessfully, to expose them to the error of their ways. More recently, the film *Hexagone* exposes viewers to the challenges faced by several friends living in the suburbs of Paris. Yet from the opening narrative that introduces us to the unemployed Slimane struggling to find work and his friend Ali "who succeeded in finding the impossible equilibrium between school and the street," it is clear that these are distinct and dissimilar characters with their own unique perspectives and personalities.[34]

Efforts to confront established and deeply anchored ways of seeing the suburbs are not always successful. Malik Chibane expressed his frustration that some journalists saw his film *Hexagone* and were "satisfied to see a beur calling other beurs delinquents." For these journalists, Chibane added, "I realized that I was helping to consolidate a certain prejudice," which prevented them from recognizing that only one minor character in the film was a delinquent—"this was only one trajectory in the film." Talking with people who saw the film Chibane was also concerned that audiences were unable to situate it within the familiar poles of either a light-hearted trouble-free movie (à l'eau de rose) or a "violent film, like American films in the black ghettos." What they didn't expect was a film that Chibane described as "profoundly European . . . like Italian cinema or the French new wave."[35]

Director Rachid Bouchareb ran into problems with the press when he tried to avoid the subject of delinquency. "The problem I had with this film (Bâton Rouge), like my second film (Cheb), was to project a different image of North African and other youths in the suburbs, one that wasn't associated with delinquency." The strategy he adopted for Bâton Rouge was "to make a film where there was this voyage to the United States so that my characters wouldn't be seen as beurs but as individuals with all their hopes and dreams." Yet Bouchareb noted that this approach was not well received by everyone. "At one point there were certain journalists who criticized it for being too nice. But I wanted to talk about this experience and to show something positive." Bouchareb added that it wouldn't be difficult for him to put together a film on drugs, delinquency, and North Africans in the suburbs. "Yes this exists and it's important to talk about it, and other directors will, but at that time . . . I wanted to distance myself from this while keeping some of the underlying elements."[36]

If representations of the suburbs by the sons and daughters of North Africans met with resistance from the French press for failing to conform to established notions of the urban periphery, they were sometimes challenged by the North African community for the opposite reason. Week-end à Nanterre's Aïssa Djabri recalled how many viewers voiced their resentment about the portrayal of immigrant youths as delinquents and criminals. In the heated debates that followed each performance viewers lashed out at the actors and demanded more positive depictions of the North African community.

> They felt like our discourse was an apology or an excuse for troubled immigrant youth. People in the community didn't want to show this side of themselves but we felt that it was better for us to do it than the media which had not yet begun to address these issues.

Yet one of the challenges faced by Week-end à Nanterre was the fact that roles were often closely patterned after the real lives of the actors. At one point, Djabri recalled, two actors had to be replaced when they were picked up by the police and incarcerated.[37]

Recounting the experiences of North African women in the suburbs was an even more sensitive task. Fathers in North African families, Saliha Amara explained, generally regarded any kind of public performance as a dishonorable activity for women with potentially damaging consequences for the family's reputation. During Kahina's performances men in the audience often hurled invectives at the female actors for daring to address the condition of women in public performances. For years Amara did not inform her father about her role in the theater company that she helped to establish.[38]

Yamina Benguigui, who described herself as the only woman from the North African immigrant community working as a documentary producer in French television, had to break away from her family to pursue her interest in film and television. Determined to bring the subject of immigration to French national television, Benguigui succeeded in airing her three-part documentary, "Femmes d'Islam," on France 2 in 1994. The objective of the documentary, which featured the condition of Muslim women in eight different countries, was to show French audiences that "Islam is not only North African or Arab countries." Yet Benguigui acknowledged that treating the condition of Muslim women in France in the first episode was not appreciated by certain segments of the North African community.

> There is a certain complex among men which is that we should show the positive side of the community. If we reveal problems we should accuse the political system; that is, we should show how France is treating immigrants and denounce the system. But to look at ourselves and to show what's happening to outsiders, that's going too far.

Showing what was happening, however, was precisely what Benguigui hoped to accomplish through a project to which she devoted two-and-a-half years of her life.[39]

Conclusion

Rather than breaking with collective sites of memory, as Nora contends, the surge of cultural productions from the North African community often borrow from and complement French representations. In the case of the suburbs the image of the *banlieues noires* is just as prevalent in accounts by immigrant youth as it has been in French imaginings since the nineteenth century. While it is true that North Africans raised in France do not regard themselves as "dangerous classes," "apaches," or ethnic versions of the "blouson noir," they do offer familiar depictions of a youth-dominated and stigmatized urban environment that generates misery and despair.

Yet the objective of these memory-charged creative works, in contrast with French renderings of the *banlieues noires*, is not to reinforce age-old notions of insiders and outsiders. Perhaps more in the tradition of the *banlieues rouges*, in novels, plays, music, movies, and television documentaries, not to mention other forms of cultural expression, they attempt to convey the complexity of the shared experiences and perspectives of North African youth raised in France. As Malik Chibane explained, if a *beur* in France "wants to have an image of what he was five or ten years ago there is nothing. He's grown up in France without leaving any trace." Chibane, like the first immigrant youth to form theater companies and music groups in the 1970s, wanted to "shatter the invisibility of this second generation."[40]

Leaving a trace does not necessarily mean abandoning or desecrating of French sites of memory. While ethnic minority cultural productions echo many of the themes of the *banlieues noires*, they are most importantly an effort to appropriate a site regarded as an important space of belonging, a *lieu d'appartenance*. If the decline of the working class has transformed the suburbs into "neighborhoods of exil," as Dubet and Lapeyronnie contend, the creative imaginings of ethnic minorities may represent an effort to reclaim them as vital spaces of inclusion and integration through shared memories.[41] Laying claim to the *banlieues* as a complex *lieu d'appartenance* will inevitably run up against challenges and opposition from inside and outside the North African community. But if we are moving into an age where official memory is losing its force, the struggle to articulate new collective forms of belonging may be a necessary and unavoidable part of what John Gillis refers to as the democratization of memory.[42]

CHAPTER 7

The Algerian War: Transcending Splintered Memories

I f the essence of the national spirit resides in shared memories, as Renan argued, how do we build a memory consensus today?[1] In *Les Lieux de Mémoire*, or *Realms of Memory* in translation, editor Pierre Nora's response is for historians to tell the old national story in a new way. Inspired by Ernest Lavisse's success in "reknitting the national garment of national history" at the end of the last century, but recognizing the impossibility of returning to outmoded, teleological, grand narratives, Nora proposes a new symbolic history of the nation.[2] Harnessing the intellectual energy of over 120 historians, Nora sets out to unearth and expose the many but now imperiled and largely forgotten national sites of memory that litter the French landscape. By revealing their inner workings and those who gave them their special symbolic charge, Nora's hope is to weave a new national tapestry held together not by the seamless narrative of an eternal France but rather by the countless sites that held special meaning for past generations.

Yet curiously, for a seven-volume, several thousand-page project spanning nearly a decade, only one chapter is devoted to France's vast imperial holdings—and even this chapter is restricted to the 1931 colonial exhibition in Paris. As for the empire proper, including prominent sites such as Indochina and Algeria where tens of thousands of French soldiers died to preserve the glory of greater France, *Realms of Memory* offers nothing but silence. The absence of Algeria, from a project so expansive that reviewer Steven Englund wondered what doesn't qualify as a *lieu de mémoire*, is particularly puzzling.[3] Algeria was unlike any other imperial territory as it was considered a legal extension of metropolitan France—which was why it was possible, in contrast to the war in Indochina, to send French soldiers as part of their national military service. Nearly an entire generation of Frenchmen from all walks of life did their required service in Algeria, approximately the same number as the United States sent to Vietnam but in a country with only one-fifth the population.[4] It was ultimately the inability of the Fourth Republic to manage the turmoil and divisions unleashed by the war that led to the recall of Charles de Gaulle and the founding of the Fifth Republic.

Does the memory of the Algerian War represent the limitations of *Realms of Memory* as a means of preserving a shared past? Are some sites of memory simply too contentious and too divisive to be enshrined and perpetuated in the kinds of symbolic sites of memory that inspire Nora's collection. Is it preferable, as Renan also argued, to forget the turbulent and traumatic events that often mark the birth of new regimes? "To forget and—I will venture to say—to get one's history wrong, are essential factors in the making of a nation; and thus the advance of historical studies is often a danger to nationality."[5]

Willful forgetting has been the primary strategy pursued by the French state toward the Algerian War, and one might add much of the imperial past. From textbooks and memorials to commemorative dates and appellations used to designate the war, successive French administrations have preferred to silence rather than recall the memory of the war. Even as another round of controversy has erupted over the use of torture during the war, the current administration refuses to support any kind of official inquiry.[6] Prime Minister Lionel Jospin expressed his support for "looking at the past and recalling even the darkest hours when our institutions failed us" and was confident that such "a search for truth would not weaken the national community." Nevertheless, he concluded, "I don't think it's up to the government to undertake this work."[7]

Splintered Memories

Paradoxically much of the attention given to the Algerian War has contributed to the perception of the conflict as a forgotten episode in French history. Stora explains that the war has been cast in films, documentaries, and academic studies as a site of perpetual rediscovery. By constantly billing themselves as the first of their kind, works on the Algerian War project the erroneous image of the conflict as an unexplored topic.[8] A few recent examples seem to bear out Stora's observation. For instance, Philippe Joutard's brief preface to Claire Mauss-Copeaux's 1998 *Appelés en Algérie* introduces the study as the first oral history on the memory of French conscripts who fought in the Algerian War. Director Alexandre Arcady's *La-bas mon pays*, released in 2000, is described as the first French film shot on Algerian soil since the war of independence. Even Stora goes to great lengths in his own work to explain how his 1991 documentary, *Les Années Algériens*, was really the first to offer a broad spectrum of memories of the Algerian War.[9]

Titles to diverse works on the war have also helped project the image of the conflict as an event without a history. From Bertrand Tavernier's 1992 documentary *La Guerre Sans Nom* (The War Without a Name) and Benjamin Stora's 1991 study *La gangrene et l'oubli* (Gangrene and Forgetting) to subtitles of studies such as *la parole confisquée* (Confiscated Words) for Mauss-Copeaux's *Appelés en Algérie*, works intended to enlighten readers or viewers on the Algerian War often anchor the image of a conflict that has escaped the labels and designations of history, silenced all voices, and inflicted a powerful form of collective amnesia. Stora observes that French media attention given to American cinematic depictions of the war in Vietnam has only strengthened the perception of Algeria as a *non-lieu de mémoire*, or a memoryless site. Time and again, French journalists respond to the release of new American films on Vietnam by chastising their own compatriots for failing to grapple with the Algerian War.[10]

In truth the war has generated a wealth of scholarship and personal accounts. In his 1985 bibliographic study, Stora found that between the end of the fighting and the middle of the 1980s approximately 1,000 works were published on the war.[11] While there is no French equivalent to the array of American blockbuster or cult films on Vietnam, the Algerian War has nevertheless made its own mark on French cinema. Between 1962 and 1982 Stora estimates that the French produced at least 30 feature and short-length films on the war.[12] In fact, the French produced more films on Algeria during the actual war years than the Americans did in the course of their war in Vietnam.[13]

What seems most characteristic of the memory of the Algerian War is not its forgetting but rather what Stora describes as its cloistered remembering. Recent studies on the memory of the war underscore how the conflict is typically remembered within a number of distinct group frameworks. Philip Dine, for example, divides his study of some 50 fictional works, out of what he estimates to be several hundred literary accounts of the war, into groups such as French conscripts, metropolitan observers, European colonizers, and colonized Algerians.[14] Naomi Greene's analysis of two films on the Algerian War, *Le crabe-tambour* and *Outremer*, is grounded in the assertion that each director represents a particular community of memory—Brigitte Rouen's *Outremer* embodies the European settler or *pied-noir* memory while Pierre Schoendoerffer's *Le crabe-tambour* evokes that of the military.[15] Benjamin

Stora's work and his television documentary, *Les Années Algériennes*, feature the testimonies of individuals ranging from retired officers and *pieds-noirs*, to ex-conscripts and former FLN officials. Yet once again each testimony represents a particular community of memory.

Works on the Algerian War publicized and promoted in terms of their novelty or unprecedented character are more accurately understood as a response to the limited and rigid recollection of the conflict caused by its cloistered remembering. Cloistered memories are "truncated, skewed and fragmentary, made up of legends and stereotypes elaborated out of the fear of telling the truth." It is precisely because so many of the groups implicated in the war cling to narrow, unchanging, and mythologized constructions of the past, argues Stora, that a "reconciliation of images" becomes so difficult. "Each group becomes the bearer of its own specific memory of Algeria and wants to see *its* film, to relive *its* own failed efforts or betrayed hopes of an event still close at hand."[16]

Stora likens the cloistered remembering of the Algerian War to ritualized forms of memory. Ritualized memory demands conformity to preestablished accounts and symbolic frameworks. It is a kind of "religious memory," in which "each event acquires meaning only in relation to a legendary organization of the past." Here Stora is critical of the kinds of sites of memory steeped in ritual and symbolism that Nora's work seeks to preserve and elevate as central elements in the shared narrative of the national past. For Stora ritualized forms of memory are harmful in that they obstruct the process of confronting the true complexity of the past. Rather than lamenting the passing of the kinds of self-enclosed, limited spaces of collective memory one finds in *Realms of Memory*, Stora calls on historians to "undertake the restitution of plural memories."[17] Such a restitution in Stora's work entails a process of revealing and challenging the multiple imaginings of the Algerian War.

In the case of both the community of French settlers and the military, long-established myths employed to interpret the Algerian past still function as powerful exculpatory or self-redeeming devices in the present. Mythical self-constructions of the *pied-noir* community as the dispossessed and damned people of Europe continue to help mitigate what Fanon denounced as the harsh reality of an inegalitarian colonial system based above all on fear and coercion. Self-victimization can function as a powerful, galvanizing form of identity that many groups are quite reluctant to discard. The 1993 assassination of Jacques Roseau, head of one of the principal *pied-noir* organizations, is evidence of the unwillingness of some elements within the former settler community to come to terms with the past. Stora reports how Roseau was gunned down outside the House of the Repatriated in Montpellier shortly after his televised dialogue with Yacef Saadi, former FLN chief of the Algiers region. For Stora, there is little doubt that Roseau was executed for his reconciliatory gestures perceived as an intolerable betrayal of the *pied-noir* community.[18]

Myths found in the accounts of former officers often emphasize the honor and nobility of those who served their country in Algeria and their betrayal by officials on the home front. It is not difficult to fathom why military officers would prefer to cloak themselves in the mythology of the civilizing mission rather than confronting the more complex and troubling reality of the past. The reluctance of the military to acknowledge its willingness to resort to uncivilized tactics in Algeria, such as the use of torture, is in keeping with its long history of denying its travesties of justice. It was not until 1993 that the French army officially cleared Captain Alfred Dreyfus of trumped up charges of treason—"103 years after the event."[19]

Here it is important to recognize that a power/knowledge relationship helps establish and sustain dominant forms of cloistered memory. Stora points out that those groups favorable to maintaining Algeria as part of France have always done more of the memory work. According to Stora, 70 percent of the works published on the war between 1962 and 1982 were written by French officers, Algerians who fought on the French side, *pieds-noirs*, and politicians—all of whom opposed Algerian independence.[20] It is the sheer accumulated weight of established ways of remembering the conflict, as Said observes in *Orientalism*, that stifles or diminishes the influence of counter-narratives.[21]

Representative associations also impose a certain degree of conformity on the memories of rank and file members. If the voices of ordinary soldiers have been confiscated, as Mauss-Copeux argues, it is not only because they have not written as many accounts of the past as the former officer class. Mauss-Copeaux's work demonstrates that many veterans of the Algerian War do not share the view that the Algerian cause was betrayed, that unscrupulous metropolitan officials sacrificed a just war that the French were winning. Nevertheless, the two leading veterans' organizations continue to project a humanitarian image of the role of the military that closely parallels the predominate recollections of the officer class. While the widespread use of torture in Algeria is openly recognized by veterans, it continues to be denied by their representative organizations.[22]

The simplified narratives of cloistered memories also tend to override or suppress the diversity of individual experiences and perspectives within groups. According to Naomi Greene when individual directors take up the topic of the Algerian War they inevitably find themselves locked into established frameworks of memory. For Greene one of the chief shortcomings of these memory constructs is that they are invariably fragmentary and incomplete, offering only a disjointed nostalgic vision devoid of new insights about the war. This seems to be the case with *La-bas mon pays*, by Axandre Aracady. Billed as the first French film set in Algeria since the war, Aracady's film succumbs to the same nostalgic vision and the same victimized portrayal of the *pied-noir* community as Brigitte Rouen's *Outremer*. At the center of the film is Pierre Nivel, who, despite his success as a television news personality, clearly lacks purpose, meaning, and passion in his life. As the drama unfolds we quickly learn that France's loss in the Algerian War uprooted the teenage Nivel from his Algerian birthplace and tore him away from his Algerian lover. Having failed in his marriage and unfulfilled by his professional life, Nivel fits the classic description of the dispossessed, downtrodden *pied-noir* forever trapped between two worlds and two eras. When Nivel receives a message to help smuggle his old girlfriend's daughter out of an Algeria now ravaged by civil war, he is irresistibly drawn into an adventure in which the chaos of the present fades into that of the past.

If the Algerian War has failed to generate a fuller range of memories, group dynamics provide only part of the explanation. Central to the difficulty of reconciling memories has been the government's inability or unwillingness to confront the Algerian past. For decades politicians from both the left and the right carefully avoided the use of the term "war" when discussing the conflict in Algeria—preferring instead to rely on alternative designations such as the events in Algeria, police operations, actions to maintain order, operations to restore civilian peace, or pacification undertakings.[23] The government has never settled on a single date to commemorate the war and it was not until the mid-1980s that the history of the conflict was integrated into high school baccalaureate exams—and even then only in a few regions.[24] In her oral history of former conscripts from the Vosges, Mauss-Copeaux finds that the absence of official memory extends to regions as well. The fact that few public squares and street names in the Vosges bear references to the Algerian War is indicative of the reluctance of local officials to confront the Algerian past.[25]

The Algerian War is subject to official amnesia because it undercut and destabilized both the left and the right representing what Stora describes as a double crisis of the Republic. For the left the war recalled the collapse of the Fourth Republic, the use of torture, and the general failure to apply its lofty egalitarian values and ideals. For the right, de Gaulle's decision to pull out of Algeria evoked memories of the military coup in Algiers, the purging of the French officers corps, the bloody campaign of terror launched by the OAS

(Secret Army Organization), and the unexpected exodus of nearly a million European settlers.[26] The response by postwar regimes, Stora argues, was to forgive and forget. Between the late 1960s and the early 1970s successive French governments passed general amnesty laws extending mass pardons to former coup participants, OAS activists, and French FLN collaborators alike.[27] Éric Savarèse adds that the story of the empire, which had grown up along side and always accompanied that of the Republic, was simply purged from public school textbooks. After 1962, Savarèse notes, silence gradually replaced the story of the empire.[28]

This official form of silence on the war extended to popular treatments of the North African community in France. After World War II demographic and economic pressures in France led to the recruitments of hundreds of thousands of workers from Morocco, Tunisia, and Algeria. By the end of the Algerian War there were already approximately 350,000 Algerians residing in France.[29] Yet in the decade after the Algerian War Savarèse observes that North Africans were treated only marginally and episodically in French films. Regardless of which side of the Mediterranean these films took place, North African characters were systematically relegated to the background and shut out of any significant role in the storyline.[30] North Africans have been in effect subject to two forms of forgetting associated with the official narrative of the national past established by the Third Republic. They are, as Savarèse shows, part of the old imperial story purged from the pages of Republican textbooks. They are also, as Gérard Noiriel demonstrates, excluded by the linear, holistic conception of the nation, established above all by the textbook writers of the Third Republic, which leaves no room for France's rich nineteenth- and twentieth-century immigration history.[31]

Ethnic Minority Memories

It is this sentiment of being invisible or denied a place in a larger story that acts as a catalyst for the emergence of memory-charged cultural initiatives by the sons and daughters of Algerian workers in France beginning in the mid-1970s. From the first theater companies and music groups to mushroom in the Paris area to more recent films and television documentaries, the children of Algerian workers have been actively laying claim to a shared past. The experience of the Algerian War certainly marked the first generation of Algerian immigrant children who often arrived or were born in France before or during the conflict. While Nora calls on historians to rally against the potentially destabilizing rise of private memory, the search for roots by second-generation Algerians can also be understood as a vital counterpoint to the excesses and oversights of existing group memories. In many respects the memory work produced by the children of North African immigrants is an important challenge to the cloistered remembering of the Algerian past on both sides of the Mediterranean.

Saliha Amara's decision to help create the theater company Kahina, in 1976, was driven by a desire to assert the presence of immigrant youth at a time when the immigrant community was still perceived strictly in terms of single, male workers. "At the time," Amara recalled "it was harder to publish than it is today, or to voice your opinions on the radio or television, so we decided to talk about ourselves and our concerns on our own." The theater company consisted of men and women, Amara explained, but the men "were in the minority and they were there above all there to play male roles, and to help us talk about our problems." The subject of Kahina's first play, "Pour que les larmes de nos mères deviennent légende" (So the Tears of Our Mothers Become Legendary), was the role of women in the Algerian War. Amara commented that the play "showed that women played an equally important role in the war of liberation in Algeria. But after independence they were silenced." "Algerian women did their duty," Amara added, "after which they fell back into anonymity, were once again subordinated, saddled with domestic work, forced into arranged marriages with a dowry and the expectation that their virginity would be in tact." Amara recalled that she personally performed one scene featuring a traditional wedding night, complete with bloodstained linens, that was particularly shocking for the public.

> We used the official [Algerian] discourse in the National Charter in between which we tried to show the reality experienced by Algerian women by means of personal testimonies of [Algerian] women living in France. This was a way of showing how our mothers lived and how we, their daughters, had no desire to live like them.[32]

By means of a classical Greek-style chorus, Amara explained, the play was performed in three languages, Arabic, Kabyle, and French, so that everyone could understand—although she added that most of the actors, including herself, were more comfortable performing in French.

Kahina's account of the war reveals the ability of ethnic minorities in France to creatively recall the past in ways that challenge the memory of both the Algerian and French communities. The subjugation of Algerian women after the war and the failure of the FLN to extend the promise of liberation to half its population was further dramatized by scenes that recounted the imprisonment and torture of women resistance fighters at the hands of the

French army. Kahina's remembering of the war runs counter to the nostalgic myths erected by *pieds-noirs* and former officers of a noble cause betrayed or a cherished way of life lost forever. At the same time it raises questions about the failure of the Algerian government to recognize the sacrifices made by women. Confronting the past was also a way for the daughters of Algerian workers to refuse to perpetuate the status of their mothers in the present or the future—this was the essence of the title of the play.

Theater offered a particularly open and interactive form of memory expression. Typical of other theater companies like Ibn Kaldoun and Weekend à Nanterre, also circulating in the Paris area during the late 1970s, Kahina's performances integrated the memories of the actors who participated in its plays. With the constant arrival and departure of actors, Amara's brother Mohand estimated that as many as 50 or 60 different people may have performed with Kahina during its six-year existence from 1976 to 1982.[33] This regular infusion of new memories meant that performances were never static. "There was a basic storyline," Saliha Amara explained, "but with the testimonies, for example, the women participating in the play could include their own personal experiences."

In stark contrast with the kinds of ritualized forms of recollection that characterize the cloistered remembering of the Algerian War, Kahina represented a more fluid, participatory form of remembrance. Ritualized memory, as Paul Connerton observes, tends to be "deliberately stylized," and subject to only a limited degree of "spontaneous variation."[34] The rigidity of rule-based ritualized memory is quite different from the openness and flexibility of Kahina's plays. While rough story lines assured a certain thematic continuity, the actual content of each performance underwent constant change and transformation depending on the memories included and conveyed. Kahina's plays are an excellent example of a collective project that lends itself to the kind of plurality of memories and critical assessment of the past advocated by Stora.

As Kahina's performances were often staged for predominantly male audiences, relating the experiences and memories of Algerian women in the past and present was no easy task. Amara recalled that the strategy frequently employed to draw spectators, especially in North African immigrant neighborhoods like Barbès in Paris, was for the actors to parade through the streets singing and dancing in traditional costumes. Expecting a concert with music and dance, Amar recalled that many of the men responded with shock and dismay at the content of the plays parachuted on them, sometimes even interrupting performances by hurling invectives at the actors. Amara recognized that these confrontational performances were quite demanding for everyone involved. "We took up topics which were taboo at the time, which everyone knew about but it was impossible to talk about." Many of the mothers disapproved of their daughters performing in public, a form of conduct regarded as sullying the family honor. It was not until four years after the founding of Kahina that Amara's father became aware of her performances.[35]

Before and in between acts many theater companies relied on local music groups to keep audiences entertained. Some of Mounsi's first concerts were in conjunction with the theater company Week-end à Nanterre. Having grown up in the Nanterre shantytown at the time of the Algerian War, music was a way of conveying his lived experiences. "I think the gravity of this history had an impact on me. Maybe when I picked up the guitar and sang, maybe it was some of this tragedy I wanted to relate."[36] When Mounsi released his first and only album, *Seconde Génération*, in 1984, his song "Batard" (Bastard) evoked his childhood memories of the war.

> Algiers . . . Paris, 1958, the Algerian War/the Nanterre Bidonville . . .
> Walls, covered with an alphabet of hate . . .
> Twist again . . .
> I remember those who wanted to throw us in the ocean.
> The ocean was too far away so they threw us in the Seine.
> It was enough to make a kid lose his mind.
> Since then . . . how much more water and how many more bodies have flowed under the bridges of the Seine.[37]

Not surprisingly confrontations between the police and the immigrant community during the war, and the Paris massacre of October 17, 1961 evoked by Mounsi in "Batard," are memories close to home that come to light in many cultural productions by second-generation North Africans. The title of Nacer Kettane's *Le Sourire de Brahim*, refers to the smile lost by the main character after his brother died in the bloody repression by the French police of Algerian protestors in October 1961. Kettane, former president of Radio Beur, recalled that it was the first to commemorate the memory of October 1961 by laying a wreath at the site.[38] October 1961 was the subject of the first commemorative effort by the Association *Au nom de la mémoire* (In the name of Memory) established in 1990. "Preventing memory from becoming fixed or frozen but always in movement," explained cofounder Samia Messaoudi, "requires groundwork that brings together many partners." It was a collaborative venture, added Messaoudi, that resulted in the film, *Le silence du fleuve* (Silence of the River) by Mehdi Lallaoui and Agnès Denis and a book by Anne Tristan. The project also gave rise to a mobile exhibition that sparked debates and discussions in 50 cities around the country.[39]

One of the more moving cinematic depictions of October 1961 is *Vivre au Paradis* (1998), directed by Bourlem Guerdjou. Although born after the war, Guerdjou's film appears to be a fulfillment of the desire expressed by the director years earlier in an interview with the author to move away from clichéd roles as an actor and to pursue new work as a director commensurate with his Algerian past.[40] The film portrays the desperate struggle of one Algerian worker, Lakhdar, at the end of the war to escape the Nanterre shantytown and to find descent housing for his wife and children. Working endlessly to save enough money to rent an apartment, ready to exploit even his closest friends, Lakdhar is clearly resentful and bitter about being pressured to make his regular payments in support of the cause of Algerian independence. When the residents of the shantytown mobilize to protest against a government-imposed curfew, Lakhdar only joins the demonstration after being shamed by a friend for betraying his Algerian identity and becoming just like the French. In the following scene, clearly labeled October 17, 1961, French police close in on and carry out a brutal repression of the demonstration. After an extended series of images of helmeted French police cornering and violently clubbing defenseless protestors trying to hide under cars or seeking shelter in apartment entranceways, the scene concludes with an explanatory note indicating that the massacre of October 17, 1961 claimed at least 200 lives.

Stora refers to October 1961 as one of the three forgotten massacres that occurred in the months leading up to the end of the war. As with the war in general, court cases and special committees set up to investigate the actions of the Paris police and their chief, Maurice Papon, were dropped with the general amnesty laws passed after the war.[41] Claude Liauzu remarks that not only is access to the archives of the Ministry of the Interior and the Paris police closed until 2021, but also many of the government records pertaining to the demonstration have simply disappeared. To this day, Liauzu regrets, it is impossible to ascertain how many people died that evening in Paris. The numbers range from Maurice Papon's unsurprisingly low estimate of 2 to as high as 200. Referring to the Society for French Historical Studies, Liauzu adds that historians in the United States have collectively expressed their objection to archival policies that obstruct access to valuable documents that might shed light on events such as October 1961. However, he laments that their counterparts in France have yet to mobilize in a similar corporative fashion.[42]

The point here is not to shower praise on American scholars but to underline the real need for the kind of memory work undertaken by second-generation Algerians. Whether it is the events of October 1961 or the use of torture during the Algerian War, the recollections offered by the progeny of Algerian workers often confront, challenge, and contradict official forms of memory and amnesia as well as the memories of other groups. This is not to suggest that one or any group has all the answers—historians included. But rather than diminishing and downplaying group memories by locking them into symbolic sites in an updated grand narrative of the nation, as Nora proposes, scholars should recognize the important role that private citizens play in helping national communities confront the true complexity of the past.

In both recent works by scholars on the memory of the war and the cultural productions by the progeny of North African workers, there seems to be a consensus about the therapeutic need to confront the past. Modernization during the 1950s and 1960s was a means of escaping and putting distance between France and its imperial past, argues Kristin Ross. The impossibility of carrying out the process of modernization without importing large numbers of North African workers has, in Ross's opinion, triggered the rise of racist violence in France today.[43] Borrowing from Henry Russo's work on Vichy France, Anne Donadey argues that in the case of Algeria the French are still bogged down in the stage of memory repression. The surge of racially motivated violence targeting the North African community since the 1980s, Donadey maintains, can be understood as a Freudian return of a still-unresolved imperial past.[44] Benjamin Stora goes as far as arguing that much of the terminology and many of the issues pertaining to the immigration debate in France today, which typically centers on the North African population, is a rehashing of similar words and preoccupations first raised in conjunction with the Algerian population during the war.[45]

The first part of this chapter should demonstrate the inappropriateness of the Freudian notion of repressed memory. While successive administrations may have tried to shut the door on the Algerian past, this has certainly never been the case for the millions of French and Algerians directly or indirectly affected by the war. Rather than being forgotten, the memory of the war, as Stora demonstrates, has been dominated by narrow, simplified, mythologized forms of cloistered memory. Yet Freud's belief that a failure to confront and work through both real and imagined memories of the past can have dire consequences in the present does seem applicable in the Algerian case. In this sense Donadey is right to challenge Renan by arguing that forgetting the divisive and turbulent events that mark the national past can also trap us into old hatreds, divisions, and destructive patterns of behavior.[46]

The power of the past to account for racial violence or discrimination in the present is evident in works by many authors of Algerian descent. For the main character in Nacer Kettane's *Le sourire de Brahim* the trigger happy, petty bourgeois responsible for racist crimes in the present are most often "former policemen or retired soldiers" driven by a certain nostalgia for the "*ratonnades*."[47] It is the racially motivated murder of Sélim, the son of a Harki, in Mehdi Charef's *Le Harki de Meriem*, that triggers a memory voyage into a still-unresolved Algerian past. Ahmed Kalaouaz's *Point Kilometrique 190* is an investigation into the brutal real-life murder of Habib Grimzi, thrown from the window of a moving train by two French Foreign Legion recruits in 1983. Flashbacks between Grimizi's gruesome demise and his birth during the violent events of the Algerian War suggest that the conflict has never really come to an end.[48]

Yamina Benguigui's 1998 television documentary *Mémoires d'Immigrés* suggests that the urban riots that have periodically exploded in France's suburbs since the early 1980s can also be understood in terms of memories from the Algerian past. After proceeding through the recollections of first-generation immigrants, the documentary concludes with the testimonies of their children who relate the scars left by the war years. One interviewee explains that it is impossible to grasp the attitude of Algerian youth toward the police in French cities today without addressing the memories of fear and confrontation dating from the war years.[49] Protests and a desire to fight back that once took the form of cultural expression and an associational movement culminating in a series of civil rights–style marches on Paris, may now, within a much-aggravated economic contest, be unleashing the kind of urban violence that typically tops the list of national preoccupations in French public opinion surveys.

Conclusion

It is better not to "awaken the memories of the war," as Maurice Faivre argues in his response to Claude Liauzu's article on October 1961. Collective memories are inevitably distorted, self-serving, and often provoke discord and disunity between groups. The best approach, advises Faivre, is to be patient until historians have had time to do their work in the archives.[50] In an interview with the author, Pierre Nora seemed to agree. After pointing out that he himself has written a book on Algeria and if the topic was left out of *Realms of Memory*, it was only due to time-management constraints and the general lack of interest in the war when the collection was underway, Nora went on to express his serious reservations about private memory. "Memory tends to particularize," explained Nora.

> This is why I'm in favor of a more unifying kind of history. The memory work and memory movements today are very dangerous instruments. Private memory for a long time functioned within a liberationist

dynamic. This is now over for most and it has since become a dynamic of self-enclosure, a lack of understanding of the other, alienation from one's own history, a means of legitimizing oneself, the loss of common ground, and very often a powerfully aggressive ethnic nationalism that sometimes even results in murder. All you need to do is to look at the role of memory in the Balkan wars. I'm very interested in memory from a historical point of view but I'm wary of the sentimental power of particularist memories. I understand it, I see it, but I'm absolutely convinced of its dangers, its pettiness, and its false legitimacy.[51]

Nora is right to remind us of the abuses and sometimes tragic uses of private memory. Historians certainly have a role to play in curbing the strife and turmoil that can result from the misuse of the past. Yet dismissing the value of private memory as a harbinger of the kinds of ethnic warfare experienced in the Balkans ignores not only the therapeutic role of group recollections but also the vital tie they can provide to the nation. Diverse forms of memory work from the North African immigrant community demonstrate how private citizens can draw attention to and promote awareness of absences and distortions in official and even scholarly accounts of the national past. Theater troupes such as Kahina and rock singers like Mounsi were calling attention to the experiences of France's North African community as early as the late 1970s, years before immigration became a mediatized, political football, and an increasingly popular topic for scholars of all stripes. Moreover, the diversity of memories found in initiatives like those of Kahina are a valuable counterpoint to the rigid, cloistered remembering of the Algerian past.

Participatory, personal forms of memory work undertaken by second-generation North Africans may reflect the same kinds of new connections between citizens and their national past that seems to be taking shape in the United States. Despite fears that Americans are losing touch with their past, the oral history work of Roy Rosenzweig and David Thelen demonstrates that the past is quite alive and well within families, among friends, and in smaller groups and places closer to home.[52] At a time when nations have lost much of their clout, when the pace of change widens the divide between old linear official histories and the lived experience of ordinary people, John Gillis argues that a revamped, participatory, hands-on form of memory may now be more suitable to the needs of the present.[53]

As older official histories increasingly lose influence and legitimacy, private citizens are required to do more of the memory work. Both Gillis and Nora recognize that assuming the task of finding meaningful connections to the past can be quite burdensome. Nora stresses how memory has become archival and we now feel compelled to store away more than we can possibly remember. Gillis points out how the burden of memory is particularly heavy on families. "Every attic is an archive, every living room a museum. Never before has so much been recorded, collected; and never before has remembering been so compulsive..."[54] Yet despite their shared concerns, Gillis is able to recognize that the privatization of memory is also a form of democratization.

> In earlier times, the past belonged only to elites, who kept heritage just as they kept offices and land—for themselves. Today the past has been democratized and we all must have our own history. What was once a luxury has become a necessity. What was once a privilege is now a right.[55]

The right to speak for themselves and to recount their own past is especially important to all those who have been marginalized or forgotten in traditional versions of official history. Rather than contributing to the splintering of memory, groups like the sons and daughters of Algerian workers in France have the capacity to create more critical, open, and truer narratives of belonging that better reflect the ideals of democratic societies.

Conclusion

The relevance of coping with ethnic diversity and coming to terms with North Africans in particular has not diminished since the end of the Mitterrand years. For *Le Monde* editor Jean-Marie Colombani the success of far-right leader Jean-Marie Le Pen in the 2002 presidential elections is evidence of France's ongoing struggle to reconcile its Jacobin assimilationist traditions with its multiethnic present. Borrowing from Benjamin Stora's *Le Transfert d'une mémoire*, Colombani describes France as a nation that has inherited the collective fears and shared sentiments of abandonment of its former settler community in Algeria. Unsure of itself in the face of its Muslim population and refusing to accept cultural diversity, France is caught in the grips of an identity crisis that September 11, with all its associated fears of an inevitable clash of civilizations, only worsened.[1]

If recognition is central to the challenge of accepting France's new demographic reality, as this book argues, the recent political record is mixed. Significant progress has been made during the presidency of Jacque Chirac. The first president to officially acknowledge France's responsibility in the Holocaust, as well as tragedies caused by other regimes such as the Armenian genocide in Turkey, Chirac has also been the first to unveil a monument to the veterans of the Algerian War and the first to make an official state visit to Algeria. Following the victory of France's soccer team in the 1998 World Cup Chirac personally hosted and toasted the French team at the Elysée Palace. For many observers the victory and Chirac's celebration of the multiethnic national team appeared to herald the coming of a new age of respect for and acceptance of diversity in French society.

Yet just three years after the euphoria of the World Cup the first ever soccer match between France and Algeria resulted in a debacle. At the start of the game, played at the Stade de France outside Paris, French fans of North African descent whistled and sounded catcalls at the Marseillaise. Chirac, in attendance and visibly disturbed by the display of irreverence, stormed out of his VIP box and refused to return until an apology was made, delaying the start of the match by half an hour.[2] When the game was finally well underway and nearing the end, Algerian supporters began hurling bottles and metal seat covers at French authorities; over a hundred fans eventually broke through security lines and spilled onto the field. In their efforts to restore order Marie-George Buffet, Minister of Youth and Sports, and Elisabeth Guigou, Minister of Labor and Solidarity, found themselves to be the targets of bottle throwers. Seventeen people were eventually taken into custody by French authorities. With fifteen minutes left in the game officials decided to call off the match and what was supposed to be a moment of reconciliation between France and Algeria ended in chaos.[3]

It is certainly possible to explain the events at the Stade de France in socioeconomic terms. The unruly behavior could be cast as a simple case of ethnic minority youth venting the kind of anger and frustration typically associated with France's beleaguered suburban populations. Disrespect for the icons, guardians, and representatives of the nation could be understood as the result of unraveling communities, the collapse of the working class as a vector of integration, or the failure of French normalizing institutions to create opportunities or a sense of hope and optimism about the future. Locked out of the political establishment and caught on the wrong side of a society of insiders and outsiders, events like the France–Algeria soccer match offer an inviting forum for the expression of pent-up grievances. "It's probably the sentiment of abandonment, revolt against discrimination, choosing the David over the Goliath that explains the whistles during the France-Algeria [match]."

Such socioeconomic accounts, however, ignore the long relationship between France and Algeria and the importance of memory to the integration process. As journalist Philippe Bernard rightly argues, the prospects for belonging and acceptance have much to do with the willingness to recognize the nation's immigration and Algerian past. To date, far too little has been done. The France–Algeria match itself coincided closely with the fortieth anniversary of October 17, 1961—when the excessive use of force by French police caused the deaths of as many as 200 peaceful Algerian protesters. Without a fuller accounting of events like October 17, 1961, we cannot expect France's Algerian youth to have much respect for the nation and its icons. For integration to succeed it is paramount to "shed light on the colonial past and in particular the Algerian War, including the murkiest and most detestable episodes."[4]

Rather than recognition, however, the order of the day seems to be repression. Following Chirac's reelection Interior Minister Nicolas Sarkozy, son of a Hungarian immigrant, has gained public notoriety through his tough stand and high-profile actions against crime and insecurity—themes that are often conflated with suburban spaces and ethnic minority youths. "In recent days, he has outlawed prostitution on the public highway, rounded up gangs of beggars and ordered police to dismantle gypsy encampments."[5] Many of Sarkozy's measures are intended to impose a greater degree of respect for French authorities. "Insulting anyone who serves the public, from firemen and bus conductors to teachers and housing estate caretakers, also becomes a punishable offense." Most striking are the proposals to criminalize forms of disrespect for icons and symbols of the French Republic. Interpreted as a direct response to the France–Algeria soccer match, the current government is now calling for offenses against the French flag and national anthem to be punishable by a fine of up to 9,000 dollars and 6 months in jail.[6]

While these measures enjoy strong public support they have provoked an outcry from certain groups. A group of 100 university professors recently drafted a petition expressing their alarm about Sarkozy's actions. Alluding to the Vichy period they suggested that such law and order policies harkens back to some of the darkest days in France's national past. "Among other measures that have already provoked justified criticism, the law on the flag and anthem inspires particular concern . . . this forced obedience to the symbols of the nation evokes unhappy past times." "Respect is earned," they declared, "it cannot be imposed."[7]

The need to earn respect through mutual recognition, and the difficulties this entails, has been at the heart of this book. It was the lack of recognition, stretching back to the interwar years and the arrival of the first North Africans in France that fueled a succession of nationalist, immigrant worker and civil rights struggles. Focusing on the rise and fall of the associational movement in the 1980s, I have tried to show that while disrespect, particularly in the form of racism and discrimination, can function as a powerful incentive for recognition struggles, it can also have a debilitating impact making it difficult for those struggles to succeed. In the case of North African youth pervasive sentiments of distrust complicated efforts to forge much-needed alliances and crippled attempts to build a national movement or ethnic lobby.

Faced with serious internal constraints the associational movement ran up against the added challenge of an increasingly hostile political context. The rise of the xenophobic far-right during the early 1980s caused both the left and the right to take a tougher stand against immigration, which became one of the leading issues of the decade. In their attempt to counter the National Front, the left and right embraced a supposedly traditional model of individual integration and belonging making governments less supportive of political projects that appeared to be rooted in particular ethnic communities. The ability of national organizations, such as SOS-Racisme and France Plus, to eclipse the associational movement in the course of the 1980s can therefore be understood as the result of the search for broad-based organizations capable of generating interest among a new generation of apolitical youth as well as the failure of associational leaders to transcend their own doubts and suspicions.

By the late 1980s ethnic minority associations receded to the local level. While activists continued to fight against various injustices and discriminatory measures affecting immigrants and ethnic minorities in France, these actions have been dispersed and limited in scope. Increasingly dependent on state subsidies, local associations continued to display a pronounced degree of distrust and suspicion toward allies both within and outside their community. In accounts by former militants it is the failure to learn and benefit from a rich history of militant experiences that continues to hinder ethnic minority associations in the present. Rather than looking at these accounts as examples of the excesses and dangers of ethnic minority memory, I have tried to argue that they represent an effort to critically assess and foster a greater degree of awareness of the benefits of learning from the past—a past that is frequently framed as an extension rather than a departure from the larger history of the nation.

Ethnic minority political and cultural actions are certainly related. Accounts of the associational movement necessarily make reference to militant theater or rock music projects that provided an important formative experience while helping activists to articulate enduring and influential viewpoints. In my own analysis I point out parallels with the associational movement, such as the significance of testimonial forms of memory and the desire to convey lived experiences to a larger public. Cultural expression has been and remains important in denouncing discriminatory policies, condemning all forms of racial intolerance, challenging stereotypes, and offering more complex and nuanced accounts of ethnic minority populations. By attempting to bring about a greater degree of understanding cultural actors have done much to improve the prospects for mutual recognition.

Yet when looking at the realm of culture I have also tried to note the difficulties involved in breaking silences. Some of the constraints also parallel those of the associational movement. For example, most of the militant theater companies have long since collapsed. Much like the associational movement, collective cultural actions became increasingly dependent on state subsidies and were often unable to reach audiences beyond the local level. Just as the militant, neighborhood-based associational movement unraveled and was eventually eclipsed by powerful professional organizations such as SOS-Racisme and France Plus, success in reaching larger audiences seemed to hinge on the ability to go professional. It was precisely this failed attempt to make the transition to professional theater that brought about the demise of several prominent companies.

The number of professional cultural actors has increased since the early 1980s. From novelists and sculptors to movie directors and cartoonists, many of these artists relate the same kinds of themes and stories found in the first theater productions and musical work. However, regardless of the content of their work, many of the ethnic minority artists I encountered were often subjected to particular pressures and constraints. Artists whose work was influenced by their ethnicity were frequently interpreted through the lens of their social and cultural origins. Those who were inspired by their roots and ethnicity often found themselves marginalized within their professional milieu. These constraints helped explain a pronounced reluctance to be too closely associated with one's community of origin and a tendency to embrace an individualistic artistic discourse that closely resembles anticommunitarian French Republican ideals.

The study of Radio Beur offers more in-depth insights into the difficulties experienced by ethnic minorities in their struggle for recognition. Radio Beur took shape within an optimistic context about the place of ethnic minority cultures in France during the early 1980s. Proclaiming itself an avatar of a new multicultural nation, Radio Beur helped fill a cultural void in the North African community. For over a decade it broadcast music from the Maghreb, helped promote aspiring and accomplished North African artists, and became an important organizer of concerts in the Paris region. Several veterans of Radio Beur claimed that the station deserved credit for introducing raï music in France. From legal advice to women's issues, Radio Beur's broadcasts offered a wealth of information and addressed a wide range of topics.

Curiously, however, for a project that adopted the label of the *beur* generation it is not clear to what extent North African youth ever identified with the station. When asked about the composition of the audience there was no consensus among former station members. Some claimed that Radio Beur always appealed to older members of the North African community nostalgic for their culture of origin. If young people listened it was only because their parents had already tuned in. Others were convinced that Radio Beur was successful in reaching a wide range of age groups. They pointed to the younger and older North Africans who turned out for concerts sponsored by the station as evidence of the broad appeal of Radio Beur. Moreover, accurate audience figures do not exist and station members always had an interest in inflating the importance of the station's following. These questions surrounding the composition and size of Radio Beur's audience reveal the difficulties of assessing the impact and influence of projects that claim to represent and promote the interests of ethnic minority populations.

While its audience remains a mystery Radio Beur's inability to achieve solidarity and unity within its own ranks is quite clear. Much like the associational movement Radio Beur's history is marred with internal divisions and discord. Early on Radio Beur was subject to charges that it was favoring the Kabyle community and Berber speakers. While denied by some, charges of cultural bias were enough for some of the founding members to leave the station. My point is that rifts within Radio Beur over the place of Berber culture reveal how ethnic divisions originating in the colonial past can migrate to the postcolonial, metropolitan present complicating efforts to achieve a greater degree of recognition.

It was the intensification of internal divisions within Radio Beur that finally brought about the demise of the station after 11 years on the air. Faced with an increasingly hostile political climate toward ethnic minority projects and the dire need for unity, Radio Beur splintered into rival clans each struggling for control over the station. Each clan leader accused the others of corruption and political intrigue while each claimed to defend the true interests and integrity of the station. My contention is that the increased importance of Radio Beur was simply too great of a temptation for ambitious station administrators who were able to rally and manipulate vulnerable rank and file members. With its first 24-hour frequency, new advertising money, and its access to the Algerian community at a time of political unrest in Algeria, the presidency and top administrative positions at Radio Beur took on an importance that was unimaginable just a few years earlier. Following a series of court cases Radio Beur finally collapsed and was replaced by Beur FM. Part of a larger commercial network, Beur FM, not unlike SOS-Racisme or France Plus, lacks the same kind of roots as Radio Beur—a project, in the words of one former president, built brick by brick by members of the North African community.

Have French cultural projects fared better in fostering a greater degree of recognition and respect for ethnic minorities in France? I try to provide answers to this question through my consideration of the 1984 Beaubourg exhibition *Les enfants de l'immigration* and the television series *La Famille Ramdam* and *Seconde B*. All of these productions represent important breakthroughs and can be taken as examples of prominent, mainstream cultural institutions offering positive forms of recognition. In the case of *Les enfant de l'immigration* one of France's most prominent cultural institutions invited immigrant youths to convey their experiences, concerns, and aspirations to mainstream audiences in the heart of the nation's capital. Several hundred thousand people who attended the three-month exhibition had the opportunity to see immigrant children as active participants in French society who respond creatively and constructively to the urban environments where they reside.

Yet when we look more closely the structure and content of the exhibition questions arise about the limits of recognition. While many scholars point out the impossibility of understanding French anxieties about North Africans today without considering the importance of the Algerian past, *Les enfants de l'immigration* tended to conflate the Algerian story with a larger immigration history. Moreover, the trajectory offered by the exhibition was a reassuring one. From the original uprooting (*arrachement*) to the inevitable re-rooting (*construction*), visitors who followed the guided path through the exhibition could feel confident that postwar communities would also find their place in French society. While such a positive message should certainly be commended, it does little to help visitors grasp the significance of the colonial past and the particular experiences of postcolonial minorities—particularities that have an important bearing on the prospects for belonging and acceptance.

It is precisely the particularity of the Algerian past that may help explain the failure of *Les enfants de l'immigration* to attract French visitors. The overwhelmingly positive response by North Africans in France, their preponderance and exceptionally active participation at the exhibition attests to the longing for and powerful appeal of the kind of institutional recognition offered by Beaubourg. Unfortunately, this kind of enthusiasm was not reciprocated by French visitors who were generally underrepresented, passive, and least likely to make a return trip to the exhibition. Despite the amalgamation of the Algerian experience with a larger immigration story and the absence of references to the Algerian War, the prominence of North Africans at the exhibition, both as visitors and participants, may simply have been too much and too early for a nation that is still struggling to contend with its colonial past and its postcolonial present.

If the French public failed to identify with the exhibition this was also true of the French establishment. Exhibition organizers complained that Beaubourg's administration showed little enthusiasm for the project, refusing to provide full funding and failing to record much of the proceedings. While Minister of Culture Jack Lang and Minister of Social Affairs Georgina Dufoix were both in attendance at the opening ceremonies, neither offered any kind of inaugural statement. At a time when immigration was becoming increasingly politicized, I suggest that the French establishment may have decided to keep a strategic distance from a project of questionable value in making them look good. The lack of support for *Les enfants de l'immigration*, the decision to cancel ambitious plans for a series of regional exhibitions, and the dismantling of agencies like the FIC and the DDC that played a key role in supporting ethnic minority cultural initiatives, may also have resulted from a shift toward projects implicating larger suburban spaces and disadvantaged populations rather than specific ethnic minority communities—a shift that was more in tune with the new Republican model based on individual forms of integration.

Similar to the Beaubourg exhibition the results of *La Famille Ramdam* and *Seconde B* are also mixed. In contrast with Britain and the United States that have a much older, although not always enviable history of television series featuring ethnic minorities, shows like *La Famille Ramdam* and *Seconde B* were pathbreakers in France. In the case of *La Famille Ramdam*, French viewers could become acquainted with a loving North African family where the parents and children have problems, hopes, and concerns that are very much like their own. In a country where public opinion polls regularly single out North Africans as a culturally alien, threatening, and inassimilable community, positive depictions of a North African family are an important achievement.

Yet true recognition and understanding cannot grow out of the elimination of differences. This, I argue, is precisely the problem with *La Famille Ramdam*. In their efforts to encourage viewers to identify with the Ramdams differences and specificities were either reduced or erased. As the series took shape and unfolded the Ramdams were upgraded from the working class to the middle class, no references were ever made to racism, discrimination or the Algerian past, and most of the plots centered on universal themes familiar to mainstream viewers. Only by walking in the shoes of the other, as Alec Hargreaves notes, does it become possible to appreciate the perspective and condition of ethnic minorities in France. In this respect, shows like *La Famille Ramdam* fall far from the mark.

This blurring or elimination of difference is certainly a common feature of television that targets broad mainstream audiences. However, in the French case we cannot ignore the importance of the Republican model that took shape during the 1980s. *Seconde B* provides clear evidence of how Republican ideals influence television depictions of ethnic minorities. From ethnic gangs to the wearing of headscarves in public schools, *Seconde B* addresses the issue of difference in numerous episodes. Yet in each case difference functions as a source of division and disorder visibly at odds with the well-being of the main characters and their classmates. When headscarves are introduced into the classroom students take the initiatives to demonstrate how chaotic schools would become if everyone chose to put their faith on display. When ethnic gangs take shape outside class they threaten to destroy the friendship of two of the main characters. In stark contrast with the public school, cast as a space of tolerance and equality, the various symbols and sources of religious or ethnic difference function solely as destabilizing and disruptive forces.

Differences are either completely neglected or are largely superficial in *Seconde B*. When Nadia suspects she is pregnant no attention is given to the particular drama this might present for a woman of North African origin. Her lifestyle and outlook are little different from those of her French classmate. When other characters take an interest in their ethnicity we quickly discover that it is for transparent reasons—typically to get the girl. *Seconde B* certainly taps into the colors and sounds of the suburbs, it even exploits the demonized image of the urban periphery, but it does little to offer insights into the identities of ethnic minority youths who reside in these spaces.

Beyond the difficulty of seeking or receiving recognition ethnic minorities are also implicated in questions pertaining to shared sites of national memory or what Pierre Nora has labeled *lieux de mémoire*. Echoing conservative anxieties about multiculturalism in the United States, Nora contends that the search for roots by ethnic minorities contributes to the privatization of memory and the weakening of common *lieux de mémoire* that bind together the nation. Nora's multivolume *Realms of Memory* is a rescue project that attempts to harness the collective energy of French historians to shore up France's shared but now endangered sites of memory by revealing their inner workings.

However, an inspection of prominent sites neglected by Nora and his collaborators, such as the suburbs or *banlieues* and the Algerian War, reveals how ethnic minorities are marginalized by, participate in, and help transcend common forms of collective memory. In the case of the *banlieues*, North African youths have been entangled in diverse forms of remembering that stretch back to the early nineteenth century. In many respects the dark images of the suburbs today and depictions of ethnic minority youths as threatening populations are recycled and revamped versions of the *banlieues noires*. It is the accumulated weight of older representations of the suburbs and the easy shorthand they provide that helps explain their continued valence in the present.

Rather than departing from established narratives, ethnic minorities often borrow from and incorporate older elements of suburban imagery into their own memory work. In novels, movies, and music by the progeny of North African workers we instantly recognize a familiar environmental lexicon and imagery that has long defined the urban periphery. Yet by shedding light on the diverse experiences of immigrant sons and daughters, revealing generational tensions and the wide array of life choices and trajectories, these cultural productions also challenge and transcend simplified or stereotypical frameworks of meanings. Borrowing from while also complicating older narratives ethnic minority cultural actors participate in and enrich shared sites of memory.

In the case of the Algerian War memory work by ethnic minorities helps transcend the limitations of fragmented or splintered sites of memory. Rather than forgotten or repressed, as some scholars posit, the Algerian War is more accurately understood as a space broken into mythologized forms of group memory. From officers to former settlers each group clings to its own self-serving reading of the past. It is this cloistered form of remembering, together with the failure or inability of the French left and right to confront the Algerian past, which perpetuates old fears and hatreds.

The ghosts of the Algerian past are omnipresent in works by the sons and daughters of North African immigrants. Time and again acts of racism and racially motivated violence are depicted as the result of an unresolved past that continues to haunt the present. Beyond alerting us to the perils of the past, the work of ethnic minorities also helps challenge and overcome the splintered and fractured remembering of the Algerian past. For example, by recalling the use of torture during the Algerian War or the failure of the Algerian government to fulfill its promise of female emancipation after independence, these works call for a truer and more honest account of the war and its aftermath on both sides of the Mediterranean. In contrast to the ritualized and static character of mythologized forms of splintered memory, ethnic minorities offer open, participatory, and fluid approaches to the past. While it is true that private memories can be a source of Balkanization, ethnic minority memory can also function as a means of liberation and enlightenment.

Rather than seeing ethnic minority memory as a form of tyranny I am inclined to adopt the perspective of John Gillis that it is part of a larger democratization of memory. For nations to serve as meaningful communities of belonging at a time when they have lost much of their influence, more open and participatory approaches to the past are necessary. Despite the difficulties of participation and recognition that I have discussed ethnic minorities in France are taking an active role in the democratization of memory. In keeping with a long French tradition of revolutionary change ushered in by marginalized groups, ethnic minorities are helping to reinvent the nation making it broader, more inclusive, and truer to its original ideals.

Notes

Introduction

1. Sylvia Poggioli, *An Islamic Journey Inside Europe: Part III Boiling Point in the Banlieues*, on National Public Radio, February 23, 2003. Alec Hargreaves, *Immigration, "Race," and Ethnicity in Contemporary France* (New York/London: Routledge, 1995), p. 119.
2. Max Silverman, *Facing Postmodernity: Contemporary French Thought on Culture and Society* (New York/London: Routledge, 1999), pp. 59–60.
3. Michel Wieviorka, "La crise du modèle français d'intégration," *Regards sur l'actualité* 161 (1990): 4. Michel Wieviorka, "Culture, société et démocratie," in Michel Wieviorka (ed.), *La Société Fragmentée? Le multiculturalisme en débat* (Paris: La Découverte, 1996), pp. 33–38.
4. Eugen Weber, *Peasants into Frenchmen: The Modernization of Rural France, 1870–1914* (Stanford, Calif.: Stanford University Press, 1976).
5. Jean-Philippe Mathy, *French Resistance: The French-American Culture Wars* (Minneapolis: University of Minnesota Press, 2000), pp. 12, 24.
6. Gérard Noiriel, "L'immigration en France: une histoire en friche," *Annales ESC* 4 (1986), p. 751.
7. INSEE, *les étrangers en France* (Paris: Hachette, 1994), p. 17.
8. Georges Mauco, *Les Étrangers en France* (Paris: Librarie Armand Colin, 1932), p. 38. Philippe Bernard, *L'immigration* (Paris: Le Monde Editions, 1993), p. 23.
9. François Dubet and Didier Lapeyronnie, *Les Quariters d'Exil* (Paris: Seuil, 1992), p. 106.
10. Gérard Noiriel, *Le creuset français: Histoire de l'immigration XIXe-XXe siècle* (Paris: Seuil, 1988), p. 261.
11. Ibid., pp. 250–257.
12. Mauco, *Les Étrangers en France*, pp. 327–334. Donald Reid, "The Limits of Paternalism: Immigrant Coal Miners' Communities in France, 1919–45," *European History Quarterly* 15 (1985), pp. 99–118.
13. Noiriel, *Le creuset français*, pp. 191–211.

14. Gérard Noiriel, "French and Foreigners," in Pierre Nora (ed.), *Realms of Memory: The Construction of the French Past*, vol. I (New York: Columbia University Press, 1996), pp. 173–178.
15. Dubet and Lapeyronnie, *Les Quariters d'Exil*, p. 83.
16. Neil MacMaster, *Colonial Migrants and Racism: Algerians in France, 1900–62* (New York: St. Martin's Press, 1997), pp. 77–78.
17. Ibid., p. 81.
18. Ibid.
19. Ibid., pp. 8–9.
20. Ibid., p. 159.
21. Ibid., p. 9.
22. Ibid., p. 197.
23. Ibid., p. 194.
24. Edward Said, *Orientalism* (New York: Random House, 1978).
25. Patrick Weil, *La France et ses étrangers. L'aventure d'une politique de l'immigration 1938–1991* (Paris: Calmann-Lévy, 1991), pp. 55–57. The preference was for Northern Europeans than Southern Europeans (particularly from Northern regions) and finally Slavic countries.
26. Catherine Wihtol de Wenden, *Les immigrés et la politique. Cent cinquante ans d'évolution* (Paris: Presses de la FNSP, 1988), p. 105. Hargreaves, *Immigration "race" and ethnicity in Contemporary France*, pp. 10–13.
27. Wihtol de Wenden, *Les immigrés et la politique*, pp. 108–109.
28. The second largest group came from the less desirable area of southern Italy. Most northern Italian immigrants in the postwar years opted for Germany or Switzerland. See, Wihtol de Wenden, *Les immigrés et la politique*, p. 132.
29. Ezzedine Mestiri, *L'immigration* (Paris: Éditions de la Découverte, 1990), pp. 30–31.
30. Mehdi Lallaoui, *Du bidonville aux HLM* (Paris: Syros, 1993), pp. 44–45.
31. MacMaster, *Colonial Migrants and Racism*, p. 194.
32. Lallaoui, *Du bidonville aux HLM*, p. 79.
33. Martin A. Schain, "The Racialization of Immigration Policy. Biopolitics and Policy-Making," in Agnes Heller and Sonja Puntscher Riekmann (eds.), *Biopolitics: The Politics of Body, Race and Nature* (Aldershot: Avebury, 1996).
34. Kathleen Paul, *Whitewashing Britain: Race and Citizenship in the Postcolonial Era* (Ithaca, N.Y.: Cornell University Press, 1997).
35. Maxim Silverman, *Deconstructing the Nation: Immigration, Racism, and Citizenship in Modern France* (New York/London: Routledge, 1992), pp. 47–48.
36. Martin A. Schain, "The Immigration Debate and the National Front," in John T.S. Keller and Martin A. Schain (eds.), *Chirac's Challenge: Liberalization, Europeanization, and Malaise in France* (New York: St. Martin's Press, 1996), p. 172.
37. James G. Shields, "Immigration Politics in Mitterrand's France," in Gino Raymond (ed.), *France During the Socialist Years* (Brookfield, Wis.: Dartmouth, 1994), pp. 225–227.

38. Weil, *La France et ses étrangers*, p. 127.
39. Schain, "The Immigration Debate and the National Front," p. 174.
40. Hargreaves, *Immigration, "Race" and Ethnicity in Contemporary France*, p. 182.
41. Schain, "The Immigration Debate and the National Front," p. 174.
42. Benjamin Stora, *Le transfert d'une mémoire: de 'l'Algérie française' au racisme anti-arabe* (Paris: La Découverte, 1999), pp. 10–11.
43. Ibid.
44. Anne Donadey, " 'Une certaine idée de la France': The Algeria Syndrome and Struggles over 'French' Identity," in Steven Ungar and Tom Conley (eds.), *Identity Papers: Contested Nationhood in Twentieth-Century France* (Minneapolis: University of Minneapolis Press, 1996).
45. Hargreaves, *Immigration, "Race" and Ethnicity in Contemporary France*, p. 157.
46. Rogers Brubaker, *Citizenship and Nationhood in France and Germany* (Cambridge, Mass.: Harvard University Press, 1992).
47. Silverman, *Deconstructing the Nation*, pp. 140–147.
48. David Beriss, "Scarves, Schools, and Segregation: The Foulard Affair," *French Politics and Society* 8.1 (1990).
49. Paul Gilroy, *Small Acts: Thoughts on the Politics of Black Cultures* (New York: Serpent's Tail, 1993), pp. 26–27.
50. Patricia M.E. Lorcin, *Imperial Identities: Stereotyping, Prejudice and Race in Colonial Algeria* (London/New York: I.B. Tauris, 1995).
51. Noiriel, "Français et Étranger," p. 178.
52. Augustin Barbara, "Beur, vous avez dit beur!" *Connexions* 58 (1991).
53. Marie-Claude Muñoz lists some 15 different terms used to designate North African youth. Marie-Claude Muñoz, *Bibliographie analytique sur les jeunes étrangers (immigrés ou fils d'immigrés)* (Paris: CIEMM, 1980), p. 7.
54. Yvan Gastaut, "Evolution des designations de l'étranger en France (1960–1990), *Cahiers de la Méditerranée* 54 (1997), pp. 18.
55. Noiriel, *Le creuset français*, p. 18.
56. Silverman, *Deconstructing the Nation*, pp. 70–94.
57. Shields, "Immigration Politics in Mitterrand's France," p. 226.
58. Véronique de Rudder, "Notes à propos de l'évolution des recherches françaises sur 'l'étranger dans la ville,' " in Ida Simon-Barouh and Pierre Jean Simon (eds.), *Les étrangers dans la ville: le regard des sciences sociales* (Paris: L'Harmattan, 1990).
59. Hargreaves, *Immigration, "Race" and Ethnicity*, p. 2.
60. Gilroy, *Small Acts*.

Chapter 1   Ethnic Minority Struggles for Recognition

1. Benjamin Stora, *Ils venaient d'Algérie: L'immigration algérienne en France 1912–1992* (Paris: Fayard, 1992), pp. 23–38.
2. Ezzedine Mestiri, *L'immigration* (Paris: La Découverte, 1990), p. 30.
3. Stora, *Ils venaient d'Algérie*, p. 160.

4. Ibid., pp. 171–177.

5. Ibid., pp. 153, 206.

6. David S. Blatt, "Immigrant Politics and Immigrant Collective Action in France, 1968–1993" (Ph.D. dissertation., Cornell University, 1995), p. 111.

7. Tahar Ben Jelloun, *Hospitalité française* (Paris: Seuil, 1994), p. 40.

8. Blatt, "Immigrant Politics," p. 141.

9. Ibid., 149. See also Mogniss H. Abdallah, *J'y suis, J'y reste!: Les lutes de l'immigration en France depuis les années soixante* (Paris: Reflex, 2000).

10. Blatt, "Immigrant Politics," p. 145.

11. Patrick R. Ireland, *The Policy Challenge of Ethnic Diversity: Immigrant Politics in France and Switzerland* (Cambridge, Mass.: Harvard University Press, 1994), p. 45.

12. Blatt, "Immigrant Politics," p. 156.

13. Ibid., pp. 154–155.

14. Saïd Bouamama, Hadjila Sad-Saoud, and Mokhtar Djerdoubi, *Contribution à la mémoire des banlieues* (Paris: Culture et liberté Ile-de-France/Editions du Volga, 1994), p. 41.

15. Catherine Polac, "Quand les immigrés prennent la parole: histoire sociale du journal Sans Frontière 1979–1985" (M.A. thesis, Institute d'Etudes Politiques de Paris, 1991).

16. Didier Lapeyronnie, "Assimiliation, mobilization, et action collective chez les jeunes chez les jeunes de la seconde generation de l'immigration maghrébine," *Revue française de sociologie* 28 (1987), pp. 287–317. François Dubet, *La galère: Jeunes en Survie* (Paris: Fayard, 1987).

17. Lapeyronnie, "Assimiliation, mobilization, et action collective," p. 293.

18. Axel Honneth, *The Struggle for Recognition: The Moral Grammar of Social Conflicts* (Cambridge, Mass.: MIT Press, 1996), pp. 131–132.

19. Ibid., p. 135.

20. Nacer Kettane, *Le Droit de réponse à la démocratie française* (Paris: La Découverte, 1986), pp. 30–31.

21. Blatt, "Immigration Politics," chap. 5.

22. Adil Jazouli, *L'Action Collective des Jeunes Maghrébins de France* (Paris: CIEMI/L'Harmattan, 1986), pp. 82–84.

23. Ireland, *The Policy Challenge of Ethnic Diversity*, p. 78. Blatt, "Immigration Politics," chap. 5.

24. Jazouli, *L'Action Collective*, pp. 75–76.

25. Blatt, "Immigration Politics," p. 112, note 3.

26. See Saïd Bouziri quoted in Djamel Khamès, "Dix ans de droit d'expression," *Arabies* (February 1992).

27. Blatt, "Immigration Politics in France," pp. 127–128.

28. Ibid., p. 129.

29. Ibid., p. 130.

30. Ibid., p. 179.

31. Ibid., pp. 179–180.

32. William Saffran, "The Mitterrand Regime and Its Policies of Ethnocultural Accommodation," *Comparative Politics* 18.1 (1985), p. 42.
33. Judith Vichniac, "French Sociaists and the Droit à la Différance: A Changing Dynamic," *French Politics and Society* 9 (1991), p. 41.
34. Blatt, "Immigrant Politics," pp. 254–255.
35. Bouzid, *La Marche* (Paris: Sinbad, 1984), p. 15.
36. Ibid., pp. 30–31.
37. Jazouli, *L'Action Collective*, p. 128.
38. Bouzid, *La Marche*, p. 15.
39. Honneth, *The Struggle for Recognition*, pp. 132–133.
40. See Sans Frontière, *La "Beur" Génération*.
41. Bouzid, *La Marche*, pp. 36, 63.
42. Jazouli, *L'Action Collective*, pp. 125.
43. Ibid., pp. 142–148.
44. Blatt, "Immigration Politics," p. 166.
45. Ibid., pp. 275–276.
46. Nelson Rodrigues et al., *La ruée vers l'égalité* (Paris: Melanges, 1985), p. 14.
47. Blatt, "Immigration Politics," chap. 6.
48. Dubet, *La Galère*, p. 363.
49. Blatt, "Immigration Politics," chap. 6.
50. Jazouli, *L'Action Collective*, pp. 150–152.
51. Blatt, "Immigration Politics," p. 323.
52. Saliha Amara and Said Idir, "Le 'Mouvement Beur' Résumé des chapitres précédents," *Hommes & Migrations* 1144 (1991), p. 25.
53. Kettane, Le *Droit de réponse*, pp. 104–105.
54. Farida Belghoul, "BHL, Barre, Gros Minet et les Autres," in Sans Frontière, *La "Beur" Génération*, pp. 40–41.
55. Vincent Geisser, "Les élus issues de l'immigration maghrébine: l'illusion de médiation politique," *Horizons Maghrébins* 20.21 (1993), pp. 69–70.
56. Vincent Geisser, *Éthnicité Républicaine: les élites d'origine maghrébine dans le système politique français* (Paris: Presses Sciences Po, 1997), pp. 168–170.
57. Jacqueline Cesari, *Être musulman en France: Associations militants et mosquées* (Paris/Aix-en-Provence: Karthala/IREMAM, 1994), p. 199, note 8.
58. Ireland, *The Policy Challenge of Ethnic Diversity*, p. 81.
59. Jan Willem Duyvendak, *The Power of Politics: New Social Movements in France* (Boulder: Westview Press, 1995), p. 128.
60. Blatt, "Immigration Politics," pp. 314–315.
61. Ibid., p. 316.
62. Miriam Feldblum, *Reconstructing Citizenship: The Politics of Nationality Reform and Citizenship in Contemporary France* (Albany, N.Y. State University of New York Press, 1999), p. 38.
63. Ibid., p. 41. See *Le Figaro*, October 25, 1985.
64. Blatt, "Immigration Politics," p. 220.

65. Ibid., pp. 225–226.
66. Weil, *La France et ses étrangers*, pp. 170–176.
67. Ireland, *The Policy Challenge of Ethnic Diversity*, p. 83.
68. Blatt, "Immigration Politics," pp. 358–359.
69. Ibid., p. 361.
70. Cesari, *Être musulman en France*, pp. 180–185.
71. Norredine Elkarati and Marie Poinsot, "Politique d'un institution: Le Fonds d'action sociale pour les travailleurs immigrés: Entretien avec Michel Yahiel, directeur du FAS," *Politix* 4.1–2 (1990), pp. 70–74. Hargreaves, *Immigration, "Race" and Ethnicity*, p. 205.
72. Interview with Saliha Amara, March 5, July 25, 1994.
73. IM'média, "Les Blues des banlieues militantes," in *Douce France* (Paris: IM'média, 1993), p. 56.
74. Kettane, *Droit de réponse*, p. 52.
75. Driss El Yazami, "Les beurs entre la mémoire et le débat," in Sans Frontière, *La "Beur" Génération*, p. 8.
76. IM'média, "Les Blues des banlieues militantes," p. 56.
77. Abdallah, *J'y suis, J'y reste!*, pp. 74–75.
78. Farid Aïchoune, *Nés en banlieue* (Paris: Ramsay, 1991), pp. 13, 21.
79. Mehdi Lallaoui, *20 ans d'affiches antiracists* (Paris: Association Black, Blanc, Beur, 1989).
80. Bouamama et al., *Contribution à la mémoire des banlieues*, p. 194.
81. Interview with Saliha Amara, July 25, 1994.
82. Bouamama et al., *Contribution à la mémoire des banlieues*, p. 199.
83. Sylvia Zappi, "Lionel Jospin annonce la création d'un musée de l'immigration," *Le Monde*, November 24, 2001.

Chapter 2 North African Cultural Expression

1. Interview with Saliha Amara, July 25, 1994.
2. Interview with Aïssa Djabri, June 28, 1994.
3. Interview with Hédi Akari, January 12, 1994.
4. Interview with Walid Bouazizi, July 3, 1994.
5. Interview with Abdelkader Khessiba, June 26, 1994.
6. Interview with Walid Bouazizi.
7. Interview with Saliha Amara.
8. Interview with Abdelkader Khessiba.
9. Interview with Jlaïel Hamadi, June 26, 1994.
10. Interview with Saliha Amara.
11. Interview with Walid Bouazizi.
12. Interview with Mounsi, January 4, 1994.
13. Blatt, "Immigration Politics," p. 200.
14. "Les lascars s'organisent: Interview de 'Rock Against Police,'" *Questions Clefs 2* (1982), pp. 52–53. Abdallah, *J'y suis, J'y reste!*, p. 58.

15. Interview with Paul Moriera, June 16, 1994.

16. Bouamama, *Contribution à la mémoire des banlieues*, pp. 45–46.

17. Abdallah, *J'y suis, J'y reste!*, pp. 56–62.

18. Jazouli, *L'Action Collective*, pp. 85–86.

19. Ahmed Boubeker and Nicholas Beau, *Chroniques Métissées: l'Histoire de France des jeunes arabes* (Paris: Alain Moreau, 1986), p. 57.

20. Blatt, "Immigration Politics," pp. 204–205.

21. Interview with Saliha Amara.

22. Interview with Walid Bouazizi.

23. Original scenario for "Faits Divers" courtesy of Saïd-Mour Laouer.

24. Chérif Chikh and Ahsène Zehraoui, *Enfants d'immigrés maghrébins* (Paris: CCI, 1984), p. 24.

25. Lebkiri, who arrived in France at the age of nine, had clearer recollections of life in Algeria than many other second-generation artists who were born or arrived in France at a much younger age.

26. Interview with Moussa Lebkiri, May 30, 1994.

27. Interview with Fatiha Mahdaoui, April 18, 1994.

28. Mounsi. *Séconde Génération*, Motor Records, 1984.

29. Paul Moreira, *Rock métis en France* (Paris: Souffles, 1987), p. 63.

30. Carrie Tarr, "Questions of Identity in Beur Cinema: From *Tea in the Harem to Cheb*," *Screen* 34.4 (1993), p. 341.

31. Maherzi Lotfi, "Il était une fois Karim Kacel," *Algérie Actualité*, June 14–20, 1984.

32. Bouziane Daoudi and Ninam Abdi, "Kacel Karim avec banlieue," *Libération*, February 25, 1988.

33. Fabrice Littamé, "Karim Kacel: à fleur de peau d'émotion et de mélodie," *L'Union*, April 14, 1992.

34. Karim Kacel, "La chanson de Kabyle," Pathé-Marconi E.M.I., 1983.

35. Karim Kacel, "Banlieue," Pathé-Marconi E.M.I., 1983.

36. Moulay Brahimi, "Musique Beur: Un look d'enfer," *Actualité de l'émigration* 92 (June 1987), p. 32.

37. Lotfi, "Il était une fois Karim Kacel."

38. Beaubourg, "Les Enfants de l'immigration," May 30, 1984, debate on "Beur Culture." I would like to thank Kamel Yanat at the Association Nouvelle Génération Immigrée for allowing me to copy this recording.

39. Interview with Mohand Amara, March 18, 1994.

40. Alec Hargreaves, *Voices from the North African Immigrant Community in France: Immigration and Identity in Beur Fiction* (New York/Oxford: Berg, 1991). Michel Laronde, *Autour du Roman Beur: Immigration et Identité* (Paris: L'Harmattan, 1993).

41. Ahmed Kalouaz, "Des écrivains à part," *Actualité de l'Emigration* 80 (November 1987).

42. Alec G. Hargreaves, "Oralité, audio-visuel et écriture: chez les romanciers issus de l'immigration maghrébine," in "itinéraires et contact de culture," *Poétiques Croisées du Maghreb* 14 (1991), pp. 175–176. Hargreaves, *Voices From the North African Immigrant Community*, pp. 126–127.

43. Sophie Ruppert, "L'Harmattan: Publishing on the Third World," *Research in African Literatures* 22. 4 (Winter 1991), p. 156. My emphasis. A few *beur* novels and plays published by L'Harmattan include: Ahmed Kalouaz, *Point Kilométrique 190* (1986), Mustapha Raïth, *Palpitations intra-muros* (1986), Arriz Tamza, *Ombres* (1989), Ferrudja Kessas, *Beur's Story* (1989), Moussa Lebkiri, *Une étoile dans l'oeil de mon frère* (1989), *Il parlait à son balai* (1992), and *Prince Trouduc en panach'* (1993).

44. Interview with Soraya Nini, March 21, 1994. I personally made this mistake when I purchased Nini's book in the immigration studies section of the FNAC. Nini's novel has been made into a movie entitled "Samia."

45. Interview with Farid Boudjellal, February 25, 1994.

46. I am drawing from Khimoune's comments in the video "Jeunesse en quête d'une culture," Ali Akika (1984) Fonds d'Intervention Culturelle. I would like to thank André Videau for allowing me to copy the recording of this debate that featured a number of North African artists and creators.

47. Interview with Rachid Khimoune, March 19, 1994.

48. Carte de Séjour, *Carte de Séjour*, CBS Records, 1982.

49. Carte de Séjour, *Rhorhomanie*, CBS Records, 1983.

50. Carte de Séjour, *Carte de Séjour 2 1/2*, Barclay, 1986.

51. Julie Kodjo, "Rachid Taha: C'est quoi le raï?" *Afrique Magazine* 107 (October 1993).

52. Interview with Rachid Taha, May 12, 1994.

53. Moriera, *Rock Métis en France*, 52, 46.

54. Interview with Malik Chibane, May 9, 1994. These figures come from Chibane.

55. Ibid.

56. This is the principal theme in Paul Gilroy's *Small Acts: Thoughts on the Politics of Black Cultures*.

57. Interview with Smaïn, April 27, 1994.

58. Alexandrine Cohen, "Le pied de nez de Smaïn," *Villes Lumières* (March 1992).

59. Colette Milon, "Smaïn: Blague à part," July 8, 1991, *Télé K7*.

60. Interview with Rachid Khimoune.

61. Kodjo, "Rachid Taha: C'est quoi le raï?"

62. Interview with Saliha Amara, July 25, 1994.

63. Kim Eling. *The Politics of Cultural Policy in France* (New York: St. Martin's Press, 1999), p. 150.

64. Ibid., see chap. 8.

Chapter 3   Radio Beur: Multiculturalism on the French Airwaves

1. Michel Rossinelli, *La liberté de la radio-télévision en droit comparé* (Paris: Publisud, 1991), pp. 93–95.

2. Raymond Kuhn, *The Media in France* (New York: Routledge, 1995), pp. 92–95.

3. François Cazenave, *Les Radios Libres* (Paris: Presses Universitaires de France, 1984), p. 8.
4. Hamida Berrahal, "Ces radios qui 'branchent' les jeunes," *Actualité de l'emigration* (October 1987), p. 10. Isabelle Nataf, "Les radios associatives en première ligne," *Le Figaro*, June 5, 1990.
5. Maryse Berdah and Emmanuelle Bouchez, "Radios Communautaires: Les Voix de la Différence," *Télérama*, February 13, 1991.
6. Jacqueline Costa-Lascoux, "Assimiler, insérer, intégrer," *Projet* 227 (1991), p. 10.
7. Bernard Stasi, *L'immigration, une chance pour la France* (Paris: Éditions Robert Lafont, 1984).
8. For a few examples of the media craze over the rise of "beur culture" see Jean Benoît, et al., "Le Style Beur," *Le Monde illustré*, May 20, 1983. François Forestier, "Aux bons beurs," *L'Express*, June 14–20, 1985. Alain Jeannet, "Le blues des petits beurs," *L'Hebdo*, June 27, 1985. Françine Rivaud, "Ces créateurs sans complèxes," *L'Express*, May 18–20, 1984.
9. FAS subsidies dossiers for Radio Beur #93059.
10. Cesari, *Etre musulman en France*, pp. 242–243.
11. Interview with Amar Bennacer, March 2, 1994.
12. Interview with Nacer Kettane, December 24, 1993, July 4, 1994.
13. For the only detailed study available of *Sans Frontière* see Catherine Polac, "Quand les immigrés prennent la parole: histoire sociale du journal *Sans Frontière*, 1979–1985." An abridged version is available in "Immigration et journalisme immigré: histoire sociale de *Sans Frontière*, 1979–1985," *Migrations Société* 6. 31 (1994), pp. 33–39.
14. Interview with Saliha Amara.
15. Interview with Nacer Kettane.
16. Interview with Amar Driff, May 9, 1994.
17. Interview with Kamel Amara, May 24, 1994.
18. Interview with Amar Bennacer.
19. Interview with Kadour Guebli, May 5, 1994.
20. Radio Beur Charter.
21. Interview with Kadour Guebli.
22. Interview with Saliha Amara.
23. Interview with Kadour Guebli.
24. Interview with Moa Abaïd, May 26, 1994.
25. Interview with Leïla Amriou, May 23, 1994.
26. Interview with Nacer Kettane.
27. Ibid.
28. Interview with Kadour Geubli. Interview with Leïla Amriou.
29. Interview with Leïla Amriou.
30. François Cazenave, *Les Radios Libres*, pp. 61–65.
31. Interview with Salah Medjani, May 3, 1994.

32. Sophie Tievant, *Les Radios de Proximité: Acteurs, produits, publics et vie locale* (Paris: Documentation Française, 1985), p. 105.

33. Letter from Michèle Cotta to Radio Beur June 7, 1983. Cotta, a former journalist, was appointed to head Radio France in August 1981 and chaired the High Authority for Audiovisual Communications between 1982 and 1986. See Kuhn, *The Media in France*, p. 176.

34. Interview with Chérif Chikh, March 31, 1994.

35. Interview with Kader Jebbouri, April 16, 1994.

36. Interview with Malika Ouberzou, April 28, 1994.

37. Radio Beur frequency application, CSA, #91PA A045 (1991), pp. 86–88.

38. Ibid., pp. 96, 98.

39. Interview with Lila Benbelaïd, April 20, 1994.

40. Interview with Aïcha Benmamar, May 13, 1994.

41. Radio Beur frequency application, CSA (1991), p. 96.

42. Interview with Fernanda da Silva, December 27, 1993.

43. Radio Beur frequency application, CSA (1991), pp. 86, 121.

44. Interview with Kadour Guebli.

45. Interview with Kamel Amara.

46. Interview with Saliha Amara.

47. Interview with Nacer Kettane.

48. Lorcin, *Imperial Identities*.

49. Fanny Colonna, *Instituers algériens: 1883–1939* (Paris: Presses de la fondation nationale des sciences politiques, 1975), p. 106.

50. Jean-Pierre Durand and Habib Tengour, *L'Algérie et ses populations* (Brussels: Éditions Complexe, 1982), p. 73. Mohand Khellil, "Kabyles en France, un aperçu historique," *Hommes & Migrations* 1179 (1994), p. 14. MacMaster, *Colonial Migrants and Racism*, p. 34. MacMaster notes that Kabyles represented 60 percent of the Algerian immigrant population in the 1950s.

51. Interview with Youcef Boussaa, May 16, 1994.

52. Interview with Kamel Amara.

53. Interview with Moa Abaïd.

54. Anne McClintock, "The Angel of Progress: Pitfalls of the Term 'Post-Colonialism,'" in Peter Hulme and Margaret Iversen (eds.), *Colonial Discourse, Postcolonial Theory* (Manchester/New York: University of Manchester Press, 1994).

55. Interview with Amar Bennacer.

56. Interview with Amar Driff.

57. Interview with Kadour Guebli.

58. Jazouli, *L'Action Collective*, p. 126.

59. Interview with Saliha Amara.

60. Interview with Samia Messaoudi, December 22, 1993, April 6, 1994.

61. Interview with Kaïssa Titous, April 14, 1994.

62. IM'média "J'ai claqué la porte de SOS-Racisme," *Quo Vadis* (Summer/Winter 1993), p. 27. René Rémond, *Notre Siècle: 1918–1988* (Paris: Fayard, 1988), p. 910.

63. Interview with Archour Fernane, April 1, 1994.

64. Interview with Mohand Dehmous, March 31, 1994.

65. Interview with Chérif Chikh.

66. Ibid.

67. Interview with Nacer Kettane.

68. Abdennasser Fattah Allah, "L'expression Beure en France: Cas de Radio Beur de Paris" (M.A. thesis, Université de droit, d'economie et de sciences sociales de Paris, Paris II, 1988), pp. 39–40.

69. Interview with Hamid Ouchène, March 2, 1994.

70. Michel Anglade, "Radio Beur" (Mémoire. Institut d'études politiques de Paris, 1989), p. 14.

71. Interview with Mohand Dehmous.

72. Interview with Nacer Kettane.

73. Radio Beur frequency application dossier, CSA (1991), p. 84.

74. Interview with Kader Jebbouri. Raï began as a form of Algerian Bedouin music whose existence can be traced back to the late nineteenth century. Since the early 1980s modern raï, transformed by a wide range of musical influences, has enjoyed considerable success among Algerian youth who represent two-thirds of the population. Its controversial lyrics that evoke themes such as sex before or outside of marriage and alcohol abuse as well as its mixture of traditional and modern electric instruments, speak to the tastes, lifestyles, and social reality of younger Algerians. Over the past decade raï has steadily gained popularity in France. However, only a few singers, such as Cheb Khaled, have attained any kind of international notoriety. For additional information on raï music see, François Bensignor, "Le raï, entre Oran, Marseille et Paris," *Hommes & Migrations* 1170 (1993).

75. Interview with Nadia Hadjeli, April 16, 1994.

76. Interview with Archour Fernane.

77. Interview with Mohand Dehmous.

78. Interview with Samia Messaoudi.

79. Interview with Nadia Kessaci, April 6, 1994.

80. Interview with Mohand Dehmous.

81. Interview with Kamel Amara.

82. Interview with Leïla Amriou.

83. Interview with Linda Amriou, May 31, 1994.

84. Interview with Kamel Amriou, April 29, 1994.

85. Radio Beur promotional information.

86. Shields, "Immigration Politics in Mitterrand's France," pp. 222–245.

87. Interview with Michel Yahiel, June 15, 1994.

88. Interview with Archour Fernane.

89. Interview with Karim Sadi-Haddad, February 10, 1994.

90. John Ruedy, *Modern Algeria: The Origins and Development of a Nation* (Bloomington, Ind.: University of Indiana Press, 1992), p. 249.

91. Alec G. Hargreaves, "Algerians in France: The End of the Line?" *Contemporary French Civilization* XIV (Summer/Fall 1990), p. 302.
92. Hargreaves, *Immigration, "race" and Ethnicity*, p. 142.
93. Hargreaves, "Algerians in France," p. 301, footnote 26.
94. Interview with Nacer Kettane.
95. Interview with Mohand Dehmous.
96. Mouloud Chalah, "Tentatives de confiscation de l'antenne Radio Beur." This quote comes from the final page of his "communiqué."
97. Interview with Nacer Kettane.
98. Interview with Malika Ouberzou.
99. Tribunal de Grande Instance de Bobigny, Prononce en Audience Publique, July 6, 1989, pp. 9–10.
100. Beur FM was subsequently awarded its first 24-hour Paris frequency. See Véronique Cauhape, "Le CSA autorise Beur FM à émettre sur 106.7 24 heures sur 24," *Le Monde*, March 26, 1996.
101. Interview with Kaissa Titous.

Chapter 4   Exhibiting Minorities: The Politics of Recognition at Beaubourg

1. Ivan Žaknić, *Le Centre Pompidou* (Paris: Flammarion, 1983), p. 77. Philippe Coulaud, "Les enfants de l'immigration et les honneurs de la cimaise: radiographie d'une exposition," Centre de Creation Industrielle, 1985, p. 3.
2. Interview with José Chapelle, December 12, 1993.
3. Interview with Véronique Hahn, June 10, 1994.
4. Interview with José Chapelle.
5. Coulaud, "Les enfants de l'immigration," pp. 46, 54.
6. Brian Rigby, *Popular Culture in Modern France: A Study of Cultural Discourse* (New York: Routledge, 1991), pp. 185–186. Bernadette Dufrêne, *La création de Beaubourg* (Grenoble: Presses Universitaires de Grenoble, 2000), pp. 36–37.
7. David L. Looseley, *The Politics of Fun: Cultural Policy and Debate in Contemporary France* (Oxford: Berg, 1995), p. 143.
8. Omar de Châtenay-Malabry, "Le Parvis des Miracles," in *Bulletin de l'agence IM'média* (1984).
9. Philippe Coulaud, "Les enfants de l'immigration," pp. 19–20.
10. Omar de Châtenay-Malabry, "Le Parvis des Miracles."
11. Carol Duncan, "Art Museums and the Ritual of Citizenship," in Ivan Karp and Steven D. Lavine (eds.), *Exhibiting Cultures: The Poetics and Politics of Museum Display* (Washington: Smithsonian Institution Press, 1991), p. 93.
12. Ibid., pp. 100–101.
13. James Clifford, *The Predicament of Culture: Twentieth-Century Ethnography, Literature and Art* (Cambridge, Mass.: Harvard University Press, 1988), chap. 9.
14. Interview with Véronique Hahn.

15. CCI, *Les enfants de l'immigration* (Paris: CCI Editions, 1984).

16. Chikh and Zehraoui, *Enfants d'immigrés maghrébins*. This quote comes from CCI director Paul Blanquart's introduction to the study.

17. Chikh and Zehraoui, *Enfants d'immigrés maghrébins*, p. 3.

18. Interview with Paul Blanquart, April 12, 1994.

19. Antonio Perotti, "L'education et le développement culturel des migrants: Étude de cas: L'Exposition: 'les enfants de l'immigration,'" Council of Europe, 1984, p. 6.

20. Interview with Paul Blanquart.

21. Chikh and Zehraoui, *Enfants d'immigrés maghrébins*.

22. Interview with Paul Blanquart.

23. André Videau, "Bilan du F.I.C. (1983–1984)," Fonds d'Intervention Culturelle, 1984.

24. Caisse des dépôts, Service des relations extérieures, "La Caisse des dépôts apporte son concours à l'exposition *les enfants de l'immigration*," January 17, 1984.

25. Interview with Paul Blanquart.

26. Interview with José Chapelle.

27. Interview with Véronique Hahn.

28. Interview with Sylvie Bessenay, December 15, 1993, April 27, 1994.

29. Interview with Véronique Hahn.

30. Ibid., José Chapelle worked for the publication *Culture au Quotidien* and was in charge of the issue *Enfants d'immigrés maghrébins*.

31. Interview with Paul Blanquart.

32. Paulo Moreira, "Ce que vous avez failli ne pas voir," *Bulletin de l'agence IM'média* (1984).

33. Interview with José Chapelle.

34. Coulaud, "Les enfants de l'immigration," p. 19.

35. Ibid., pp. 24, 28, 51, 58, 29, 46.

36. Donadey, "'Une Certaine Idée de la France,'" pp. 216, 222.

37. Ibid., p. 223.

38. Naomi Greene, *Landscapes of Loss: The National Past in Postwar French Cinema* (Princeton, N.J.: Princeton University Press, 1999), p. 135.

39. MacMaster, *Colonial Migrants and Racism*, chaps. 4, 8, 9.

40. Hargreaves, *Immigration, "Race," and Ethnicity*, p. 2.

41. Gérard Noiriel, *Qu'est-ce que l'hisoire contemporaine?* (Paris: Hachette, 1998), pp. 222–223.

42. Chikh and Zehraoui, *Enfants d'immigrés maghrébins*.

43. Interview with Véronique Hahn.

44. Perotti, "L'education et le développement culturel des migrants," p. 19.

45. Mogniss Abdallah, "Le new deal culturel à Beaubourg," *Bulletin de l'agence IM'média* (1984).

46. Interview with Sylvie Bessenay.

47. Sylvie Bessenay, "Evaluation de la Manifestation 'Toulouse Multiple,'" Inter-Service Migrants, 1986.

48. Interview with Sylvie Bessenay, April 27, 1994.

49. Bessenay, "Evaluation de la Manifestation 'Toulouse Multiple.' "
50. Interview with Sylvie Bessenay.
51. Bessenay, "Evaluation de la Manifestation 'Toulouse Multiple.' "
52. Ibid.
53. Interview with Sylvie Bessenay.

Chapter 5   French Television in the Age of Multiculturalism

1. Laurent Joffrin, "Les vérités qui dérangent,"*Le Nouvel Observateur*, September 13–19, 1990, p. 6. The survey, taken from August 18–22, 1990, was based on a sample of 1,000 people representative of the general population ages 18 and older.
2. It was not until the mid-1990s that the Institut National d' Audiovisuel, the government agency that manages the largest archival holdings of audiovisual materials in France, began reorganizing to accommodate independent researchers.
3. Marie-Françoise Lévy, "L'immigration dans la production documentaire, le magazine, la fiction française. Variations autour d'un thème, 1975–1991," in Claire Frachon and Marion Vargaftig (eds.), *Télévisions d'Europe et Immigration* (Paris: Institut National de l'Audiovisuel/Association Dialogue Entre les Cultures, 1993), pp. 57–65. Lévy analyzed some 275 shows with immigration as the central theme.
4. Timour Muhidine, "Beurs Mais Pas Groseilles: Les Arabs à l'Écran," *Arabies* (April 1991), pp. 76–79.
5. For a review of the films by Djabria and Lahouassa, see Hedi Dhoukar "Aïssa Djabri et Farid Lahouassa: Témoigner sur le quotidien et en sortir," *CinémAction* 95 (1990), pp. 172–173.
6. Interview with Aïssa Djabri and Farid Lahouassa, January 24, 1994.
7. Alec G. Hargreaves, "La Famille Ramdam: un sit-com 'pur beur' "? *Hommes & Migrations* 1147 (1991), p. 65. I would like to thank Alec Hargreaves for sending me the original scenario of *La Famille Ramdam*.
8. Interview with Thierry de Navacelle, February 2, 1994.
9. Interview with Martine Lheureux, February 1, 1994. Lheureux is an executive producer at IMA. She was responsible for the scripts and relations with the writers and M6 during the production of *La Famille Ramdam*.
10. Interview with Thierry de Navacelle.
11. M6 test study for La Famille Ramdam. I would like to thank Thierry de Navacelle for sending me this study.
12. Original scenario for *La Famille Ramdam*, 1988. Alec Hargreaves notes that Suzanne and Jean-Noël were added upon the advice of Françoise Verney who felt that the series needed additional characters with whom French viewers could identify. See Alec Hargreaves, "La Famille Ramdam: un sit-com 'pur beur?' " p. 65.
13. See two episodes, "Papy fait de la résidence" and "Amour Minitel."
14. Alec Hargreaves, "La Famille Ramdam: un sit-com 'pur beur?' " p. 66.

15. Pied-Noirs were the Europeans settlers of French-controlled Algeria.
16. M6 test study for *La Famille Ramdam*.
17. An accord between the French and Algerian governments provided some solace by allowing children of Algerian descent to complete their military service in either country.
18. Richard L. Derderian, "Daughters in Conflict: The Brother/Sister Relationship in Ferrudja Kessas's *Beur's Story*," *Journal of Maghrebi Studies* 1–2.1 (1993).
19. Alec Hargreaves, "La Famille Ramdam: un sit-com 'pur beur' "? pp. 61–62.
20. Interview with Farid Boudjellal, February 25, 1994.
21. Interview with Aïssa Djabri.
22. Médiamétrie ratings for *La Famille Ramdam*.
23. Interview with Thierry de Navacelle. The decision to air only one episode a week was the result of the series starting while it was still in the production stage and had yet to accumulate a backlog of episodes.
24. Interview with Amay Urtizverea, February 23, 1994.
25. Interview with Lahouassa and Djabri.
26. The findings of the *Seconde B* section are based on a viewing of 34 of the first 52 episodes and interviews with executives from France 2, Flach Film, and Vertigo Productions.
27. *Centre France*, May 12, 1993.
28. "Seconde" is the first year in a three-year high school system. The average age of students in the "seconde" year is 16. The specific classification, "Seconde B," no longer exists.
29. The series was filmed at the Lycée Jean Monnet in Franconville.
30. The series introduction notes that Jamin's character was modeled in part after the character played by Robin Williams in *The Dead Poet's Society*.
31. Interview with Simone Girard, June 15, 1994.
32. The *tchador* is a black headscarf and full body robe associated with Iranian fundamentalists. Consciously or not, the writers did not choose to dress Malika in a less provocative and more typical Muslim religious garment. In the press coverage of the real headscarves affair French journalists often confused or manipulated the symbolic meaning of various garments worn by women in Muslim countries. The Iranian tchador frequently represented the oppression of women in regressive Muslim nations and the religious threat to French secular (and Judeo-Christian) traditions.
33. Interview with Claude Chauvat, June 17, 1994.
34. Bible for *Seconde B*. The bible is the term used in the French television and movie industries for the book that contains character, setting descriptions, and plot summaries. I would like to thank Marie-France Le Texier at France 2 for providing me with the bible for *Seconde B*.
35. Interview with Aïssa Djabri. Smaïn is a well-known comedian of Algerian descent. Raised in France, Smaïn frequently employs ethnic stereotypes in his movies and standup performances.
36. Interview with Claude Chauvat.

37. Médiamétrie ratings for *Seconde B*. I would like to thank Claude Chauvat for sending me the series ratings as well as the test study for *Seconde B*.
38. Interview with Claude Chauvat.
39. Test study of *Seconde B* for France 2, SORGEM, May 19, 1993.
40. Interview with Claude Chauvat.
41. Médiamétrie ratings for *Seconde B*.

Chapter 6   Les Banlieues: *Suburban Space and National Identity*

An earlier version of chapter 6 appeared as "*The Banlieues as Lieux de mémoire:* Urban Space, Memory, and Identity in France," in *The Geopolitics of Globalization and South East Asia/Europe Relations*, ed. Pierre Lagayette (ed.), Paris: Presses de l'Université de Paris-Sorbonne, 2003: 107–120.

1. Dubet and Lapeyronnie, *Les Quartiers d'Exil*.
2. Maurice Agulhon, "Paris: A Traversal from East to West," in Pierre Nora (ed.), *Realms of Memory: The Construction of the French Past*, vol. III (New York: Columbia University Press, 1998).
3. Henri Boyer and Guy Lochard, *Scènes de télévision en banlieues: 1950–1994* (Paris: L'Harmattan: Institut National d'Audiovisuel, 1998), p. 19.
4. Annie Fourcault, "Banlieues d'hier: les 'zoniers' de Paris," *Panoramiques* 2.12 (1993), p. 15.
5. Pierre Nora, "Between Memory and History," in Pierre Nora (ed.), *Realms of Memory: The Construction of the French Past*, vol. I, p. 2.
6. Boyer and Lochard, *Scènes de télévision en banlieues*, p. 40.
7. John Merriman, *The Margins of City Life: Explorations on the French Urban Frontier, 1815–1851* (New York: Oxford University Press, 1991), pp. 4–5.
8. Liisa Malakki, "National Geographic: The Rooting of Peoples and the Territorialization of National Identity among Scholars and Refugees," in Geoff Ely and Ronad Grigor Suny (eds.), *Becoming National: A Reader* (New York: Oxford University Press, 1996).
9. Nicholas Green, *The Spectacle of Nature: Landscape and Bourgeois Culture in Nineteenth-Century France* (Manchester: Manchester University Press, 1990), pp. 46, 53, 55. Andrew Lees, *Cities Perceived: Urban Society in European and American Thought, 1820–1940* (New York: Columbia University Press, 1985), p. 70.
10. David P. Jordan, *Transforming Paris: The Life and Times of Baron Haussmann* (Chicago, Ill.: University of Chicago Press, 1995), pp. 188–191. Merriman, *The Margins of City Life*, p. 44.
11. Fourcault, "Banlieues d'hier," p. 16.
12. Michelle Perrot quoted in Merriman, *The Margins of City Life*, p. 81. Roger Icart, "Des origines à 1930: La banlieue dans le cinéma français muet," *Cahiers de la Cinémathèque* 59.60 (1994), p. 16.

13. Jean-Paul Dollé, "Villes et banlieues dans le cinéma français," *Cahiers de la Cinémathèque* 59.60 (1994), p. 75.

14. Dubet and Lapeyronnie, *Les Quartiers d'Exil*, pp. 49–65.

15. Boyer and Lochard, *Scènes de télévision e banlieues*, pp. 67–68.

16. Norma Evenson, *Paris: A Century of Change, 1878–1978* (New Haven, Conn.: Yale University Press, 1979), pp. 238, 246.

17. Dubet, *La galère*, pp. 23–24. Adil Jazouli, *Les Années Banlieues* (Paris: Seuil, 1992), p. 141.

18. Weber, *Peasants into Frenchmen*, chap. 1.

19. Loïc J.D. Wacquant, "Pour en finir avec le myth des 'cité-ghettos': Les differences entre la France et les Etats-Unis," *Annales de la recherche urbaine* 52 (1992).

20. Boyer and Lochard, *Scènes de télévision en banlieues*, p. 153.

21. Marie-Claude Taranger, "Télévision et 'western urbain': enjeux et nuances de l'information sur les banlieues," *Revue d'histoire du cinema* 50.60 (1994), p. 60.

22. T.J. Clark, *The Painting of Modern Life: Paris in the Art of Manet and His Followers* (Princeton, N.J.: Princeton University Press, 1984), chap. 3. Christain-Marc Bosséno, "Années 30–60: le cinema français invente la banlieue," *Cahiers de la Cinémathèque* 59.60 (1994), pp. 27–28. Boyer and Lochard, *Scènes de télévision en banlieues*, pp. 47–48.

23. Lees, *Cities Perceived*, pp. 78–81.

24. Richard L. Derderian, "Radio Beur, 1981–1992: L'échec d'un multiculturalism à la française," *Hommes & Migrations* 1191 (1995), p. 55.

25. Richard L. Derderian, "Social Realism, Suburban Culture and Ethnic Diversity on French Television. A Case Study of Seconde B," *Contemporary French Civilization* 21.1 (1997), p. 44. Richard L. Derderian, "Popular Music From the North African Immigrant Community: Multiculturalism in Contemporary France, 1945–1994," *Contemporary French Civilization* 20.2 (1996), p. 213.

26. "Banlieue" (1983) Pathé Marconi.

27. Mehdi Charef, *Le thé au harem d'Archi Ahmed* (Paris: Mercure de France, 1983), pp. 24–25.

28. Mounsi, *Second Génération*, Motor Records, 1984.

29. *Hexagone* transcript. Transcript courtesy of Malik Chibane.

30. Mounsi, *La Cendre des villes* (Paris: Éditions Stock, 1993).

31. "Banlieue" (1983) Pathé Marconi.

32. Interview with Aïssa Djabri, June 28, 1994.

33. Interview with Saliha Amara, July 25, 1994.

34. *Hexagon* transcript.

35. Interview with Malik Chibane.

36. Interview with Rachid Bouchareb, May 11, 1994.

37. Interview with Aïssa Djabri.

38. Interview with Saliha Amara.

39. Interview with Yamina Benguigui, July 2, 1994.

40. Interview with Malik Chibane, May 9, 1994.

41. Dubet and Lapeyronnie, *Les Quartiers d'Exil.*
42. John R. Gillis. "Memory and Identity: The History of a Relationship," in John R. Gillis (ed.), *Commemorations: The Politics of National Identity* (Princeton, N.J.: Princeton University Press, 1994).

Chapter 7   The Algerian War: Transcending Splintered Memories

Chapter 7 was originally published as "Algeria as a *lieu mémoire*: Ethnic Minority Memory and National Identity in Contemporary France." *Radical History Review* 83(2002): 28–43. I would like to thank the editors of *Radical History Review* for granting copyright permission.

1. Ernest Renan, "What is a Nation?" in Omar Dahbour and Micheline R. Ishay (eds.), *The Nationalism Reader* (Atlantic Highlands: Humanities Press, 1995).
2. Pierre Nora, "From *Lieux de Mémoire* to Realms of Memory," in Pierre Nora (ed.), *Realms of Memory: The Construction of the French Past*, vol. I, p. xix.
3. Steven Englund, "Ghost of the Nation Past," *Journal of Modern History* 64 (June 1992), p. 305.
4. Benjamin Stora, *La Gangrène et l'oubli: La mémoire de la guerre d'Algérie* (Paris: La Découvert, 1991), pp. 293–294.
5. Renan, "What is a Nation?" p. 145.
6. "The Chagrin and the Belated Pity," *Economist*, May 12, 2001.
7. "Les déclarations du premier ministre," *Le Monde*, May 7, 2001.
8. Benjamin Stora, *Imaginaires de guerre: Algérie-Viêt-nam en France et aux Etats-Unis* (Paris: Editions de la Découverte, 1997), p. 25.
9. Ibid., pp. 199–202.
10. Ibid., pp. 25–28.
11. Stora, *La gangrène et l'oubli*, p. 238.
12. Ibid., p. 248.
13. Stora, *Imaginaires de guerre*, p. 134.
14. Dine, *Images of the Algerian War: French Fiction and Film, 1954–1992* (Oxford: Oxford University Press, 1994).
15. Greene, *Landscapes of Loss.*
16. Stora, *Imaginaires de guerre*, 190–191. Stora's emphasis.
17. Ibid.
18. Stora, *Le transfert d'une Mémoire*, pp. 64–65.
19. "The Chagrin and the Belated Pity."
20. Stora, *La gangrène et l'oubli*, p. 239. Said, *Orientalism.*
21. Said, *Orientalism.*
22. Claire Mauss-Copeaux, *Appelés en Algérie: La parole confisquée* (Paris: Hachette, 1998), p. 50.
23. Donadey, "'Une Certaine Idée de la France,'" p. 215.
24. Ibid., see footnote 5.
25. Mauss-Copeaux, *Appelés en Algérie*, p. 47.

26. Stora, *La gangrene et l'oubli*, chap. 5.
27. Ibid., pp. 281–282. For an extended treatment of the political divisions created by the war see Todd Shepard, "Decolonizing France: Reimagining the Nation and Redefining the Republic at the End of Empire" (Ph.D. dissertation, Rutgers University, New Brunswick, 2001).
28. Éric Saverèse, *Histoire coloniale et immigration: Une invention de l'étranger* (Biarritz: Séguier, 2000), pp. 164–166.
29. Mestiri, *L'immigration*, p. 30.
30. Saverèse, *Histoire coloniale et immigration*, p. 44.
31. Noiriel, *Le Creuset Français*, chap. 1.
32. Interview with Saliha Amara, March 5, 1994.
33. Interview with Mohand Amara.
34. Paul Connerton, *How Societies Remember* (Cambridge: Cambridge University Press, 1992), p. 44.
35. Interview with Saliha Amara.
36. Derderian, "Popular Music From the North African Immigrant Community," p. 210.
37. Mounsi, "Batard," in *Seconde Génération* (Motor Records, 1984). Author's translation.
38. Interview with Nacer Kettane, July 4, 1994. See also Richard L. Derderian, "Radio Beur, 1981–1992: L'échec d'un multiculturalism à la française."
39. Samia Messaoudi, "Au nom de la mémoire," *Hommes & Migrations* 1175 (April 1994), p. 41.
40. Interview with Bourlem Guerdjou, July 4, 1994.
41. Stora, *La gangrène et l'oubli*, p. 100.
42. Claude Liauzu, "Voyage à Travers La Mémoire et L'Amnésie: Le 17 Octobre 1961," *Hommes & Migrations* 1219 (May–June 1999), pp. 57–61.
43. Kristin Ross, *Fast Cars, Clean Bodies: Decolonization and the Reordering of French Culture* (Cambridge, Mass.: MIT Press, 1996).
44. Donadey, "Une Certain Idée de la France."
45. Stora, *Le Transfert d'une Mémoire*, p. 90.
46. Donadey, "Une Certain Idée de la France," pp. 227–228.
47. Nacer Kettane, *Le Sourire de Brahim* (Paris: Denoël, 1985), p. 132. The *Petit Larousse* defines *ratonnades* as punitive expeditions carried out against North Africans.
48. Alec G. Hargreaves, *Voices from the North African Immigrant Community*, pp. 62–66.
49. Yamina Benguigui, *Mémoires d'Immigrés: L'Heritage Maghrébin* (Canal+ Video, 1998).
50. Maurice Faivre, Courrier, *Hommes & Migrations* 1220 (1999), p. 132.
51. Interview with Pierre Nora, December 7, 2000.
52. Roy Rosenzweig and David Thelen, *The Presence of the Past: Popular Uses of History in American Life* (New York: Columbia University Press, 1998).
53. John R. Gillis, *A World of Their Own Making: Myth, Ritual, and the Quest for Family Values* (Cambridge, Mass.: Harvard University Press, 1996), pp. 232–233.

54. Gillis, "Memory and Identity: The History of a Relationship," pp. 13–14.
55. Gillis, *A World of Their Own Making*, p. 4.

Conclusion

1. Jean-Marie Colombani, "La blessure," *Le Monde*, April 23, 2002.
2. Jon Henley, "French Back New Law to Punish Lack of Respect for Icons of the Republic," *The Guardian*, February 7, 2003.
3. Jo Johnson, "Violence Halts Algeria-France Soccer Match," *Financial Times* (London), October 8, 2001. "Algerian Soccer Fans get Suspended Jail Sentence," *Agence France Press*, November 26, 2001.
4. Philippe Bernard, "Du match France-Algérie au 17 Octobre 1961," *Le Monde*, October 26, 2001.
5. Matthew Cambell, "France Applauds Crime Crusade: Reforms Make Politician a National Hero," *Times of London*, December 26, 2002.
6. Charles Bremner, "French Face Jail for Insulting the Flag," *The Times* (London), February 15, 2003.
7. Ibid.

Bibliography

Primary Sources

Bessenay, Sylvie. "Evaluation de la Manifestation 'Toulouse Multiple,'" Inter-Service Migrants, 1986.

Bible for *Seconde B*, Flach Film.

Caisse des dépôts, Service des relations extérieures. "La Caisse des dépôts apporte son concours à l'exposition *les enfants de l'immigration*," January 17, 1984.

Chakchouka. "Faits Divers," 1981.

Chalah, Mouloud. "Tentatives de confiscation de l'antenne Radio Beur," 1991.

Conseil Supérieur de l'Audiovisuel, Paris, #91PA A045 Radio Beur frequency application, 1991.

Cotta, Michèle. Letter to Radio Beur, June 7, 1983.

Fonds d'Action Sociale pour les Travailleurs Immigrés et leurs Familles, #93059 Radio Beur subsidies dossier

Kahina. "Pour que les larmes de nos mères deviennent une légende," 1976.

——— "La famille Ben Djelloul en France depuis 25 ans," 1979.

Médiamétrie ratings for *La Famille Ramdam*.

Médiamétrie ratings for *Seconde B*.

M6 test study for *La Famille Ramdam*.

Radio Beur Charter, 1981.

SORGEM. Test study of *Seconde B* for France 2, May 19, 1993.

Tribunal de Grande Instance de Bobigny, Prononce en Audience Publique, July 6, 1989.

Vertigo Production, Original Scenario for *La Famille Ramdam*, 1988.

Videau, André. "Bilan du F.I.C. (1983–1984)," Fonds d'Intervention Culturelle, 1984.

Audiovisual Material

Akika, Ali. *Jeunesse en quête d'une culture*, Fonds d'Intervention Culturelle, 1984.

Benguigui, Yamina. *Les Femmes d'Islam*, France 2, June 8, 15, 22, 1992.

Benguigui, Yamina. *Mémoires d'Immigrés: L'héritage maghrébin*, Canal+ video, 1998.

Bouchareb, Rachid. *Bâton Rouge*, 1985.

Carte de Séjour, *Carte de Séjour*, CBS Records, 1982.

——— *Rhorhomanie*, CBS Records, 1983.

——— *Carte de Séjour 2 1/2*, Barclay, 1986.

Charef, Mehdi. *Le thé au harem d'Archimède*, 1985.

Chiban, Malik. *Hexagone*, 1994.

Kacel, Karim. "Banlieue," Pathé-Marconi E.M.I., 1983.

——— "La chanson de Kabyle," Pathé-Marconi E.M.I., 1983.

"La Culture Beur." Beaubourg, *Les Enfants de l'immigration*, May 30, 1984.

La Famille Ramdam, M6.

Mounsi. *Séconde Génération*, Motor Records, 1984.

Poggioli, Sylvia. *An Islamic Journey Inside Europe: Part III Boiling Point in the Banlieues*, on National Public Radio, February 23, 2003.

Seconde B, France 2.

Taha, Rachid. *Barbès*, Barclay, 1990.

——— *Rachid Taha*, Barclay, 1993.

Week-end à Nanterre, (1980).

Interviews

Abaïd, Moa, Paris, May 26, 1996.

Akari, Hédi, Paris, January 12, 1994.

Amara, Kamel, Telephone, March 24, 1994.

Amara, Mohand, Aubervilliers, March 18, 1994.

Amara, Saliha, Paris, March 5, 1994, July 25, 1994.

Amriou, Kamel, St. Ouen, April 29, 1994.

Amriou, Leïla, Paris, March 23, 1994.

Amriou, Lila, Paris, April 20, 1994.

Amriou, Linda, Bobigny, March 31, 1994.

Benbelaïd, Lila, Paris, April 20, 1994.

Benguigui, Yamina, Paris, July 2, 1994.

Benmamar, Aïcha, Paris, May 13, 1994.

Bennacer, Amar, Paris, March 2, 1994.

Bessenay, Sylvie, Paris, December 15, 1993, April 27, 1994.

Blanquart, Paul, Paris, April 12, 1994.

Bouazizi, Walid, Paris, July 3, 1994.

Bouchareb, Rachid, Paris, May 11, 1994.

Boudjellal, Farid, Paris, February 25, 1994.

Boussaa, Youcef, Paris, May 16, 1994.

Chapelle, Josée, Paris, December 12, 1993.

Chauvat, Claude, Paris, June 17, 1994.

Chibane, Malik, Sarcelles, May 9, 1994.

Chikh, Chérif, Paris, March 31, 1994.
da Silva, Fernanda, Paris, December 27, 1993.
de Navacelle, Thierry, Paris, February 2, 1994.
Dehmous, Mohand, Paris, March 31, 1994.
Djabri, Aïssa, Paris, January 1, 1994, June 28, 1994.
Driff, Amar, Paris, May 9, 1994.
Fernane, Archour, Paris, April 1, 1994.
Girard, Simone, Paris, June 15, 1994.
Guebli, Kadour, Aubervilliers, May 5, 1994.
Guerdjou, Bourlem, Paris, July 4, 1994.
Hadjeli, Nadia, Paris, April 16, 1994.
Hahn, Véronique, Paris, June 10, 1994.
Hamadi, Jlaïel, Gennevilliers, June 26, 1994.
Jebbouri, Abdelkader, Paris, April 16, 1994.
Kessaci, Nadia, Paris, April 6, 1994.
Kettane, Nacer, Paris, December 24, 1993, July 4, 1994.
Khessiba, Abdelkader, Gennevilliers, June 26, 1994.
Khimoune, Rachid, Paris, March 19, 1994.
Lahouassa, Farid, Paris, January 1, 1994.
Lebkiri, Moussa, Fontenay-Sous-Bois, May 30, 1994.
Lheureux, Martine, Paris, February 1, 1994.
Mahdaoui, Fatiha, Telephone, April 18, 1994.
Medjani, Salah, Paris, May 3, 1994.
Messaoudi, Samia, Paris, December 22, 1993, April 6, 1994.
Moreira, Paul, Paris, June 16, 1994.
Mounsi, Paris, January 4, 1994.
Nini, Soraya, Paris, March 21, 1994.
Nora, Pierre, Paris, December 7, 2000.
Ouberzou, Malika, St. Denis, April 28, 1994.
Ouchène, Hamid, Paris, March 2, 1994, April 6, 1994.
Sadi-Hadad, Karim, Paris, February 10, 1994.
Smaïn, Paris, April 27, 1997.
Taha, Rachid, Paris, May 12, 1994.
Titous, Kaïssa, Paris, April 14, 1994.
Urtizverea, Amaya, Paris, February 23, 1994.
Videau, André, Paris, February 2, 1994.
Yahiel, Michel, Paris, June 15, 1994.

Secondary Sources

Abdallah, Mogniss H. *J'y suis, J'y reste!: Les lutes de l'immigration en France depuis les années soixante*. Paris: Reflex, 2000.
——— "Le new deal culturel à Beaubourg," *Bulletin de l'agence IM'média*, 1984.

Agulhon, Maurice. "Paris: A Traversal from East to West." In *Realms of Memory: The Construction of the French Past*, vol. III. Pierre Nora (ed.). New York: Columbia University Press, 1998.

Aïchoune, Farid. *Nés en banlieue*. Paris: Ramsay, 1991.

Anglade, Michel. "Radio Beur," Mémoire. Institut d'études politiques de Paris, 1989.

Amara, Saliha and Idir, Said. "Le 'Mouvement Beur' Résumé des chapitres précédents," *Hommes & Migrations* 1144 (1991): 19–26.

Begag, Azouz. *Le gone du Chaâba*. Paris: Seuil, 1986.

Ben Jelloun, Tahar. *Hospitalité française*. Paris: Seuil, 1994.

Bernard, Philippe. *L'immigration*. Paris: Le Monde Editions, 1993.

Blatt, David. "Immigration Politics and Immigrant Collective Action in France, 1968–1993," Ph.D. dissertation, Cornell University, Ithaca, 1995.

Body-Gendrot, Sophie. "Migration and the Racialization of the Postmodern City in France." In *Racism, the City and the State*, Malcolm Cross and Michael Keith (eds.). New York: Routledge, 1993.

Bouamama, Saïd, Hadjila Sad-Saoud, and Mokhtar Djerdoubi. *Contribution à la mémoire des banlieues*. Paris: Culture et liberté Ile-de-France/Editions du Volga, 1994.

Boubeker, Ahmed and Nicholas Beau. *Chroniques Métissées: l'Histoire de France des jeunes arabes*. Paris: Alain Moreau, 1986.

Bouzid. *La Marche*. Paris: Sindbad, 1984.

Boyer, Henri and Guy Lochard, *Scènes de télévision en banlieues: 1950–1994*. Paris: L'Harmattan: Institut National d'Audiovisuel, 1998.

Brubaker, Rogers. *Citizenship and Nationhood in France and Germany*. Cambridge, Massachusetts: Harvard University Press, 1992.

Cazenave, François. *Les Radios Libres*. Paris: Presses Universitaires de France, 1984.

CCI, *Les enfants de l'immigration*. Paris: CCI Editions, 1984.

Cesari, Jocelyne. *Etre musulman en France: Associations, militants et mosquées*. Paris: Éditions Karthala et Iremam, 1994.

Charef, Mehdi. *Le thé au harem d'Archi Ahmed*. Paris: Mercure de France, 1983.

Chikh, Chérif and Ahsène Zehraoui. *Enfants d'immigrés maghrébins*. Paris: CCI, 1984.

Clark, T.J. *The Painting of Modern Life: Paris in the Art of Manet and His Followers*. Princeton, New Jersey: Princeton University Press, 1984.

Clifford, James. *The Predicament of Culture: Twentieth-Century Ethnography, Literature and Art*. Cambridge, Massachusetts: Harvard University Press, 1988.

Colonna, Fanny. *Instituteurs algériens: 1883–1939*. Paris: Presses de la fondation nationale des sciences politiques, 1975.

Connerton, Paul. *How Societies Remember*. Cambridge, United Kingdom: Cambridge University Press, 1992.

Couloud, Phillippe. "Les enfants de l'immigration et les honneurs de la cimaise: radiographie d'une exposition," Centre de Création Industrielle, Paris, 1985.

Dine, Philip. *Images of the Algerian War: French Fiction and Film, 1954–1992*. Oxford: Oxford University Press, 1994.

Donadey, Anne. "'Une certaine idée de la France': The Algeria Syndrome and Struggles over 'French' Identity." In *Identity Papers: Contested Nationhood in Twentieth-Century France*, Steven Ungar and Tom Conley (eds.). Minneapolis: University of Minneapolis Press, 1996.

Dubet, François. *La Galère: Jeunes en Survie*. Paris: Fayard, 1987.

Dubet, François and Didier Lapeyronnie. *Les Quartiers d'Exil*. Paris: Éditions du Seuil, 1992.

Dufrêne, Bernadette. *La création de Beaubourg*. Grenoble: Presses Universitaires de Grenoble, 2000.

Duncan, Carol. "Art Museums and the Ritual of Citizenship." In *Exhibiting Cultures: The Poetics and Politics of Museum Display*, Ivan Karp and Steven D. Lavine (eds.). Washington: Smithsonian Institution Press, 1991.

Durand, Jean-Pierre and Habib Tengour. *L'Algérie et ses populations*. Brussels: Éditions Complexe, 1982.

Duyvendak, Jan Willem. *The Power of Politics: New Social Movements in France*. Boulder, Colorado: Westview Press, 1995.

Eling, Kim. *The Politics of Cultural Policy in France*. New York: St. Martin's Press, 1999.

Evenson, Norma. *Paris: A Century of Change, 1878–1978*. New Haven, Connecticut: Yale University Press, 1979.

Fattah Allah, Abdennasser. "L'expression Beure en France: Cas de Radio Beur de Paris," Mémoire de DEA. Science de l'information et de la communication. Université de Droit, d'Economie et de Sciences Sociales de Paris, Paris II, 1988.

Feldblum, Miriam. *Reconstructing Citizenship: The Politics of Nationality Reform and Citizenship in Contemporary France*. Albany: State University of New York Press, 1999.

Geisser, Vincent. *Éthnicité Républicaine: les élites d'origine maghrébine dans le système politique français*. Paris: Presses Sciences Po, 1997.

Gillis, John R. "Memory and Identity: The History of a Relationship." In *Commemorations: The Politics of National Identity*, John R. Gillis (ed.). Princeton, New Jersey: Princeton University Press, 1994.

———*A World of Their Own Making: Myth, Ritual, and the Quest for Family Values*. Cambridge, Massachusetts: Harvard University Press, 1996.

Gilroy, Paul. *Small Acts: Thoughts on the Politics of Black Cultures*. New York: Serpent's Tail, 1993.

Green, Nicholas. *The Spectacle of Nature: Landscape and Bourgeois Culture in Nineteenth-Century France*. Manchester: Manchester University Press, 1990.

Greene, Naomi. *Landscapes of Loss: The National Past in Postwar French Cinema*. Princeton, New Jersey: Princetown University Press, 1999.

Hargreaves, Alec G. *Voices from the North African Immigrant Community in France: Immigration and Identity in Beur Fiction*. Oxford: Berg, 1991.

———*Immigration, "Race" and Ethnicity in Contemporary France*. New York: Routledge, 1995.

Honneth, Axel. *The Struggle for Recognition: The Moral Grammar of Social Conflicts*. Cambridge, Massachusetts: MIT Press, 1996.

INSEE. *Les étrangers en France*. Paris: Hachette, 1994.

Ireland, Patrick R. *The Policy Challenge of Ethnic Diversity: Immigrant Politics in France and Switzerland*. Cambridge, Massachusetts: Harvard University Press, 1994.

Jazouli, Adil. *L'Action Collective des Jeunes Maghrébins de France*. Paris: CIEMI/L'Harmattan, 1986.

——— *Les Années Banlieues*. Paris: Seuil, 1992.

Jordan, David P. *Transforming Paris: The Life and Times of Baron Haussmann*. Chicago, Illinois: University of Chicago Press, 1995.

Kettane, Nacer. *Le Sourire de Brahim*. Paris: Denoël, 1985.

——— *Le Droit de réponse à la démocratie française*. Paris: La Découverte, 1986.

Kuhn, Raymond. *The Media in France*. New York: Routledge, 1995.

Lallaoui, Mehdi. *20 ans d'affiches antiracists*. Paris: Association Black, Blanc, Beur, 1989.

——— *Du bidonville aux HLM*. Paris: Syros, 1993.

Laronde, Michel. *Autour du Roman Beur: Immigration et Identité*. Paris: L'Harmattan, 1993.

Lees, Andrew. *Cities Perceived: Urban Society in European and American Thought, 1820–1940*. New York: Columbia University Press, 1985.

Lévy, Marie-Françoise. "L'immigration dans la production documentaire, le magazine, la fiction française. Variations autour d'un thème, 1975–1991." In *Télévisions d'Europe et Immigration*, Claire Frachon and Marion Vargaftig (eds.). Paris: Institut National de l'Audiovisuel/Association Dialogue Entre les Cultures, 1993.

Looseley, David L. *The Politics of Fun: Cultural Policy and Debate in Contemporary France*. Oxford: Berg, 1995.

Lorcin, Patricia M.E. *Imperial Identities: Stereotyping, Prejudice and Race in Colonial Algeria*. London/New York: I.B. Tauris, 1995.

MacMaster, Neil. *Colonial Migrants and Racism: Algerian in France, 1900–62*. New York: St. Martin's Press, 1997.

Malakki, Liisa. "National Geographic: The Rooting of Peoples and the Territorialization of National Identity among Scholars and Refugees." In *Becoming National: A Reader*, Geoff Ely and Ronad Grigor Suny (eds.). New York: Oxford University Press, 1996.

Mathy, Jean-Philippe. *French Resistance: The French-American Culture Wars*. Minneapolis: University of Minnesota Press, 2000.

Mauco, Georges. *Les Étrangers en France*. Paris: Librairie Armand Colin, 1932.

Mauss-Copeaux, Claire. *Appelés en Algérie: La parole confisquée*. Paris: Hachette, 1998.

McClintock, Anne. "The Angel of Progress: Pitfalls of the Term 'Post-Colonialism.'" In *Colonial Discourse, Postcolonial Theory*, Peter Hulme and Margaret Iversen (eds.). Manchester/New York: University of Manchester Press, 1994.

Merriman, John. *The Margins of City Life: Explorations on the French Urban Frontier, 1815–1851*. New York: Oxford University Press, 1991.

Mestiri, Ezzedine. *L'immigration*. Paris: Éditions La Découverte, 1990.

Moreira, Paul. *Rock métis en France*. Paris: Souffles, 1987.

Mounsi. *La Cendre des villes*. Paris: Éditions Stock, 1993.

Muñoz, Marie-Claude. *Bibliographie analytique sur les jeunes étrangers (immigrés ou fils d'immigrés)*. Paris: CIEMM, 1980.

Noiriel, Gérard. *Le creuset français: Histoire de l'immigration XIX-XX siècles*. Paris: Seuil, 1988.

——— "French and Foreigners." In *Realms of Memory: The Construction of the French Past*, vol. I, Pierre Nora (ed.). New York: Columbia University Press, 1996. 145–178.

——— *Qu'est-ce que l'histoire contemporaine?* Paris: Hachette, 1998.

Nora, Pierre. "From *Lieux de Mémoire* to Realms of Memory." In *Realms of Memory: The Construction of the French Past*, vol. I, Pierre Nora (ed.), New York: Columbia University Press, 1996.

——— "Between Memory and History." In *Realms of Memory: The Construction of the French Past*, vol. I, Pierre Nora (ed.). New York: Columbia University Press, 1996.

Paul, Kathleen. *Whitewashing the Britain: Race and Citizenship in the Postcolonial Era*. Ithaca, New York: Cornell University Press, 1997.

Perotti, Antonio. "L'education et le développement culturel des migrants: Étude de cas: L'Exposition: 'les enfants de l'immigration,'" Council of Europe, 1984.

Polac, Catherine. "Quand les immigrés prennent la parole: histoire sociale du journal Sans Frontière, 1979–1985," Mémoire présenté pour le Dîplôme d'Etudes Approfondies d'Etudes politiques de Paris. Institute d'études politiques de Paris, 1991.

Renan, Ernest. "What is a Nation?" In *The Nationalism Reader*, Omar Dahbour and Micheline R. Ishay (eds.). Atlantic Highlands: Humanities Press, 1995.

Rigby, Brian. *Popular Culture in Modern France: A Study of Cultural Discourse*. New York: Routledge, 1991.

Rodrigues, Nelson, Josée Chapelle, Olga Najgeborn, and José Vieira. *La ruée vers l'égalité*. Paris: Melanges, 1985.

Rosenzweig, Roy, and David Thelen. *The Presence of the Past: Popular Uses of History in American Life*. New York: Columbia University Press, 1998.

Ross, Kristin. *Fast Cars, Clean Bodies: Decolonization and the Reordering of French Culture*. Cambridge, Massachusetts: MIT Press, 1996.

Rossinelli, Michel. *La liberté de la radio-télévision en droit comparé*. Paris: Publisud, 1991.

Rudder, Véronique de. "Notes à propos de l'évolution des recherches françaises sur 'l'étranger dans la ville.'" In *Les étrangers dans la ville: le regard des sciences socials*, Ida Simon-Barouh and Pierre Jean Simon (eds.). Paris: L'Harmattan, 1990.

Ruedy, John. *Modern Algeria: The Origins and Development of a Nation*. Bloomington: University of Indiana Press, 1992.

Said, Edward. *Orientalism*. New York: Ramdom House, 1978.

Saverèse, Éric. *Histoire coloniale et immigration: une invention de l'étranger*. Biarritz: Séguier, 2000.

Schain, Martin A. "The Racialization of Immigration Policy. Biopolitics and Policy-Making." In *Biopolitics: The Politics of Body, Race and Nature*, Agnes Heller and Sonja Puntscher Riekmann (eds.). Aldershot: Avebury, 1996.

———"The Immigration Debate and the National Front." In *Chirac's Challenge: Liberalization, Europeanization, and Malaise in France*, John T.S. Keller and Martin A. Schain (eds.). New York: St. Martin's Press, 1996.

Shepard, Todd. "Decolonizing France: Reimagining the Nation and Redefining the Republic at the End of Empire," Ph.D. dissertation, Rutgers University, New Brunswick, 2001.

Shields, James G. "Immigration Politics in Mitterrand's France." In *France During the Socialist Years*, Gino Raymond (ed.). Brookfield: Dartmouth, 1994.

Silverman, Maxim. *Facing Postmodernity: Contemporary French Thought on Culture and Society*. New York: Routledge, 1999.

——— *Deconstructing the Nation: Immigration, Racism and Citizenship in Modern France*. New York/London: Routledge, 1992.

Stasi, Bernard. *L'immigration: une chance pour la France*. Paris: Éditions Robert Laffont, 1984.

Stora, Benjamin. *La Gangrène et l'oubli: La mémoire de la guerre d'Algérie*. Paris: La Découvert, 1991.

——— *Ils venaient d'Algérie: L'immigration algérienne en France 1912–1992*. Paris: Fayard, 1992.

——— *Imaginaires de guerre: Algérie-Viêt-nam en France et aux États-Unis*. Paris: La Découverte, 1997.

——— *Le transfert d'une mémoire: de "L'Algérie française" au racisme anti-arabe*. Paris: La Découverte, 1999.

Tievant, Sophie. *Les Radios de Proximité: Acteurs, produits, publics et vie locale*. Paris: Documentation Française, 1985.

Weber, Eugen. *Peasants into Frenchmen: The Modernization of Rural France, 1870–1914*. Stanford, California: Stanford Unversity Press, 1976.

Weil, Patrick. *La France et ses étrangers. L'aventure d'une politique de l'immigration 1938–1991*. Paris: Calmann-Lévy, 1991.

Wieviorka, Michel. "Culture société et démocratie." In *La Société Fragmentée? Le multiculturalisme en débat*, Michel Wieviorka (ed.). Paris: La Découverte, 1996.

Wihtol de Wenden, Catherine. *Les immigrés et la politique. Cent cinquante ans d'évolution*. Paris: Presses de la FNSP, 1988.

Žaknić, Ivan. *Le Centre Pompidou*. Paris: Flammarion, 1983.

Articles, Journals, and Newspapers

Abdallah, Mogniss H. "Le new deal culturel à Beaubourg," *Bulletin de l'agence IM'média*, 1984.

Barbara, Augustin. "Beur, vous avez dit beur!" *Connexions* 58 (1991): 141–156.

Belghoul, Farida. "BHL, Barre, Gros Minet et les Autres," in *La "Beur" Génération*. Paris: Sans Frontière, 1984: 39–41.

Berdah, Maryse and Emmanuelle Bouchez, "Radios Communautaires: Les Voix de la Différence," *Télérama*, February 13, 1991.

Bernard, Philippe. "Du match France-Algérie au 17 octobre 1961," *Le Monde*, October 26, 2001.

Beriss, David. "Scarves, Schools, and Segregation: The Foulard Affair," *French Politics and Society* 8.1 (1990): 1–13.

Berrahal, Hamida. "Ces radios qui 'branchent' les jeunes," *Actualité de l'emigration* 10 (October 1987).

Bosséno, Christain-Marc. "Années 30–60: le cinema français invente la banlieue," *Cahiers de la Cinémathèque* 59.60 (1994): 27–32.

Brahimi, Moulay. "Musique Beur: Un look d'enfer," *Actualité de l'émigration* 92 (June 1987).

Bremner, Charles. "French Face Jail for Insulting the Flag," *The Times* (London), February 15, 2003.

Cambell, Matthew. "France Applauds Crime Crusade: Reforms Make Politician a National Hero," *Times of London*, December 26, 2002.

Centre France, May 12, 1993.

Châtenay-Malabry, Omar de. "Le Parvis des Miracles," in *Bulletin de l'agence IM'média* (1984).

Cohen, Alexandrine. "Le pied de nez de Smaïn," *Villes Lumières* (March 1992).

Colombani, Jean-Marie. "La blessure," *Le Monde*, April 23, 2002.

Costa-Lascoux, Jacqueline. "Assimiler, insérer, intégrer." *Projet* 227 (1991): 7–15.

Daoudi, Bouziane, and Ninam Abdi. "Kacel Karim avec banlieue," *Libération*, February 25, 1988.

Derderian, Richard L. "Daughters in Conflict: The Brother/Sister Relationship in Ferrudja Kessas's *Beur's Story*," *Journal of Maghrebi Studies* 1–2.1 (1993): 72–78.

——— "Radio Beur, 1981–1992: L'échec d'un multiculturalism à la française," *Hommes & Migrations* 1191 (1995): 55–59.

——— "Popular Music from the North African Immigrant Community: Multiculturalism in Contemporary France, 1945–1994," *Contemporary French Civilization* 20.2 (1996): 205–219.

——— "Social Realism, Suburban Culture and Ethnic Diversity on French Television. A Case Study of Seconde B," *Contemporary French Civilization* 21.1 (1997): 38–51.

Dollé, Jean-Paul. "Villes et banlieues dans le cinéma français," *Cahiers de la Cinémathèque* 59.60 (1994): 75–80.

El Yazami, Driss. "Les beurs entre la mémoire et le débat," in *La "Beur" Génération*. Paris: *Sans Frontière*, 1984: 7–9.

Elkarati, Nourredine and Poinsot, Marie. "Politique d'une institution: Le Fonds d'action sociale pour les travailleurs immigrés: Entretien ave Michel Yahiel, directeur du FAS," *Politix* 4.1–2 (1990): 70–74.

Englund, Steven. "Ghost of the Nation Past," *Journal of Modern History* 64 (1992): 299–320.

Faivre, Maurice. Courrier, *Hommes & Migrations* 1220 (1999): 132.

Fourcault, Annie. "Banlieues d'hier: les 'zoniers' de Paris," *Panoramiques* 2.12 (1993): 14–17.

Gastaut, Yvan. "Evolution des designations de l'étranger en France (1960–1990)," *Cahiers de la Méditerranée* 54 (1997): 15–24.

Geisser, Vincent. "Les élus issus de l'immigration maghrébine: l'illusion de médiation politique," *Horizons Maghrébins* 20.21 (1993): 60–79.

Hargreaves, Alec G. "Algerians in France: The End of the Line?" *Contemporary French Civilization* 14.2 (1990): 292–306.

———"La Famille Ramdan: un sit-com 'pur beur?'" *Hommes & Migrations* 1147 (1991): 60–66.

———"Oralité, audio-visuel et écriture: chez les romanciers issus de l'immigration maghrébine." *Poétiques Croissée du Maghreb* 14 (1991): 170–176.

Henley, Jon. "French Back New Law to Punish Lack of Respect for Icons of the Republic," *The Guardian*, February 7, 2003.

Icart, Roger. "Des origines à 1930: La banlieue dans le cinéma français muet," *Cahiers de la Cinémathèque* 59.60 (1994): 15–25.

IM'média. "J'ai claqué la porte de SOS-Racisme," *Quo Vadis* (1993): 44–47.

———"Les Blues des banlieues militantes," *Quo Vadis* (1993): 56.

Joffrin, Laurent. "Les vérités qui dérangent,"*Le Nouvel Observateur*, September 13–19, 1990.

Johnson, Jo. "Violence Halts Algeria-France Soccer Match," *Financial Times* (London), October 8, 2001.

Kalouaz, Ahmed. "Des écrivains à part," *Actualité de l'Emigration* 80 (November 1987).

Khamès, Djamel. "Dix ans de droit d'expression," *Arabies* (February 1992).

Khellil, Mohand. "Kabyles en France, un aperçu historique," *Hommes & Migrations* 1179 (1994): 12–18.

Kodjo, Julie. "Rachid Taha: C'est quoi le raï?" *Afrique Magazine* 107 (October 1993).

Lapeyronnie, Didier. "Assimiliation, mobilisation, et actions collective chez les jeunes de la second génération de l'immigration maghrébine," *Revue française de sociologie* 28 (1987): 287–317.

"Les déclarations du premier ministre," *Le Monde*, May 7, 2001.

"Les lascars s'organisent: Interview de 'Rock Against Police.'" *Questions Clefs* 2 (1982): 52–63.

Liauzu, Claude. "Voyage à travers la mémoire et l'amnésie: le 17 octobre 1961," *Hommes & Migrations* 1219 (1999): 56–61.

Littamé, Fabrice. "Karim Kacel: à fleur de peau d'émotion et de mélodie." *L'Union*, April 14, 1992.

Lofti, Maherzi. "Il était une fois Karim Kacel," *Algérie Actualité*, June 14–24, 1984.

Maier, Charles S. "A Surfeit of Memory? Reflections on History, Melancholy and Denial," *History and Memory* 5.2 (1993):136–152.

Messaoudi, Samia. "Au nom de la mémoire," *Hommes & Migrations* 1175 (1994): 41.

Milon, Colette. "Smaïn: Blague à part," *Télé K7*, July 8, 1991.

Moreira, Paul. "Ce que vous avez failli ne pas voir," *Bulletin de l'agence IM'média,* 1984.

Muhidine, Timour. "Beurs Mais Pas Groseilles: Les Arabs à l'Écran," *Arabies* (April 1991): 76–79.

Nataf, Isabelle. "Les radios associatives en première ligne," *Le Figaro,* June 5, 1990.

Noiriel, Gérard. "L'immigration en France: une histoire en friche," *Annales ESC* 4 (1986).

Polac, Catherine. "Immigration et journalisme immigré: histoire sociale de Sans Frontière, 1979–1985," *Migrations Société* 6.31 (1994): 33–39.

Reid, Donald. "The Limits of Paternalism: Immigrant Coal Miners' Communities in France, 1919–45," *European History Quarterly* 15 (1985): 99–118.

Ruppert, Sophie. "L'Harmattan: Publishing on the Third World," *Research in African Literatures* 22.4 (1991): 155–159.

Saffran, William. "The Mitterrand Regime and Its Policies of Ethnocultural Accommodation," *Comparative Politics* 18.1 (1985): 41–64.

Taranger, Marie-Claude. "Télévision et 'western urbain': enjeux et nuances de l'information sur les banlieues," *Revue d' histoire du cinema* 50.60 (1994): 59–71.

Tarr, Carrie. "Questions of Identity in Beur cinema: From *Tea in the Harem to Cheb*," *Screen* 34.4 (1993): 321–342.

"The Chagrin and the Belated Pity," *Economist,* May 12, 2001: 57.

Vichniac, Judith. "French Sociaists and the Droit à la Différance: A Changing Dynamic," *French Politics and Society* 9 (1991): 41–56.

Wacquant, Loïc J.D. "Pour en finir avec le myth des 'cité-ghettos': Les differences entre la France et les Etats-Unis," *Annales de la recherche urbaine* 52 (1992): 20–30.

Wieviorka, Michel. "La crise du modèle français d'intégration," *Regards sur l'actualité* 161 (1990): 3–15.

Zappi, Sylvia. "Lionel Jospin annonce la création d'un musée de l'immigration," *Le Monde,* November 24, 2001.

Index